The Transnational Media Corporation
Global Messages and Free Market Competition

LEA'S COMMUNICATION SERIES
Jennings Bryant/Dolf Zillmann, General Editors

Selected titles include:

Christ • Media Education Assessment Handbook

Dennis/Wartella • American Communication Research: The Remembered History

DeWerth-Pallmeyer • The Audience in the News

Gershon • The Transnational Media Corporation: Global Messages and Free Market Competition

Vorderer/Wulff/Friedrichsen • Suspense: Conceptualizations, Theoretical Analyses, and Empirical Explanations

Webster/Phalen • The Mass Audience: Rediscovering the Dominant Model

For a complete list of other titles in LEA's Communication Series, please contact Lawrence Erlbaum Associates, Publishers

The Transnational Media Corporation
Global Messages and Free Market Competition

Richard A. Gershon
Western Michigan University

Routledge
Taylor & Francis Group
New York   London

Copyright © 1997, by Lawrence Erlbaum Associates, Inc.
All rights reserved. No part of the book may be reproduced in any form, by photostat, microform, retrieval system, or any other means, without the prior written permission of the publisher.

First published by:

Lawrence Erlbaum Associates, Inc., Publishers
10 Industrial Avenue
Mahwah, New Jersey 07430

This edition published 2012 by Routledge:

Routledge
Taylor & Francis Group
711 Third Avenue
New York, NY 10017

Routledge
Taylor & Francis Group
2 Park Square, Milton Park
Abingdon, Oxon OX14 4RN

Cover design by Kristin Alfano

Library of Congress Cataloging-in-Publication Data

Gershon, Richard.
　The transnational media corporation : global messages and free market competition / Richard A. Gershon
　　　p. cm.
　Includes bibliographical references and index.
　ISBN 978-0-80582-425-4 (cloth)
　　1. Telecommunication—Case studies. 2. International business enterprises—Case studies. 3. Free market—Case studies. 4. Competition, International—Case studies. I. Title.
　HE7631.G34 1996
　384.3'1—dc20　　　　　　　　　　　　　　　　96-20813
　　　　　　　　　　　　　　　　　　　　　　　　CIP

For Casey and Matthew

Contents

About the Author ix

Preface xi

I The Transnational Media Corporation: Business and Economic Considerations 1

1 The Transnational Media Corporation and Foreign Direct Investment 3

2 Deregulation, Privatization, and the Changing Global Media Environment 20

3 The Globalization of Television Trade and Distribution 38

4 The Transnational Advertising Agency: Global Messages and Free Market Competition 60

5 Telecommunications and Intelligent Networks: Managing the Transnational Corporation 77

6 Expanded Cable and Open Video Systems: Establishing a Blueprint for Broadband Residential Services 97

7 The Transnational Media Corporation: Cultural Trespass and Challenges to National Sovereignty 116

II Transnational Media: The Players 133

8 Time Warner, Inc. 135

9 The Sony Corporation 154

10 Bertelsmann A.G. 166

11	The Walt Disney Company	178
12	News Corporation Ltd.	195
Postscript		212
Author Index		221
Subject Index		223

About the Author

Richard A. Gershon, PhD (Ohio University, 1986) is Associate Professor of Telecommunications Management in the Department of Communication at Western Michigan University. Dr. Gershon specializes in the field of telecommunications and organizational planning. He teaches courses in telecommunications management, law and regulations; communication technology; and international communication. His articles have appeared in such publications as *Telecommunications Policy, Communication and the Law, Journal of Media Economics,* and *Telephony* Magazine. In addition, he serves as a consultant and has presented seminars on behalf of Logtel Communication in Santiago, Chile, and Johns Hopkins University and Polytechnic University in the United States. Dr. Gershon also served as the Chair of the International Division of the Broadcast Education Association from 1994 to 1996.

Preface

This is a book about one of the major power brokers of our time—the transnational media corporation. Starting in the early 1980s, the combination of international deregulation and privatization trends coupled with advancements in computer and communication technology have transformed the conduct of international business. The result has been a consolidation of players in all aspects of business, including banking, aviation, insurance and mass media.

The decades of the 1980s and 1990s will long be remembered as a time of rapid growth and expansion for international business. It was a period characterized by major mergers and leveraged buyouts. Much of the financing was accomplished through easy credit by the world's leading financial institutions and corporate willingness to assume major amounts of debt. The purchase and acquisition of media properties must be understood in the context that it was a part of a much larger set of international business dealings. Time Inc.'s 1989 purchase of Warner Communications for $11.2 billion and Walt Disney's 1996 purchase of Capital Cities/ABC for $19.5 billion are highly illustrative of this trend. The transnational media corporation (TNMC) has indeed become a salient feature of today's global economic landscape.

I first became interested in transnational media during the winter of 1990 when I began teaching a course on international telecommunications policy. At the time, I became interested in the question, what makes a global corporation global? And second, to what extent does the TNMC affect the marketplace of ideas? Part I of this book examines the regulatory and economic reasons prompting the formation of the TNMC. It seeks to explain why such companies have come into being and further considers how transnational operations affect the development of new media products in terms of cost, quality, and availability.

The TNMC is unique among global corporations given the fact that its primary business is the creation of information and entertainment products. This book also examines the highly complex relationship between TNMCs and the host nations in which they operate. It further considers such specific issues as cultural trespass, transborder data flow, and the effects of transnational media on the marketplace of ideas.

During the past decade, scholars and media critics alike have become increasingly suspicious of the better known, high-profile media mergers. Such suspicions give way to a number of myths about the intentions of the TNMC and the people who run them. One of the prevalent myths concerning TNMCs is that such companies are monolithic in their approach to business. In fact just the opposite is true. The business strategies and corporate culture of a TNMC are often a direct reflection of the person (or persons) who were responsible for developing the organization and its business mission. Part II of this book provides a series of case study analyses of five leading TNMCs, including Time Warner Inc., Sony Inc., Bertelsmann A.G., the Walt Disney Company, and News Corporation Ltd. Specific attention is given to the history, business philosophy, and economic performance of the aforementioned companies.

The merger and acquisition boom of the 1980s and 1990s has fundamentally transformed the media marketplace for the future. The 21st century promises a very different set of media industry players than was the case in past years. The difficulty in writing such a book is that no sooner have you completed a chapter or case study than the information becomes quickly dated. This was especially true in the summer of 1995 when I was putting the finishing touches on the Walt Disney case study. No sooner had I turned off the printer than the Walt Disney Company announced its plans to purchase Capital Cities/ABC. A few days later, Time Warner announced its intentions to purchase Turner Broadcasting. The material is volatile to say the least. And yet nothing speaks more directly to change and the future of media and telecommunications than the global partnering of the TNMC.

ACKNOWLEDGMENTS

This book was 5 years in the making. During that time, I have been greatly appreciative of Western Michigan University and WMU Research and Sponsored Programs for their financial support and assistance. In particular, I want to thank Dr. Diether Haneicke, President of Western Michigan University, and Dr. Douglas Ferraro, the former Dean of the College of Arts and Sciences, for their financial and professional support of this project. There are several people who have been especially helpful in the development of this book. First, I want to thank Dr. James Gilchrist, Chair of the Department of Communication, for providing me with the release time and technical support that enabled me to finish this project. Jim is one of those rare and special people who knows how to clear the field. Thanks go to the managers and representatives at Time Warner, Sony Inc., Bertelsmann A.G., Walt Disney, and News Corporation Ltd. who provided me with important information and documentation related to their business operations. I also wish to thank several graduate students who provided invaluable assistance in the preparation of this manuscript: Heidi Holwerda, Tsutomu Kanayama, Gerfried Kroeger, Al Snyder, and Nizam Osman.

Special thanks goes to Dr. Rod Rightmire, Indiana University, and Dr. Mike Wirth, University of Denver, for their helpful comments and suggestions. Their insights made this book immeasurably better. In particular, I want to take this opportunity to thank Rod for his many years of friendship and support.

I am indebted to the editorial staff at Lawrence Erlbaum Associates who have been instrumental in making this project possible. They include: Kathleen O'Malley (my editor), Hollis Heimbouch (formerly of LEA), Teresa Horton, production editor, and Sara Scudder, editorial assistant. In addition, a number of people listened to me talk through the ideas contained in this book or provided support in a variety of ways: Carol Levin, Raj Kumar, Nancy Rightmire, James Jaksa, Paul Yelsma, Alicia Yeagley, and Cynthia Bergeon. My special thanks to all of them.

Finally, I want to thank my wife Casey who read every word of this manuscript as we traveled the Canadian highways during the summer of 1995. I so appreciate her grace, wisdom, and loving support. This book could never have happened without her. Last but not least, I want to thank my son Matthew who is forever teaching his Dad slick moves.

Richard A. Gershon

I

The Transnational Media Corporation: Business and Economic Considerations

1

The Transnational Media Corporation and Foreign Direct Investment

The multinational corporation is a nationally based company with overseas operations in two or more countries. It is a salient feature of today's global economic landscape. The origins of the multinational corporation can be traced back to the early 19th century.[1] However, today's multinational corporation is one of the important economic legacies of the post-World War II period. The postwar setting provided the right conditions for its rapid growth and development.[2]

In the decade that followed, there was a paradigmatic shift away from nationalistic economic policies of the 1930s, toward an internationally free-market economy. The shift was in large measure supported by the establishment of the World Bank and the International Monetary Fund. Both organizations were created for the purpose of making financial loans and the settlement of trade disputes more dependable. In addition, the cause of international free trade was greatly enhanced by the United States, which provided billions of dollars in financial aid and investment in the reconstruction of both allies and former enemies.[3] The decade of 1950s saw the beginning of what would become a truly global economy.

Since then, the multinational corporation has become a major force in shaping the world's economy. It is the multinational corporation that has been particularly instrumental in organizing world trade as well as the allocation of resources. In describing the multinational corporation of the 1970s, Jacoby (1984) wrote:

> The multinational corporation, is among other things, a private government, often richer in assets and more populous in stockholders and employees than are some of the nation states in which it carries on its business. It is simultaneously a "citizen" of several nation states, owing obedience to their laws and paying them taxes, yet having its own objectives and being responsive to a management located in a foreign nation.[4]

Vernon and Wells (1981) suggested that the multinational corporation is linked by ties of common ownership and is thus able to draw on a common set of resources, including managerial talent, financing, information systems, and patents.[5] Roche (1992) contended that the multinational corporation is the most aggressive when it comes to employing the newest and best technology. One indication of this is the use of advanced telecommunications technology as a way to move information around the globe instantaneously.[6] Telecommunications technology has fundamentally changed the conduct of international business trade and operations. Voice, data, and video communications using satellite and/or fiber optic transmission has virtually eliminated the time differential that once separated nations and business. Such technology allows the world to operate in real time and gives true meaning to the term *global village*.

THE TRANSNATIONAL MEDIA CORPORATION

Most contemporary research uses the term *transnational* in place of *multinational*. Often, the terms are used interchangeably without precise definitions and distinctions. The transnational corporation (TNC) as a system of organization represents a natural evolution beyond the multinational corporation of the 1960s and 1970s. One distinctive feature of the TNC is that strategic decision making and the allocation of resources is predicated on economic goals and efficiencies with little regard to national boundaries. Often, the national identity or (corporate center) is unknown to the general public.[7]

At the same time, very few companies operate in all markets of the world. Instead, the TNC tends to operate in preferred markets with an obvious preference (and familiarity) toward one's home market. Equally important is the fact that TNCs do not operate uniformly in their approach to business.[8] The business strategies and corporate culture of a TNC is often a direct reflection of the person or persons who were responsible for developing the organization and its business mission. The Sony Corporation, for example, is very much a Japanese company. The company's board of directors is mostly Japanese and all strategic decision making occurs in Tokyo. Alternatively, Bertelsmann A.G. is a transnational media corporation that reflects the business philosophy and media interests of its founder, Reinhard Mohn, who believed in the importance of decentralization. Yet, when it comes to test marketing a new product or service, Bertelsmann will usually conduct the first set of tests in its native Germany before introducing it internationally.

The problem of divergent goals between multinational corporations and host governments has long been the subject of analysis. Nowhere is the problem of divergent goals more apparent than in the area of mass media products and services. What distinguishes the transnational media corporation (TNMC) from other types of TNCs is that the principle commodity being sold is information and entertainment. Yet, the financial imperatives that drive TNMCs are not always compatible with the political and economic objectives of the host nation. At issue is the control over the international marketplace of ideas, challenges to national sovereignty, the potential loss of national culture, and technological and product dependency. Bagdikian (1991) argued that in the United States alone, 23 corporations control most of the business of daily newspapers, magazines, television, books, and motion pictures.[9]

The decade of the 1980s saw the world's economy become more fully privatized. Current trends in privatization and free market economies have led to an international consolidation of media companies. The trend toward consolidation has begun to emerge worldwide. According to the late Steven Ross, former co-chief executive officer, Time Warner: "In order to succeed in business today, you must be in all the major markets of the world."[10] Similarly, the late Robert Maxwell fully expected to be 1 of 10 TMNCs responsible for the majority of worldwide news and entertainment. In a 1987 interview, Maxwell stated, "I expect to be one of ten surviving global publishing companies. Once you understand that, you understand what I've been driving at."[11]

This chapter considers the reasons prompting the formation of TNMCs as well as the reasons for engaging in foreign direct investment (FDI). Special attention is given to five leading TNMCs including Time Warner Inc., Sony Inc., Bertelsmann A.G., The Walt Disney Company, and News Corporation Ltd.

THE PURPOSE OF A GLOBAL MEDIA STRATEGY

Foreign Direct Investment

Foreign Direct Investment (FDI) refers to the ownership of a company in a foreign country. This includes the control of assets. As part of its commitment, the investing company will transfer some of its managerial, financial, and technical expertise to the foreign-owned company.[12] Most major corporations become foreign direct investors through a process of gradual evolution rather than by deliberate choice. Later, as pressures arise from various international operations, the company begins to recognize the need for a more comprehensive global strategy.[13] Historically, the TNMC began as a company very strong in one or two areas. Bertelsmann A.G. began as a mail-order book distributor, whereas Time Inc. (prior to its merger with Warner) was in the business of magazines and pay cable television.

The decision to invest abroad can be a risky proposition because the TNC is subject to the laws and regulations of the host country. It is vulnerable to any future changes in the host country's politics and policies. Dymsza (1984) wrote that FDI can only occur if the host country is perceived to be politically stable, provides sufficient economic investment opportunities, and has business regulations considered to be reasonable.[14] In short, the opportunities for FDI in mass media are strongly correlated to the level of openness in which the host country operates. This is most likely to occur in western democracies with stable governments.

The TNMC engages in FDI for many of the same reasons that other TNCs do.[15] When considering the TNMC, in particular, five reasons can be cited:

1. Proprietary assets and natural resources.
2. Foreign market penetration.
3. Production and distribution efficiencies.
4. Overcoming regulatory barriers to entry.
5. Empire building.

Proprietary Assets and Natural Resources

Some TNCs invest abroad for the purpose of obtaining specific proprietary assets and natural resources. The ownership of talent or specialized expertise can be considered a type of proprietary asset. Sony Corporation's purchase of CBS Records in 1988 and Columbia Pictures in 1989 has made the company a formidable player in music and entertainment. The Sony Corporation purchased proprietary assets in the form of exclusive contracts with some of the world's leading musicians and entertainers. The company also holds the copyrights to various music recordings and films.

The company's 1975 introduction of its Betamax videocassette recorders underscored the point that hardware design was not enough to ensure consumer acceptance.[16] The Sony Corporation firmly believes that ownership of music and entertainment will provide the company with greater leverage in promoting its technical business. One indication of this is Sony's entry into digital autotape (DAT) and multimedia equipment. The goal, according to Sony's former American Vice-Chairman, Michael Schulhof, is to build synergies between entertainment programming and technical development.[17] Sony's purchase of both CBS Records and Columbia Studios is very consistent with their desire to cultivate foreign markets. In 1994, approximately 72.6% of its revenues were derived from foreign sales.[18]

Foreign Market Penetration

Some TNCs invest abroad for the purpose of entering a foreign market and serving it from that location. The TNC's decision to invest is based on the profitability of the market, growth potential, and the existing competitive situation.[19] The market may exist or may have to be developed. The ability to buy an existing media property is the easiest and most direct method for market entry. This was the strategy employed by the French based Hachette SA Corporation that wanted to establish a U.S. presence.

Hachette first entered the United States in 1985 with the launching of *Elle*, the U.S. equivalent of a highly successful French magazine. A year later, Hachette President Jean-Luc Lagardere bought Curtis Circulation Company, the second-largest magazine distributor in the United States. In 1988, Hachette became a major force in U.S. publishing by paying $716 million to

Diamandis Communications Inc. for 12 magazines. Within a few weeks of the Diamandis purchase, Hachette paid $450 million for Grolier Publications, which included such American titles as *Encyclopedia Americana, Disney's Wonderful World of Reading,* and *Dr. Seuss's Beginning Readers Programs.*[20]

A variation on direct-market entry approach is for the TNMC to become an international contractor. According to Grosse and Kujawa (1988), the TNC will sometimes elect to license or franchise a special product or process, rather than investing in costly plant and equipment.[21] The Disney Corporation is able to successfully trade on its name worldwide. It is a name that is clearly differentiated from all other entertainment products and services. The Disney Corporation, through its consumer products division, licenses more than 16,000 items of merchandise worldwide. Similarly, the formation of Tokyo Disney is based on a limited partnership agreement. The Walt Disney Company leases the company name and its characters in exchange for 10% of all gate fees and 5% from food and merchandise sales.

Production and Distribution Efficiencies

The costs of production and labor are important factors in the selection of foreign locations. The TNC may find it more cost effective to produce and distribute selected goods and services from a foreign location. The foreign country enables the TNC to achieve a comparative advantage whereby a product or service can be produced for less cost than that which is produced locally.[22] Wilson (1990) cited the example of Ireland, where data processing has become a cottage industry to service a variety of information requirements for several leading US based companies. "Offshore data and information processing is divided into two sources: American firms establishing their own facilities that focus on internal needs; and local firms that contract out data services to U.S. and other users."[23]

Some TNCs invest abroad for the purpose of creating production and distribution efficiencies. The world's leading newspaper and magazine industries will invest and operate foreign publishing sites as a way to achieve such efficiencies. *Time Magazine* and the *Wall Street Journal* are typical of major news publications that distribute their news content via satellite to various international publishing sites where they are locally published and distributed.

Overcoming Regulatory Barriers to Entry

Some TNCs invest abroad for the purpose of entering into a market that is heavily tariffed. It is quite common for governments to impose some measure of regulatory control on foreign imports. This is done in order to protect local companies from foreign competition that is perceived to be highly aggressive. One way to overcome regulatory barriers to entry is to promote joint partnerships or create foreign subsidiaries. A highly effective TNC is one that smoothly integrates itself into the local economy by becoming national companies, or at least giving that appearance.

In October 1989, the European Community (EC) adopted its Television Without Frontiers directive that requires member states to ensure "where practical and by appropriate means that broadcasters reserve for European works majority proportion of their transmission time."[24] EC officials have long been concerned with the amount of imported U.S. and foreign programming. The EC Directive (as well as the completed 1993 General Agreement on Tariffs and Trade) includes plans for limiting the number of foreign television and film imports. Present efforts to establish program quotas are an attempt to respond to both cultural and economic pressures. One way to overcome regulatory barriers to entry is to promote joint partnerships and/or create foreign subsidiaries.

The U.S. television and film industries have already begun forming joint partnerships with European television and media industries. An indication of this is Capital Cities/ABC's 50% investment in Telemunchen, a German television production house. Similarly, Viacom International, in a joint venture with British Telecom (and the former Maxwell Mirror Group), has combined efforts to launch *Music Television (MTV) Europe*. In spite of such attempts to impose import quotas, the privatization of Western Europe offers considerable opportunities for FDI.

Empire Building

FDI can sometimes be prompted by reasons that go beyond simple business considerations. This seems to be especially true for mass media companies that are privately held. The research into the personal motivations and influence wielded by major owners over their respective media holdings is well documented.[25] News Corporation President Rupert Murdoch has sometimes been characterized as an empire builder in the tradition of the press barons of the 19th century.[26] Similarly, the words *media mogul* and *magnate* were used to describe the late Robert Maxwell, whose international deal making was well known.[27] Author Ben Bagdikian referred to the current generation of media businessmen like Murdoch, Berlusconi, and Lagardere as the "Lords of the Global Village."[28]

Today's generation of transnational media owners are consummate businessmen who are engaged in a level of international deal making never before seen in the history of media and telecommunications. They are risk takers at the highest level, willing and able to spend billions of dollars in order to advance the startup of a new program venture or to execute a highly complex business merger. Such men as Ted Turner, Rupert Murdoch, Michael Eisner, and Gerry Levin (to name only a few) possess a level of interest in media and telecommunications that goes well beyond the issue of straight profitability. For them, success is also measured in terms of business gamesmanship and the art of deal making.

INTERNATIONAL MERGERS AND ACQUISITIONS

The decade of the 1980s witnessed an unprecedented number of international mergers and acquisitions that has brought about a major realignment of business players. In one industry after another, companies are announcing strategic alliances or outright mergers that would have been unthinkable in past years. The concerns for antitrust violations seem to be overshadowed by a general acceptance that such changes are inevitable in a global economy. The result has been a consolidation of players in all aspects of business, including banking, insurance, aviation, and mass media. The combination of worldwide privatization trends coupled with advancements in new media and telecommunications technology has significantly contributed to the creation of the TNMC. Table 1.1 compares the five leading TNMCs identified in this book for the years 1992 and 1994, based on general sales revenues and net income.

During the 1980s, an estimated $1.3 trillion was spent in the transfer and sale of corporate assets worldwide.[29] Much of the financing was accomplished through easy credit by the world's leading financial institutions and corporate willingness to assume major amounts of debt. Between the years 1985 and 1992, the United States became a prime market for FDI in media properties. Table 1.2 provides a listing of major FDIs and acquisitions of U.S. media corporations during this time period.

TABLE 1.1
Five Leading Transnational Media Corporations 1992 and 1994 Revenues (in Millions)

Transnational Media Corporation	World Headquarters	Revenues & Net Income 1992	Revenues & Net Income 1994	Principal Business
Time-Warner	United States	$13,070 / $86	$15,905 / (91)[a]	Magazines, cable, and film
Bertelsmann A.G.	Germany	$11,006 / 392	$10,955 / 476	Book and record publishing, printing, and manufacturing
Sony	Japan	$28,733 / 903	$36,250 / 149	Electronic equipment, recorded music, and film
Walt Disney Co.	United States	$7,504 / 816	$10,055 / 1,110	Film, theme parks, product licensing
News Corporation Ltd.	Australia	$7,811 / 385	$7,985 / 917	Newspapers, DBS, magazines, television, and film

Note. Source: Company reports.
[a]Loss.

TABLE 1.2
Foreign Direct Investment in US Media Corporations (1985–1992) (in Millions)

TNMC	Country	FDI/Acquisition Target	Year	Amount
Bertelsmann	Germany	Doubleday Book Publishing	1986	$475
		RCA Records	1986	$350
C. Itoh, Toshiba	Japan	Time Warner Equity Stake	1992	$1,000
Hachette	France	Diamandis Communication	1988	$712
		Grolier Publications	1988	$450
Matsushita	Japan	MCA	1990	$6,200
Maxwell Com.	Great Britain	Tribune Co. (NY Daily News)	1991	—
		Macmillan Inc.	1988	$2,600
		Official Airlines Guide	1988	$750
		Science Research Assoc.	1988	$150
News Corp.	Australia/ United States	Triangle Publications	1988	$2,085
		Harper & Row	1987	$300
		20th Century Fox	1986	$1,055
		Seven Metromedia Stations	1986	$1,500
Sony	Japan	Columbia Pictures	1989	$4,950
		CBS Records	1987	$2,000

Note. Source: Company reports.

TRANSNATIONAL MEDIA OWNERSHIP: ECONOMIC CONSIDERATIONS

The Theory of Comparative Advantage

The results of research conducted during the 1960s and 1970s have shown that the successful multinational enterprise is a company that exhibits some form of comparative advantage. Specifically, such companies possess a type of proprietary asset; that is, a highly specialized production process or ownership of talent that enables it to achieve higher revenues and/or lower costs than its competitors.[30]

The Walt Disney Company. In the world of television and film entertainment, the name Walt Disney is a highly prized proprietary asset. It is a name that is clearly differentiated from all other entertainment products and services. This, in turn, has allowed the company to create an ongoing relationship with the public. The Walt Disney Company trades on its name whenever a new project is begun, whether it be the Disney Channel, a pay-cable television service, or the start-up of Disney's more than 350 retail store outlets worldwide.

The Disney name allows for certain marketing efficiencies by enabling the company to introduce new products without having to educate the consumer. The consumer products division, for example, ties into the Disney proprietary trade name by licensing its characters, literary properties and music to various manufacturers, publishers, and retailers worldwide. Disney's production of the now-famous *Lion King* movie is available in a variety of media formats and tie-ins. They include the film on videotape for rental or purchase, the Lion King exhibit at Walt Disney World, t-shirts and stuffed animals at all Disney Stores, the Lion King music licensing, and the Lion King video game. As a result, the Walt Disney Company has earned in excess of $1 billion on the creation of one idea and multiple product spinoffs.

Vertical Integration Strategies

There are several ways that a major corporation can strategically plan for its future. One common growth strategy is vertical integration whereby a company will control most or all of its operational phases. The rationale is that vertical integration will allow a large-sized company to be more efficient and creative by promoting combined synergies between its various operating divisions.

The Time Warner Corporation. In July 1989, Time Inc. and Warner Communications completed a corporate merger that would make it the largest media company in the world. The Time Warner merger was conceived as a global strategy in order to position the company to compete head to head with the world's leading media companies. Company strategists believe that by the year 2000, there will be an international oligopoly of six or seven TNMCs.[31]

The Time Warner merger has taken the philosophy of vertical integration to a whole new level in terms of strategic planning at the international level.[32] In principle, Time Warner can control an idea from its appearance in a book or magazine to its debut in domestic and foreign movie theaters, as well as later distribution via cable and/or videocassette. To fully appreciate the opportunities for vertical integration, it is important to consider what both companies brought to the 1989 merger agreement. The opportunities for vertical integration (and combined synergy) can be seen in Table 1.3.

News Corporation Ltd. Rupert Murdoch's News Corp. Ltd. has also used a vertical integration strategy as the basis for launching new businesses. Murdoch entered the U.S. market in 1985 with the purchase of seven TV stations from Metromedia Inc. for $2 billion. A year later, he purchased 20th

TABLE 1.3
Creating Time Warner (1989): What Each Player Brought to the Merger Agreement

Time	Warner
Magazines	**Films and Television**
Time	Warner Brothers
Fortune	Warner Brothers Television
Sports Illustrated	Lorimar Television
Money	Warner Home Video
People	
Southern Living	**Records and Music**
Life	Warner Brothers Records
	Atlantic Records
Cable Programming	Elektra Entertainment
Home Box Office	WEA
Cinemax	Warner/Chappell Music
HBO video	
The Comedy Channel	**Cable Television**
	Warner Cable Communications
Cable Television	
American Telecomm. Inc.	**Publishing**
	Warner Books
Books	DC Comics
Time-Life Books	*Mad Magazine*
Little Brown	
Book-of-the-Month Club	
Oxmoor House	
Scott-Foresman	

Note. Source: Time Inc. and Warner Communication 1988 Annual Reports.

Century Fox for $1.55 billion. The combining of a steady source of programming with ready-made distribution outlets provided the company with an ability to overcome economic barriers to entry. The Fox Television Network was in a position to lay the groundwork for a possible fourth U.S. television network. In April 1987, Murdoch launched the Fox Television Network with 108 affiliates.[33]

The result is that News Corp. is able to produce films and television programs that can be sold or aired on the Fox Television Network or the company's British- and Asian-based direct broadcast satellite (DBS) services, including British Sky Broadcasting and Star Television, respectively. In 1988,

News Corp. purchased *TV Guide* and several other magazines from Triangle Publications for $3 billion. *TV Guide* provides a powerful vehicle for promoting the Fox Network and its programs.[34] In May 1994, Fox improved its affiliate position by paying New World Communications $500 million to break their 12-station affiliation agreement with the three major U.S. networks and to join Fox Broadcasting instead. As a result, Fox increased its VHF penetration rate from 25% to 40% and ensured greater viewer access in such key U.S. markets as Dallas, Detroit, Atlanta, Cleveland, Phoenix, and Kansas City to name only a few.

Does vertical integration always work? The answer depends largely on the company and the nature of the work being performed. For TNMCs like Disney and News Corporation Ltd., the answer is yes. For TNCs like AT&T and IBM, size has proven to be a major obstacle because internal departments are seemingly unable to work together. Even Time Warner has not fully addressed the issue of internal synergies, especially when it comes to film production. Cooperative efforts between Warner films and HBO did not materialize long after the merger agreement. There are several reasons why companies are unable to achieve the once-hoped-for internal synergies. In some cases, subsidiaries or divisions feel handicapped at having to purchase materials from a sister company that is arguably more expensive or less efficient than a competitor. The lack of synergy can also result from complex heirarchial decision making or even turf wars. In order to address such problems, some TNCs are fundamentally restructuring their operations. On September 20, 1995, AT&T announced that it would subdivide its worldwide operations into three separate business units, including AT&T Services, AT&T Network Equipment and AT&T Global Information Systems. The overriding objective is to streamline each company and make them more globally competitive. It should be noted that the reorganization is in part due to AT&T's 1991 purchase of NCR Corporation at a cost of $7.5 billion. Instead of improving AT&T's entry into computers, the NCR debacle has cost the company an additional $144 million in pretax losses and will result in the elimination of 8,500 positions.

Decentralization

Information is a strategic imperative for TNCs. The ability to transmit and receive information efficiently is a key part of the equation. The advent of computer and communication technology has virtually eliminated the time lag that once separated corporate headquarters and their worldwide affiliates. Instead, such technology allows international business to operate in real time and gives true meaning to the term *transnational*. One direct consequence of such instantaneous information has been the decentralization of management and operations. This has greatly affected strategic decision making.

Bertelsmann A.G. Bertelsmann A.G. is the second largest TNMC in the world. The company's central headquarters is based in Gutersloh, Germany.

Bertelsmann A.G. is the most transnational of the world's leading mass media companies. The company's management style is highly decentralized. Two thirds of its business is done outside Germany. The company owns Gruner & Jahr, which produces 37 magazines in five countries, including *Stern* and *Brigette* in Germany, *Parents* in America, *Best* and *Prima* in Britain, and *Femme Actuelle* in France.

In the United States alone, Bertelsmann owns Bantam Books, Doubleday Corporation, Dell Publishing, the Literary Guild, and RCA Records. The company adheres to a strict philosophy of autonomy that allows each subsidiary to determine its own performance objectives. Each subsidiary retains its own name, which may partly explain why the parent company is not well known to the general public.[35]

High Risk and Financial Solvency

The business of media and telecommunications are industries characterized by high start-up costs and high risk. The decisions to publish a new magazine or launch a direct broadcast satellite service are high-risk ventures with few guarantees. Such efforts require a long-term view toward investment. The TNMC is arguably better able to sustain long-term investments and achieve economic efficiencies than most nationally based companies. Researchers Ozanich and Wirth (1992) identified the importance of size and reputation of a TNC as the basis for being able to raise capital in a foreign market.[36] The globalization of capital markets enables such companies to obtain loans and issue securities. Waterman (1991) argued that "any risk of anticompetitive behavior must be balanced by the greater efficiency benefits of large size that chain operations can now realize."[37]

The decade of the 1980s will long be remembered as a time of rapid growth and expansion for international business. It was a period characterized by major mergers and leveraged buyouts. The basic financing was accomplished through easy credit by the world's leading financial institutions, and corporate willingness to assume major amounts of debt. The FDI in media properties must be understood in the context that it was a part of a much larger set of international business dealings. As Carvath (1992) pointed out, the assumption of debt was not used for the purpose of reinvestment, but rather, the paying off of shareholders. Such companies increased their own vulnerability through acquisitions or stock buybacks.[38]

Beginning in the early 1990s, the world's economy confronted a major recession that unleashed a set of forces that caused a serious decline in revenues for many leading TNCs. The recession was especially difficult for the media and telecommunication industries, which are highly dependent on advertising.[39] The problem was further compounded by the enormous debt that these companies were carrying. Such companies were confronted with a peculiar dilemma. On the one hand, the TNMC (like any other company) needs to remain financially solvent and meet its short-term debt obligations.

On the other hand, the unique business of media and telecommunications requires a constant commitment to reinvest in new media products, services, and equipment. The problems associated with debt financing and the TNMC can be seen in the following examples.

Maxwell Communication: A Cautionary Tale. Robert Maxwell was once described as the consummate dealmaker. He spent the better part of the 1980s building Maxwell Communications with the expectation that his company would achieve revenues of $8 billion by 1990. Maxwell Communications never achieved this financial objective, nor did the company benefit from the presumed synergies that were said to exist within the company's diverse media holdings. Instead, the Maxwell holdings remained a loose confederation of companies without linked resources and a strategic plan.[40]

On November 5, 1991, Maxwell died at sea in what was reported as an accidental drowning. Maxwell's controversial death left his two sons, Kevin and Ian, wrestling with both a family tragedy and the urgent need to restructure the company and its enormous debt. At the time of Maxwell's death, Maxwell Communications was faced with $3 billion worth of debt. In order to meet short-term loan obligations, the company sold Pergamon Press PLC for $764.9 million. Pergamon had long been considered one of the company's strongest assets.

Creditors are presently seeking payment for past debts and financial obligations. The company faces the daunting task of selling off additional assets in order to meet short-term loans. The problem is especially vexing because the selling prices did not equal the high prices Maxwell paid only a few years before.

Time Warner Corporation. If given a choice, Time Inc. would have much preferred to consummate its merger with Warner Communications under the terms of the original agreement; that is, an all-stock exchange (no cash) deal. Instead, a hostile takeover attempt by Paramount Communication forced Time Inc. to come up with an alternative, albeit more costly, approach to financing its merger/acquisition of Warner Communications. Time Inc.'s willingness to purchase Warner Communications for $14.9 billion and assume an $11.2 billion debt load came at a time when market conditions were aggressive and being highly leveraged was considered an acceptable business practice for long-term financing.

The merging of Time Warner was originally expected to generate synergies that would ultimately boost the value of the combined stock. The merger agreement called for a plan to forge massive alliances in Europe and Asia as a way to enter these markets. The plan would require that these partners invest in a limited partnership as a way to gain an equity stake in Time Warner's assets. The plan to sell limited partnerships has only been partially successful to date. In November 1991, Time Warner entered into an agreement with Japan's Toshiba Corporation and C. Itoh, a well-respected trading company. The latter companies agreed to purchase a 12.5% stake in Time Warner for $1 billion.

Through this arrangement, Time Warner has obtained an important source of capital as well as gaining greater access to Japanese markets.[41] In May 1993, Regional Bell Operating Company US West paid $2.5 billion for a 25% interest in Time Warner's Entertainment, which includes the company's cable and programming properties.

In September 1995, Time Warner announced that it would merge with Turner Broadcasting Systems, involving an $8 billion stock swap. In exchange, Ted Turner would receive $2.5 billion and a 11.3% stake in Time Warner, thus making him the company's largest stockholder.[42] In addition, Turner would serve as vice chairman of Time Warner and will remain CEO of Turner Broadcasting Systems. Through its affiliate, Liberty Media, John Malone's TCI would emerge as Time Warner's second-largest shareholder.

Shortly after the agreement was announced, US West filed a lawsuit in an attempt to block the proposed merger. US West cited numerous conflicts of interests and a concern that the value of its 25% interest in Time Warner Entertainment would be substantially devalued. For company stockholders (and industry analysts), a bigger question remains—namely, Time Warner's ability to absorb added debt at a time when its finances are just beginning to stabilize. In the aftermath of the Time Warner merger, the company's debt financing proved difficult enough. Between 1990 and 1994, Time Warner experienced a net income loss 4 out of 5 years. Their current long-term debt is $8.8 billion. The purchase of Turner Broadcasting will add an additional $2 billion to the company's total debt for a total of $10.8 billion.

News Corp. Ltd. News Corp. President Rupert Murdoch may well be considered the most ambitious of the media magnates. In the late 1980s, News Corp. financed several ambitious projects including the start-up of the Fox Television Network in the United States and Europe's first DBS service, SkyChannel. Both investments were accomplished with short-term bank loans. Both ventures have proven to be a major drain on the company's resources. This, in addition to its other financial obligations, forced the company to seek a major restructuring of its $8.3 billion debt. In 1991, a lending group consisting of 146 banks gave News. Corp. $600 million to meet its financial commitments. The result was a major downgrading of News Corp. stock.[43]

It has taken 4 years for News Corporation Ltd. to climb out of its financial hole. The company is quite solvent once again, but even Rupert Murdoch concedes that he is not prepared to bet the company as he did in the early 1990s.

DISCUSSION

Since the late 1970s, there has been a worldwide shift toward economic privatization of domestic and international business. Nowhere is this more evident than in the fields of mass communication and telecommunications. The merger and acquisition boom of the past decade has produced a very different set of media industry players than was the case in past years.

In a transnational economy, media decision making and FDI are largely based on economic efficiencies with little regard for national boundaries. The decision to engage in FDI is based on the profitability of the market and future growth potential. The TNMC is, therefore, more likely to view transnational expansion and its effects in the context of whether it makes good business sense. This chapter has identified five reasons for engaging in FDI: natural resources and proprietary assets, foreign market penetration, production and distribution efficiencies, overcoming regulatory barriers to entry, and empire building.

In a transnational economy, corporate size becomes an important consideration when it comes to FDI strategies and achieving economic efficiencies. Several TNMCs, including Time Warner, News Corporation Ltd., and Disney have adopted vertical integration strategies as a way to build internal efficiencies. Corporate size also becomes important for the purpose of underwriting the cost of new products and services. Communication technologies such as cable television, DBS, and high definition television require high capitalization and/or commitment to sophisticated equipment.

The TNMC is arguably better able to achieve economic efficiencies and sustain long-term investment than most nationally based companies. The TNMC, given its size and name recognition, is able to exercise investment opportunities around the world. The globalization of capital markets allows TNCs to access a variety of funding mechanisms including banks, securities, and insurance. It is for these reasons that the TNC and the TNMC are perceived to be companies without a discernible corporate center and where political allegiances are secondary to the business of profitability.

NOTES

[1] Although much smaller in size, the origins of the multinational corporation can be traced back to the early 19th century. Strong nationalistic economic policies combined with the two World Wars precluded the possibility of such corporations from ever becoming too large. Some researchers have argued that it was such policies that largely contributed to both the economic depression of the 1930s and World War II itself.

[2] William A. Dymsza, "Trends in Multinational Business and Global Environments: A Perspective," *Journal of International Business Studies*, (Winter 1984), p. 25.

[3] Leonard Glynn, "Multinationals in the World of Nations," *The Multinational Enterprise in Transition*, (Eds.) Phillip Grub, Fariborz Ghadar, and Dara Khambata, (Princeton, NJ: Darwin Press, 1984), pp. 63–64.

[4] Neil H. Jacoby, "The Multinational Corporation," in *The Multinational Corporation in Transition*, (Eds.) Phillip D. Grub, Fariborz Ghadar, and Dara Khambata, (Princeton, NJ: Darwin Press, 1984), p. 3.

[5] R. Vernon and L. Wells, *Manager in the International Economy*, 4th ed. (Englewood Cliffs, NJ: Prentice-Hall, 1981), p. 4.

[6] Edward M. Roche, *Managing Information Technology*, (New York: MacMillan, 1992), p. 1.
[7] Specifically, the multinational corporation has been understood by most scholars to mean a nationally based company with overseas operations. The transnational company is market driven; where the allocation of resources is predicated on economic goals and efficiencies with little regard to national boundaries. See Peter F. Drucker, *The New Realities*, (New York: Harper & Row, 1989), pp. 115–139; and "The Stateless Corporation," *Business Week*, 14 May, 1990, p. 98.
[8] Debra Fleenor, "The Coming and Going of the Global Corporation," *Columbia Journal of World Business* (28)4, 1993, pp. 8–10.
[9] Ben Bagdikian, *The Media Monopoly*, 3rd ed. (Boston: Beacon Press, 1990), p. 4.
[10] "The Worldwide Web Steve Ross is Weaving," *Business Week*, 13 May, 1991, pp. 82–83.
[11] "Robert Maxwell," *Forbes*, 5 October, 1987.
[12] Robert E. Grosse and Duane Kujawa, *International Business: Theory and Application*, (Homewood, IL: Irwin, 1988), p. 87.
[13] Stefan H. Robock and Kenneth Simmonds, *International Business and Multinational Enterprises*, 4th ed. (Homewood, IL: Irwin, 1989), pp. 195–197.
[14] Dymsza, pp. 32–33.
[15] Jack N. Behrman and Robert E. Grosse, *International Business and Governments: Issues and Institutions*, (Columbia: University of South Carolina Press, 1990), pp. 36–49; See also Grosse and Kujawa, pp. 87–93.
[16] The United States acceptance of VHS as a de facto videocassette standard was largely determined by the greater availability of rental films on VHS as compared to Beta (the standard that was promoted by Sony). In the final analysis, software availability proved to be more of a critical issue than questions pertaining to technical superiority.
[17] One indication of this is Sony's entry into High Definition Television. Sony is using its Columbia Studios as a place to build and promote its HDTV editing facilities. "Sony: The Media Colossus," *Business Week*, 25 March, 1991, pp. 64–70.
[18] Sony Corporation, *1994 Annual Report to Stockholders*, (Tokyo: Sony Corporation Inc.).
[19] Behrman and Grosse, p. 42
[20] Stewart Toy, "Can Hachette's Dream Survive its Debt?" *Business Week*, 25 February, 1991, pp. 62–63; and "Hachette Says Over Half of its Earnings Come From Outside France," *Publishers Weekly*, 11 August, 1989, p. 335.
[21] Grosse and Kujawa, p. 25.
[22] Glynn, "Multinationals in the World of Nations," pp. 70–71.
[23] Mark Wilson, "The Impact of Communication Technology on the Offshore Relocation of Services: Data Processing in Ireland," A presentation given to the International Communication Association Conference, Dublin, Ireland, June 1990, p. 1.
[24] The EC Council Directive Concerning the Pursuit of Television Broadcasting Activities (the "Directive"), adopted by the EC Council of Ministers in Luxembourg on October 3, 1989, article 4.
[25] David Halberstam, *The Powers That Be*, (New York: Knopf, 1979), p. 122; Gay Talese, *The Kingdom and the Power*, (New York: Anchor Press/Doubleday, 1978); Hank Whittemore, *CNN: The Inside Story*, (Boston: Little, Brown, 1990).
[26] Anthony Smith, *The Age of the Behemoths: The Globalization of Mass Media Firms*, (New York: Priority Press Publications, 1991), p. 21.
[27] "Media Mogul Maxwell Reveled in Growth, Now Must Scale Back," *Wall Street Journal*, 13 September, 1991, pp. A1–A4.
[28] Ben H. Bagdikian, "The Lords of the Global Village," *The Nation*, 12 June, 1989, p. 805.
[29] Two of the more notable acquisitions included Kohlberg, Kravis, and Roberts' acquisition of RJR Nabisco for $24.7 billion. Similarly, Phillip Morris consolidated its food holdings by paying $5.6 billion for General Foods and $12.6 billion for Kraft Foods.

[30] A. L. Cavet, "A Synthesis of Foreign Direct Investment Theories of the Multinational Firm," *Journal of International Business Studies*, (Spring/Summer 1981), pp. 43–59.

[31] Bill Saporito, "The Inside Story of Time Warner," *Fortune*, 20 November, 1989, p. 27.

[32] Time Warner Inc., *1989 Annual Report to Stockholders*, (New York: Time Warner Inc., 1989), p. 1.

[33] Laurie Thomas & Barry Litman, "Fox Broadcasting Company, Why Now? An Economic Study of the Rise of the Fourth Network," *Journal of Broadcasting and Electronic Media*, 35(2), 1991, pp. 139–157.

[34] "Fox Owner Buys the Henhouse," *U.S. News and World Report*, 22 August, 1988, p. 42.

[35] "Reinhard Mohn," *The Nation*, 12 June, 1989, p. 810.

[36] Gary Ozanich and Michael Wirth, "Trends in Globalization: Direct Foreign Investments in Media Companies 1985–1991," A presentation given to the 37th Annual Broadcast Education Association, Las Vegas, NV, April 12, 1992.

[37] David Waterman, A New Look at Media Chains and Groups 1977–1989. *Journal of Broadcasting and Electronic Media*, 35(2), 1991, pp. 167–177.

[38] Rod Carvath, "The Reconstruction of the Global Media Marketplace," *Communication Research*, 19(6), 1992, p. 708.

[39] During times of recession, companies look to streamline their cost of operations. The advertising budget is usually one of the first things to go. In the United States alone, television network advertising fell 7.1% in the first half of 1991 as compared to the same period in 1990. Similarly, magazine ad revenue was down 5% for the first half of 1991 and newspaper ad revenue was down 7%. "What Happened to Advertising?" *Business Week*, 23 September, 1991, p. 23.

[40] "Media Mogul Maxwell Reveled in Growth, Now Must Scale Back," *Wall Street Journal*, pp. A1–A4.

[41] Time Warner Inc., *1991 Annual Report to Stockholders*, (New York, NY: Time Warner Inc., 1991).

[42] "It's TBS Time," *Broadcasting & Cable*, 25 September, 1995, pp. 8–10.

[43] "A Chastened Man," *The Economist*, 19 January, 1991, pp. 60–61.

2

Deregulation, Privatization, and the Changing Global Media Environment

Today, the level of economic restructuring and consolidation is unprecedented in the history of international business and commerce. The globalization of economic activity has forced many nations of the world to carefully consider their national economic policies. The once sacrosanct government monopolies, including airlines, steel, and telecommunications, are feeling the international winds of change. There is a growing realization that if such government-protected monopolies do not move fast enough in providing advanced services at the right cost, they will soon find themselves being outperformed by their international rivals. The result is a worldwide movement to deregulate government involvement in business and to privatize or sell off state-owned companies.

In a transnational economy, the allocation of resources is predicated on market goals and efficiencies. This is especially true in the field of telecommunications, which is a business characterized by high start-up costs and considerable financial risk. It is also a business that is decidedly global in which success is largely dependent on the free flow of trade across national borders. This book argues that the combination of international deregulation and privatization trends coupled with advancements in new media and telecommunications technology has forever changed the global media landscape. Specifically, this chapter examines the first set of factors and how they have transformed the conduct of international businesses and media trade.

DEREGULATION, PRIVATIZATION, AND ECONOMIC CHANGE

The changing telecommunications and mass communication structures of the United States, Great Britain, and Japan are highly illustrative of deregulation and privatization trends worldwide. Likewise, European Community (EC) efforts to eliminate nonessential regulation and trade barriers represent a large-scale effort to promote the cause of competition. Even *perestroika*, the one time answer to Soviet privatization, was an attempt to reform a failed economic policy. The common motivation behind such regulatory and economic reforms was the perceived inefficiency of central planning and government-protected monopolies. Government-owned enterprises tend to be inefficient operations and can be characterized by:

- Poor financial performance.
- Overstaffing.
- Dependence on government subsidies.
- Highly centralized and politicized organizations.
- Exclusionary dealings with competitive imports.
- Strong adherence to rules and regulations.
- Poor export performance.
- Inefficience and technical noncompetitiveness.

Privatization is a highly political process that involves the conversion and/or selling off of state-owned enterprises (SOEs) into the private sector. The primary objective is to allow a market economy to flourish and thereby create opportunities and incentives for economic development. The successful privatization of SOEs is intended to improve the quality of goods and services while reducing the role of the state in the economy. The selling off of SOEs, in particular, represents a way for government to raise cash that can be applied toward the reduction of the government's operating deficit. Likewise, the same money can be used toward other government-supported services. Another related objective of privatization is to promote the development of new technologies and services through FDI. The resulting competition would increase productivity and operating efficiency.[1]

A nation that decides to privatize must create the proper conditions for the stable transfer of valued assets into the private sector. As Lieberman (1993) pointed out, one of the biggest challenges associated with privatization is institutional failure; that is, the inability on the part of government in knowing how to manage the process. Government ministries charged with the responsibility of privatizing select SOEs often lack the expertise and budget to carry out their mission. This includes everything from being able to evaluate the proper worth of select assets to knowing how to mount an effective public relations campaign in order to attract the right kind of private investors.[2]

The challenge of regulatory reform and privatization will be especially difficult for those countries whose planning structures were once highly centralized. Specifically, the conversion to a market economy will be most disruptive for those government agencies and people that have long been insulated from inefficient practices. In order to minimize the disruptive effects, these countries will need to mobilize domestic savings, infuse their economies with foreign cash, and create new job opportunities. The TNC is likely to be a major force in organizing such efforts.

The United States and Economic Deregulation

Beginning in the early 1980s, the United States under the Reagan administration actively promoted a policy of economic deregulation. The policy was designed to foster greater economic competition by allowing the marketplace to establish priorities and professional standards of business conduct rather than needless government intervention. The resulting cost savings was expected to spur productivity and new product development. As part of that effort, the Reagan administration reduced the stringency of many industrial standards required by such government agencies as the Securities Exchange Commission (SEC) and the Environmental Protection Agency (EPA), to name only a few.

Perhaps no one championed the cause of deregulation more than the Federal Communications Commission (FCC) under the leadership of its former Chairman, Mark Fowler. As one *Business Week* commentator noted: "The FCC has become Washington's most advanced laboratory for the antiregulation theories of the Reagan administration."[3] It was during Fowler's tenure at the FCC that the U.S. telecommunications industry experienced the most dramatic effects of deregulation put into practice.[4] Such deregulatory efforts included the breakup of AT&T,[5] the passage of the Cable Communications Policy Act of 1984,[6] and most recently, the passage of the Telecommunications Act of 1996.

Table 2.1 provides a brief overview of the more significant deregulatory measures supported by the FCC during the period between 1980 and 1996.

The Telecommunications Act of 1996

On February 1, 1996, after months of lengthy debate and negotiations, the U.S. Congress overwhelmingly passed the Telecommunications Act of 1996 (henceforth, referred to as the Act). The Act was signed into law by President Bill Clinton on February 8, 1996 and its provisions become effective immediately. The Telecommunications Act of 1996 is the first comprehensive rewrite of the Communications Act of 1934 and dramatically changes the ground rules for competition and regulation in virtually all sectors of the communications industry, including:

1. Radio and television broadcasting.[7]
2. Cable television.
3. Local and long-distance telephony.
4. Telecommunications equipment manufacturing.
5. The Internet and online computer services.

The Act represents a major step forward in the development of U.S. telecommunications policy. The Act is clearly deregulatory in nature and adopts competition as the basic charter for all telecommunications markets.

TABLE 2.1
The FCC and U.S. Deregulation of Telecommunication Services (1980–1996)

Telephone equipment and long-distance service (1984)	Supported the breakup of AT&T, the premiere local and long-distance telephone monopoly in the United States. This, in turn, promoted long-distance competition by permitting the entry of alternative long distance carriers, including MCI, Sprint, and others.
Cable television deregulation (1984)	Supported the passage of the Cable Communications Policy Act, which significantly deregulated the cable industry. Cable operators were given greater control in the selection of programming and the establishment of subscriber rates.
Expanded broadcast station ownership (1984) and (1992)	The FCC raised the limit on broadcast ownership of TV, AM, and FM stations from 7 each to 12. In 1992, the commission discontinued duopoly rules in order to permit ownership of more than two AM or FM stations within the same community.
Broadcast licensing	Abandoned lengthy comparative renewal hearings in favor of a more streamlined process. Current broadcasters could presume that reasonable past performance would lead to a renewal of their broadcast license.
Obscenity and indecency	Relaxed rules concerning the use of potentially obscene and indecent programming in both radio and TV.
Telephone entry into cable (1996)	The passage of the Telecommunications Act of 1996 allows U.S. telephone companies to provide cable television as a cable operator, common carrier, or under an open video systems scenario.
Cable entry into telephone (1996)	The passage of the Telecommunications Act of 1996 also permits cable entry into telephone communication.

The underlying rationale is that competition will encourage both lower rates for consumers and creative new approaches toward the development of telecommunications products and services. Prior to the Act, major segments of the U.S. telecommunications marketplace adhered to strict marketplace regulation, thus creating protected markets (or de facto monopolies). As a consequence of the Act, merger and concentration rules have been relaxed and telephone and cable cross-market entry rules have been eliminated altogether.

Great Britain and Privatization

Monopolies, by their very nature, have little incentive to be innovative. The lack of competition causes them to be satisfied with the status quo. Although they ensure adequate levels of service, they are by no means willing to promote the adoption of new products and costly services. This was a major reason that brought about the eventual breakup of AT&T. It was also the same reason prompting regulatory reform in Great Britain, as well as in other European Post Telephone and Telegraph (PT&T) systems. Not even the best managed

PT&Ts can keep up with the changing demands of corporate users, who require leading-edge technology.

The problem is further complicated by the fact that the PT&T is highly dependent on government support and is just one of several agencies competing for limited or scarce financial resources. Regardless of its perceived importance, telecommunications is simply another allocation within a much larger scheme of governmental priorities, including health, education, defense, and transportation.

The case of British Telecom is highly illustrative. In late 1985, British Prime Minister Margaret Thatcher authorized the sale of 51% of the country's nationally owned common carrier, British Telecom, to the private sector. The Thatcher administration's decision to privatize was but one example of a much larger economic mandate to privatize several nationally-owned industries, including airlines and steel.

In past years, British Telecom had acquired a reputation for poor service and waste. British Telecom was plagued by apathetic management, which delayed replacement of antiquated equipment, including electronic telephone exchanges that covered only one fifth of the country. British Telecom was reputed to have one of the lowest productivity records in the Western world; the result of extensive featherbedding where up to three grades of engineers were required to install a single telephone line.

The privatization of British Telecom was seen as the best solution to spur competition and efficiency into the marketplace. After privatization, a major shipment of electronic switches was purchased from Sweden's Ericsson Corporation, thereby putting pressure on lax British equipment manufacturers who were not accustomed to having to compete in what was otherwise a guaranteed market. The British government subsequently licensed Mercury Communications to offer alternative voice and data services in direct competition with British Telecom. In a matter of 7 years, British Telecom reemerged as one of the world's leading telecommunication companies, currently offering telecommunication services to large corporate users in 20 of the world's largest cities. This includes a $1 billion investment in a highly advanced international telephone network called Cyclone.[8]

The Thatcher administration likewise served notice to the British Broadcasting Corporation (BBC) that it no longer wanted to subsidize domestic radio and television production. The cost of television production had risen steadily at a time when there were competing demands for public finance. There was also a perception among government officials that the cost of producing television in Great Britain had become generally inflated. This was especially true at the independent television (ITV) companies whose market power and lack of incentives encouraged the system to be overstaffed and inefficient.[9]

A 1988 white paper called the Peacock Report was highly critical of the current state of British broadcasting. The report cited how the existing four-channel system had led to an abuse of market power, resulting in higher costs and less viewing options.[10] Prime Minister Thatcher was reported to have called the ITV companies "the last bastions of restrictive practices."[11]

The Thatcher administration subsequently took procompetitive steps to clear the way for new cable and satellite program suppliers. In addition, the British government gave its support to the start up of two DBS ventures. Both Robert Maxwell and Rupert Murdoch began pan-European DBS operations in 1987. Despite heavy financial losses, Murdoch's Sky Television absorbed Maxwell's British Satellite Broadcasting and was reorganized under a newly created DBS service called British Sky Broadcasting.

Japan and Privatization

In Japan, it is sometimes hard to distinguish between private industry and the government itself. The name *Japan Inc.* has come to symbolize the close working relationship between government and industry. Starting in the early 1980s, the Japanese government, through the Ministry of Posts & Telecommunications (MPT), established an advisory committee to investigate the possibility of reform in telecommunications. Japan's domestic telephone provider, Nippon Telegraph and Telephone (NTT), a public corporation, became the subject of an important internal review.

The advisory committee solicited opinions from both the business and industrial sectors. NTT had received high marks for enabling the government to offer universal telephone service to its citizens.[12] Japan then had the second largest number of telephones in service after the United States. At the same time, there was a growing sentiment that NTT would not be able to keep pace with the changing demands of corporate users, or be able to successfully offer new and diverse services. The internal call for greater competition was quite strong. A direct result of those meetings was the adoption of the following principles:

1. An acceptance in principle to abolish the telecommunications monopoly (NTT) in order to introduce competition.
2. A plan to reorganize NTT, a government institution (and public corporation), into the private sector.

In the meantime, there was external pressure as well. The United States was applying pressure to crack Japan's estimated $32 billion telecommunications market. Both sets of forces prevailed on April 1, 1985, when Japan liberalized their telecommunications trade policies. The passage of the NTT company bill resulted in NTT losing its monopoly status in exchange for being allowed to enter new fields of communication.[13] Japan's PT&T was authorized to sell 33% of its 66% ownership of NTT to private domestic investors. The Japanese government subsequently licensed four common carriers to offer basic telephone service in competition with NTT. In addition, 17 carriers now provide value added services.[14]

Perestroika: The Soviet Answer to Privatization

As early as 1982, former Soviet leader Mikhail Gorbachev came to the sobering realization that his country was suffering from a failed economic policy. In a country that had long held to the principles of centralized planning, there came the realization that unless the country was prepared to economically restructure, the world was going to pass them by. To further complicate matters, the Soviet Union was severely handicapped by the staggering cost of its foreign obligations, most notably in the area of defense spending The economic solution would require a Soviet version of privatization.

The successful conversion to a market economy would require more than just economic restructuring. In a country where a simple photocopier was off limits to the average citizen, there would have to be a corresponding openness in the free flow of information. To this end, Gorbachev coined the term *Glasnost*. Throughout his tenure as president, Gorbachev expressed the need for a qualitatively new state of Soviet society. The policy of *Glasnost* could be felt on all levels, ranging from greater openness in news coverage to the phasing out of controls on information technology.

Journalists were better able to express themselves and critique the actions of government in a manner never before seen in that country. One example was the close scrutiny paid to the Soviet rescue and relief effort following the December 1988 earthquake in Armenia. The opportunities for self-expression stood in marked contrast to the cold silence that had blanketed the nuclear disaster at Chernobyl only 2 years before.

In the area of computer technology, Soviet planners came to the inescapable conclusion that either they foster nationwide computer literacy or be relegated to a secondary status in the transnational world of the future. The decision to become more computer literate, however, would pose a real dilemma for a country that was highly restrictive in its use of information. The Soviet Union could not expect to be a major player in the worldwide telecommunications revolution while trying to control the use of new communication technology based on ideological concerns. In short, the Soviet government could not expect its citizens to be creative in their use of advanced information technology while trying to impose restrictions on its use.

Gorbachev was a practical man who came to this realization early on in his tenure. He recognized that many of his country's problems, including a stalled economy and a trade imbalance with the west, could only be solved within the context of an international framework. Gorbachev's plan was to convert to a market economy by redistributing national resources and by relying on the country's internal strengths. One area that held significant promise for the future was space communications and the country's successful history of deploying satellites.

The successful redistribution of national resources would require significant cuts in military spending. Naturally, better relations with the U.S. and the Western allies became a top priority. Events surrounding the failed coup attempt and the subsequent breakup of the Soviet Union are well documented. The new Commonwealth of Independent States finds itself having to sort through many of the same economic issues that confronted the former Soviet Union. The conversion to a market economy has not been easy. The newly formed republics are now forced to rebuild their media facilities and adopt policies within the context of an uncertain political climate. According to Young and Launer (1991):

> Today the impending conversion to a market economy and the combative uncontrollable press have rendered the social scene almost unrecognizable. It is difficult to perceive any remnant of those tentative, cautious policy conceptions that ushered in the new age of Soviet political culture. Indeed, one seldom even hears the term glasnost.[15]

Deregulation, Privatization, and European Unification

The 12 countries that comprise the European Community (EC) are combining the best features of deregulation and privatization as part of a larger strategy for improving economic growth. In 1985, the EC heads of state agreed to a program that would lift all economic restrictions now separating those countries. The result of that effort was the passage of the European Community Act, which provides the legal framework for future political and economic cooperation among member nations. The new Europe is first and foremost the product of a continentwide economic deregulatory movement where the rigid rules of government bureaucracy are finally being swept away. At the same time, the newly evolving EC is an attempt to create an internal trading zone that favors the products and services of its member nations.

Some of the more prominent deregulatory features of the EC plan call for the free flow of products and services between EC members, the elimination of taxes on imports between EC members, the elimination of excessive documentation now required of EC members during the transport of products across national borders, and mutually recognized university degrees and vocational certificates among EC member states.

Nowhere are the proposed changes more profound than in the area of telecommunications in general, and television broadcasting in particular. The European Community Act calls for the stated willingness to share scientific and artistic expertise among EC nations. The EC Act encourages the free movement of products and services across national boundaries. Specifically, EC Directive 89/552 is designed to permit an open market for television broadcasting by reducing barriers and restrictions placed on cross-border transmissions.

The EC set an original date of 1992 in order to allow sufficient time for EC nations to enact their own legislation that would bring them into compliance with the EC plan. However, major political events including German unification, the breakup of the Soviet Union, and the Yugoslavian civil war have significantly altered the original time frame for European unification.

The EC council subsequently met in July 1993 and established a new date of January 1, 1998 as the proposed date when the full liberalization of telecommunication services could be expected. The EC's primary objective from the outset was to create an internal market in which competition was not distorted. In past years, however, telecommunications has been highly regulated with state owned PT&Ts being given exclusive monopoly rights in the provision of broadcast and telephone service. Thus any proposed solution for the future would have to be gradually phased in so as not to destabilize the PT&T's financial stability.[16]

At the time of the council's meeting, there was a clear recognition that broadcasting, cable, and telephony have adhered to separate forms of regulation. Europe's future information economy, however, is expected to be built on the convergence of different communication media and would thus require a comprehensive policy framework. In December 1993, the EC issued a white paper entitled *Growth, Competitiveness, Employment—The Challenges and Ways Forward into the 21st Century*. The paper asserts the importance of establishing a comprehensive policy that addresses all sectors of the information economy.[17]

In response to the report, a high-level group of experts chaired by Martin Bangemann was invited by the EC in December 1993 to examine these issues and to make specific recommendations toward achieving a comprehensive plan. The group submitted its report entitled *Europe and the Global Information Society* to the European Council of Corfu in June 1994. The Bangemann report proposes the development of enhanced information networks and telecommunications services based on a partnership between the public and private sectors. The report further recommends that the financing of both infrastructure and services should be accomplished in the private sector. Specifically, the Bangemann report identifies a number of projects that are vital to an advanced information economy, including distance learning, health care networks, telecommuting, and a trans-European public administration network.[18]

The Bangemann report also asserts the need for an improved and more flexible approach to telecommunications regulation. The first two recommendations are highly deregulatory in nature:

1. The opening up of telecommunications infrastructure and services to competition.
2. The gradual removal of political constraints (and subsidies) of monopoly service providers.
3. The establishment of a European regulatory authority to supervise telecommunications operations within the EC.

ECONOMIC CONCENTRATION AND THE MARKETPLACE OF IDEAS

In response to the Bangemann report, the EC Council adopted an action plan entitled *Europe's Way to the Information Society*, which underscores the necessity of a coordinated approach for the implementation of enhanced telecommunications networks and services.[19] The Bangemann report and the EC's action plan provide the framework for the European Community's future transition to an information economy.

ECONOMIC CONCENTRATION AND THE MARKETPLACE OF IDEAS

The combination of deregulation and privatization has transformed the conduct of international business. The TNMC is the most powerful economic force for global media activity that the 1980s has produced. Through a process of FDI, the TNMC actively promotes the use of advanced media technology including VCRs, cable television, multimedia, and DBS. Such efforts have ignited the transborder flow of media products worldwide. The resulting globalization of media activity has forced both governments and policymakers alike to consider the long-term implications. The concluding section of this chapter considers the issue of economic concentration and the marketplace of ideas. For it is this issue, above all others, that will affect the cause of media diversity and free expression.

In principle, deregulation and privatization are supposed to foster competition and thereby open markets to new service providers. The example of U.S. and British telecommunications equipment manufacturers are often cited as examples to support this position. Moscow (1990), however, presented a series of arguments that attempted to show how deregulation can sometimes lead to economic consolidation and thereby limit competition and new product development. He cited the example of the U.S. airline industry.[20] In 1978, the U.S. airline industry was composed of 11 major airline carriers. Since then, the number of active airline carriers has been significantly reduced. Not only is there less competition, but there is widespread concern over what an oligopoly means to professional standards, including price, customer service, and safety.

The Business of Information and Media Entertainment

The problem of economic concentration poses some unique problems for the TNMC whose principal product is information and entertainment. The real question is what transnational media ownership means to the future of new and diverse media products and services? According to Bagdikian (1990), the major issue is one of influence. Bagdikian's central argument is that a small set of dominant media corporations exercise a disproportionate effect over the marketplace of ideas:

Market dominant corporations in the mass media have dominant influence over the public's news, information, public ideas, popular culture, and political attitudes. The same corporations exert considerable influence within government precisely because they influence their audiences' perceptions of public life, including perceptions of politics and politicians as they appear—or do not appear—in the media.[21]

Implicit in such arguments is that the TNMC should be treated differently from other TNCs because of their unique ability to influence public opinion. Corporate size is presumed to limit the availability or diversity of media products and ideas in favor of promoting some type of corporate agenda. Accordingly, a policy of privatization and deregulation, if taken to its logical conclusion, will sometimes create the very problems they were meant to solve. When all that is left is a de facto monopoly, the result can be a lack of competition and a serious breakdown in professional standards. Equally important is that the company can engage in a variety of anticompetitive practices and/or exert undue influence on the marketplace. The stakes become higher when the same business activity occurs at the international level.

In all areas of media and telecommunications, there has been a move toward consolidation of companies. The increase in group and cross-media ownership is the direct result of media corporations looking for ways to promote greater internal efficiencies.[22] The ownership of broadcast stations in the United States, for example, is increasingly becoming the domain of group broadcasters whereas cable television is largely controlled by multiple system operators (MSOs). Ten MSOs control over 70% of the U.S. cable marketplace. In computer software, Microsoft Corporation is responsible for 80% of the world's PC operating system software. In Australia, News Corporation Ltd. is responsible for 66% of all newspaper production. Sony Corporation is responsible for 48% of the world's television sets. The Disney Corporation has a virtual lock on children's animated films.

Do such companies exhibit the classic forms of behavior of monopolies and/or oligopolies? Not exactly. It would be more accurate to say that most of these companies are market leaders within well-defined information boundaries. Researchers like de Sola Poole and Compaine reject many of the traditional arguments associated with economic concentration. They take the position that advancements in new media technologies including converging media formats and multiple distribution channels preclude the possibility of a few dominant media companies controlling the marketplace of ideas. Compaine cited the VCR industry as an example of a media technology that is moving faster than the ability of government and business to control its distribution and use. Similarly, the rapid emergence of the Internet is moving well beyond any one company's ability to dominate the content that is exhibited and exchanged between the millions of people who access it daily. Compaine wrote:

ECONOMIC CONCENTRATION AND THE MARKETPLACE OF IDEAS 31

The empirical evidence indicates that the media structure in the United States is by far more open, diverse, and responsive to public needs and wants than at any time in history, notwithstanding the contrary sense that is suggested by headlines created when media companies merge.[23]

Group Ownership Patterns and Media Production

In the United States, the history of chain newspapers is a well-documented phenomena and may serve to illustrate the implications for other mass media. Chain newspapers allow for production efficiencies, whereby news gathering, marketing, and research can be performed on a large scale. Corporate management is able to impose its financial expectations on its newspaper subsidiaries by promoting the common sharing of editorial and marketing resources.[24] The reasons that once prompted the formation of chain newspapers are largely the same reasons prompting group ownership patterns in other mass media. Specifically, the marketplace for media products has become increasingly competitive as have the costs for doing production.

Cross-Media Ownership

There has also been a steady increase in cross-media ownership patterns as well. The convergence of media and telecommunications has prompted today's TNMC to engage in a combination of news, entertainment, and enhanced information services. Cross-media ownership allows for a variety of expanded efficiencies, including:

1. Sharing and recycling of news information.
2. Cross-marketing among the different media outlets.
3. Bulk buying and group discount (i.e., paper, supplies, computer equipment, newswire services, etc.).
4. Sharing of resources, including journalists, market researchers, management, consulting, and so on.
5. Offering clients package discounts in advertising. TNMCs like Time Warner, Bertelsmann, and News Corp. routinely offer clients package discounts in advertising that cut across several of the company's owned print and electronic media.
6. Sharing of printing and distribution efficiencies. News Corp. prints several of its British newspapers out of one publishing center located in the Wapping district of London. Similarly, Turner Broadcasting uses the same set of satellites for all its cable feeds.
7. The ability to advance complementary technologies.

The once clear lines that separated media and telecommunications are becoming less distinct. The result is a convergence of modes whereby technologies and services are becoming more fully integrated.[25] The TNMC and

Transnational Telecommunications Corporation (TNTC) are positioning themselves to become full-service providers. For companies like Time Warner, Bell Atlantic, British Telecom, and TCI, the long-term goal is to be able to offer consumers a full range of media and telecommunication services. Such companies are equally capable of delivering broadband services to the home, including voice, data, video, and utility-based communication. The full-service provider will operate as a kind of electronic supermarket that will carry both house products as well as those of other software distributors. Under this arrangement, a subscriber might elect to receive their cable services from Time Warner, their voice communication from MCI, and their energy monitoring service from Niagara Power and Electric.

TNMC Concentration and Political Influence

Critics argue that the TNMC will use its power and influence to affect the outcome of political elections and/or involve itself in political decision making. There is no simple answer to this question. The history of newspapers is filled with examples of strong publishers who used their newspapers to influence national politics. From William Randolph Hearst to William Buckley, individual newspapers and magazines have and will continue to endorse political candidates. The problem is not a uniquely transnational media issue. If anything, TNMCs like Time Warner and Bertelsmann are far too diverse to impose a unified political agenda.

At the same time, there are some exceptions. News Corporation's Rupert Murdoch (and the late Robert Maxwell) are perhaps the most notorious CEOs for injecting themselves into the political landscape. All through the 1980s, Murdoch became increasingly more conservative in his politics. Several of News Corp.'s newspapers and broadcast media were highly supportive of former British Prime Minister Margaret Thatcher and U.S. President Ronald Reagan. Murdoch routinely met with both leaders and was very supportive of their political campaigns, as well as their efforts to promote a new brand of conservatism. News Corp. played an important role in defining the political spirit of Thatcherism and the Reagan Revolution. The late Charles Douglas Home, Editor of News Corp's *Times* of London, acknowledged that Murdoch and Thatcher would consult regularly on important matters of policy.[26]

Both Prime Minister Thatcher and U.S. President Reagan responded in like kind. The Thatcher government backed Murdoch and News Corp. all during the company's stand-off with the British printing unions. Similarly, when Murdoch sought to purchase seven Metromedia stations in 1985, the FCC granted him a waiver in direct violation of its cross-ownership rules by allowing the common ownership of a broadcast station and newspaper in the same market. The Reagan-appointed FCC granted Murdoch a series of interim waivers in both the New York and Boston markets.[27] Rather than selling the New York *Post*, Murdoch did everything in his power to have the waivers extended and made permanent.

In the final analysis, Murdoch's politics are very pragmatic. Murdoch is first and foremost a businessman. He is not someone who spends a lot of time engaging in politics. His interest in politics is to a large extent directly related to his ability to conduct his business. It is for this reason that Murdoch is quite capable of supporting a Democratic mayor in New York City and a Republican president for the United States.

There is only limited evidence to suggest that the TNMC will use its vast editorial and creative facilities to regularly promote a corporate philosophy and/or to challenge the politics and policymaking of a foreign government. Instead, the TNMC is more likely to use its influence when important business issues are at stake. CEOs like Katharine Graham of the *Washington Post* have been known to use their considerable influence in advancing telecommunications policy designed to restrict both AT&T and the Bell Operating Companies from entering into electronic publishing following the breakup of AT&T in 1984. The *Washington Post* and several leading U.S. newspapers ran editorials advocating a position strongly opposed to telephone entry into electronic publishing. On such occasions, however, the TNMC or news organization is arguably no different than any company or trade organization trying to affect a political or regulatory outcome.

Advertising Source Control and Self-Censorship

Do potential advertisers impose a type of pressure on what is said by the TNMC and its many subsidiaries? The issues of advertising source control and self-censorship pose a unique problem for companies engaged in the production of information and entertainment. The marketing and editorial staffs of most commercial media are keenly aware of advertising sensitivities. One of those sensitivities is the unstated expectation that the said media will not write or televise stories that are highly critical of a major advertiser or any of its subsidiaries. There is a tacit understanding that the said advertiser is to be thought of as a valued customer. Once again, this is not uniquely a TNMC phenomenon.

In the case of the TNMC, however, the financial stakes are considerably higher. The prospective advertiser has the ability to selectively pull its advertising from any or all of the TNMCs print media and video outlets. A related problem is financial interlocking whereby senior executives of the TNMC sit on the board of directors of leading companies, and vice-versa. Many of these senior heads are from companies that are important advertisers. The situation poses a unique conflict of interest for a news organization when it comes to reporting about that company and/or its subsidiaries. In the end, it comes down to a type of self-censorship.

The problem of self-censorship can also occur when media and nonmedia properties are owned by the same corporate parent. Jean-Luc Lagardere is CEO of Hachette SA as well as Matra SA, one of France's largest defense contractors. Similarly, General Electric is parent company to the NBC television network in the United States. There is an unstated pressure and expectation that the news media division is careful when it comes to reporting about the parent company and its advertisers.

Turow's (1992) investigation of Time Warner Inc. prompted him to rework Elizabeth Noelle-Neuman's spiral of silence to describe self-censorship tendencies when it comes to reporting about internal organizational matters. According to Turow, such efforts to report about the parent organization and internal operations went largely unrewarded. Turow concluded that such efforts can in fact generate the opposite reaction from superiors who are not appreciative of self-disclosure reporting.[28]

Transnational Media and Content Neutrality

By far the most serious problem facing today's TNMC is that such companies have become content neutral. In a deregulated free market economy, profitability and market potential have become the true test of whether a creative work makes it. The TNMC, given its diverse worldwide media activities, is unlikely to impose professional or moral restraints on the production of creative works, regardless of whether such efforts are obscene, violent, or result in the invasion of privacy.

Critics argue that the TNMC needs to recognize its civic responsibility when it comes to the production of music and films that are highly sexist, violent, and profane. For example, Time Warner and Bertelsmann have come under increased scrutiny for their failure to exercise self-restraint when it comes to the marketing of select forms of rap music. It is not surprising, therefore, that members of the political establishment and citizen groups alike are taking aim at TNMCs that fail to exercise some degree of critical judgment. U.S. Senator Bob Dole and former GOP Education Secretary William Bennett are leading an effort to curb the abuses of the entertainment industries that they feel have become irresponsible in the music that is presented to the public. In June 1995, C. Delores Tucker, Head of the National Political Congress of Black Women, met with then Warner Music Group chairman Michael Fuchs. She handed him several lyrics from songs that appear on several of Time Warner's recording labels. One such lyric came from the song "Mind of a Lunatic" from the rap group Geto Boys. The lyric reads: "Her body's beautiful so I'm thinkin rape/Grabbed the bitch by her mouth slam her down on the couch./She begged in a low voice: 'Please don't kill me.'/I slit her throat and watch her shake like on TV."

Activists like Tucker have threatened to boycott Time Warner music, movies, and cable TV properties. Said Tucker, "They're pimping pornography to children for the almighty dollar. Corporations need to understand: What does it profit a corporation to gain the world but lose its soul. That's the real bottom line."[29]

The concern about public reaction is very real. On September 26, 1995, Time Warner announced that it would divest itself of its 50% interest in

Interscope records, the recording label for many prominent U.S. rap musicians.

DISCUSSION

Current trends toward deregulation and free-market economies have led to an economic concentration of media companies. The trend, however, is part of a larger worldwide movement toward transnational economic consolidation. In a highly deregulated free-market economy, strategic decision making and the allocation of resources is based on the profitability of the market and future growth potential.

International deregulation has enabled the TNMC to exercise investment opportunities around the world. In the process, media decision making and FDI is largely based on economic efficiencies with little regard for national boundaries. In assessing the potential dangers of economic concentration, the TNMC is unlikely to use its creative and editorial facilities to promote a corporate agenda. TNMCs like Time Warner or Bertelsmann are far too diverse in their business operations. There is limited evidence to support the argument that the TNMC will engage in power politics. Even Murdoch's News Corp., although admittedly conservative, is first and foremost a business. The company's primary objective is profitability, and not the worldwide imposition of a corporate or political agenda. Such efforts would be counterproductive to an open marketplace of ideas.

The real problem is diametrically opposite. Today's TNMC has effectively become content (software) neutral. The desire for profitability has made the modern TNMC unwilling or unable to impose critical judgment as to whether such media works are appropriate for public consumption. The proliferation of tabloid journalism, soft-core pornography, sexist rap music, and television and film violence underscore their commercial viability. In an open marketplace of ideas, the TNMC does not stop to ask whether such materials are suitable for the public. Company officials are more likely to cite the phrase, "We're only giving the public what it wants."

As the world's economy becomes more fully privatized, the goal of nation states and the goal of TNMCs will increasingly find themselves on a collision course. For it is the purpose of nation states to strengthen the cause of political and economic sovereignty whereas the goal of the TNC is profitability. By failing to exercise critical judgment, the TNMC has squarely placed itself in direct confrontation with government regulators and citizen groups alike.

There are few international laws to govern the conduct of transnational media corporations. Countries like China, Malaysia, and Saudi Arabia (to name only a few) have taken it on themselves to exercise critical judgment when it comes to media imports. They establish program quotas or standards based on religious or cultural codes of conduct. Yet these same countries are strong adherents to free-market economies. For such countries, there is no apparent conflict. International deregulation and privatization is admittedly a delicate balancing act that requires government and its representative agencies to properly function as the nation's defenders of the public interest and moral codes while participating in an interdependent global economy.

NOTES

[1] Ira W. Lieberman, "Privatization: The Theme of the 1990's," *Columbia Journal of World Business* (28)1, Spring, 1993, pp. 10–11.

[2] Ibid.

[3] "Has the FCC Gone Too Far?" *Business Week*, 5 August, 1985, p. 48.

[4] It is important to note that the deregulatory efforts of the Reagan administration were not simply confined to the United States. In November 1984, the Reagan administration, in conjunction with the FCC, declared its support for privately owned international satellites. In keeping with its deregulatory philosophy, the United States issued its so-called "open skies" policy by supporting the development of separate satellite systems with the proviso that such systems pose no economic threat to the future viability of Intelsat. See Richard A. Gershon, "Intelsat: Global Cooperation in an Era of Deregulation," (14)7 June 1990.

The U.S. administration's adoption of an open-skies policy was consistent with three earlier regulatory activities: In *Re Applications of Microwave Communications Inc*, 18 FCC 2d 953 (1969); FCC Report and Order, Docket # 19528; and *United States v American Telephone and Telegraph Company, Western Electric Company Inc, and Bell Telephone Laboratories Inc*, US District Court (DC Cir. 1974), Civil Action 74-1698, Civil Action No. 82-0192 ("Modified Final Judgment," 1982). In all three actions, the intention was to promote greater competition in the provision of telecommunication products and services.

[5] *United States v AT&T*, 552 F Supp 131 (DDC 1982), *Maryland v United States*, 460 US 1001 (1983).

[6] Cable Communications Policy Act of 1984, 47 U.S.C. (1984).

[7] The Telecommunications Act of 1996. The following are just a few of the more significant highlights.

Under the terms of the Act, national broadcast ownership limits have been significantly reduced. It also relaxes local ownership caps. The rules follow a step ladder approach, whereby the larger the market, the more stations one company may own. All license renewal applications for both radio and television are now extended to 8 years. (The former license renewal procedure was 5 years for television and 7 years for radio.) The Act also streamlines the renewal process. Barring a serious violation, a radio or television broadcaster can expect that their license will be renewed.

The Act substantially relaxes rules governing cable television systems resulting from the passage of the 1992 Cable Act. Rate regulation restrictions will be removed effective March 1, 1999 on all cable systems except the basic tier that includes all over-the-air channels and public and educational channels. Pricing freedom is available sooner for cable television companies that face effective competition from local telephone companies or other video service providers.

The Telecommunications Act of 1996 is also important with respect to who can provide cable and telephone service in the United States The Act repeals all statutory bans against telephone companies from providing video programming in their own service areas. Telephone companies can elect to become cable operators or they can function as common carriers or open video systems providers. Likewise, cable operators are now able to provide telephone service both inside and outside their areas. The Act, however, does not allow cable companies to buy telephone companies (or vice versa), except in nonurban areas with fewer than 35,000 people and under other limited circumstances.

[8]"The Sun Never Sets on British Telecom," *Business Week*, 7 December, 1992, p. 54.

[9]Peter Dunnett, "United Kingdom: A Declining Role for Auntie," *The World Television Industry*, (London: Routledge, 1990), pp. 130–133.

[10]Ibid., p. 140.

[11]One indication of the perceived inefficiency was the 1987 case involving Thames television. After a labor dispute, a controversial production that involved 30 technicians being paid triple time was later reproduced with seven technicians at time and a half.

[12]The formation of the NTT public corporation in 1952 made possible the remarkable recovery of telecommunications facilities from the destruction caused by WWII. It enabled Japan to offer universal telephone service to its citizens.

[13]Richard A. Gershon, "Reform of Japan's Telecommunications Operations," *Telecommunications Magazine*, December, 1984, p. 82.

[14]The four common carriers are collectively referred to as Type I carriers. Three offer basic telephone service between Tokyo and Osaka and include Japan Telecom Company, Teleway Japan Corporation, and Daini-Denden Inc. Another carrier, the Tokyo Telecommunications network, a subsidiary of the electric utility monopoly of Tokyo's Kanto district, provides local services in that area. See Tsuruhiko Nambu, Kazuyuki Suzuki, and Tetsushi Honda, "Deregulation in Japan," *Changing the Rules: Technological Change, International Competition and Regulation in Communications*, (Eds.) R. Crandall and K. Flamm, (Washington, DC: Brookings Institution, 1989), pp. 150–151.

[15]Marilyn Young and Michael Launer, "Redefining Glasnost in the Soviet Media? The Recontextualization of Chernobyl," *Journal of Communication* 41(2), Spring, 1991, pp. 102–124.

[16]Hans Schoof and Adam Watson Brown, "Information Highways and Media Policies in the European Union," *Telecommunications Policy*, 19(4), 1995, pp. 325–338.

[17]European Commission, *Growth, Competitiveness, Employment—The Challenges and Ways Forward into the 21st Century*, White paper, COM(93), 700, December 5, 1993.

[18]*Europe and the Global Information Society*, A report of the High Level Group on the Information Society, Martin Bangemann, Chair, submitted to the European Community Council, June 1994.

[19]Schoof and Brown, pp. 329–330.

[20]Vincent Moscow, "The Mythology of Telecommunications Deregulation," *Journal of Communication*, 40(1), Winter, 1990, pp. 43–45.

[21]Ben Bagdikian, *The Media Monopoly*, 3rd ed. (Boston: Beacon Press, 1990), pp. 4–5.

[22]Hollywood has likewise adopted formula approaches to the making of movies that include numerous sequels to those movies that have developed a proven track record. The result is an endless repeat of tried and true movie sequels, including *Rocky I-V, Star Trek I-V, Beverly Hills Cop I-III, Home Alone I* and *II*, and so on.

[23]Benjamin M. Compaine, "The Expanding Base of Media Competition," *Journal of Communication*, 35(3), Summer, 1985.

[24]The Gannett Corporation is the largest newspaper chain in the United States and is often cited as an example of what is best and worst in newspaper production. Critics of newspaper chains are quick to point out how formula (or recipe) approaches to media production result in a similarity of format between one chain newspaper and the next. Gannett newspapers have sometimes been described as the journalistic equivalent of fast food.

[25]Richard A. Gershon, "Is Videodialtone the Future of Telephone Programming?" *Telephony*, 9 November, 1992, pp. 20–26.

[26]William Shawcross, *Murdoch*, (New York: Simon & Schuster, 1992), p. 199.

[27]"Court Comes Down for Murdoch on Crossownership," *Broadcasting*, 4 April, 1988, pp. 40–41.

[28]Joseph Turow, "Organizational Tensions and Journalistic Norms," A presentation given to the 42nd International Communication Association Conference, Miami, FL, May 23, 1992.

[29]"Gunning for Gangstas," *Business Week*, 19 June, 1995, p. 41.

3

The Globalization of Television Trade and Distribution

In the years that followed World War II, the global economy grew at an unprecedented rate. It was expected that the period of the 1950s would be a time of considerable growth as war-damaged economies throughout the world began the process of rebuilding. In fact, however, growth rates far exceeded most expectations. Growth rates were especially impressive in the area of manufacturing. Between the years 1948 and 1968, international trade showed a steady rate of increase as indicated: 1948 to 1953, 6.7%; 1958 to 1963, 7.4%; 1963 to 1968, 8.6%.[1]

International economic growth was suddenly disrupted with the onslaught of a worldwide recession. A major contributing factor was the OPEC decision in 1973 to increase oil prices by 400%. Other contributing factors were increased labor costs among several industrialized nations, as well as international exchange rates becoming increasingly unstable. The recovery was slow and uneven. It was not until the early 1980s that the world's economy began to flourish.

What has emerged is a world economy that is fundamentally different than the period immediately following World War II. Since the mid-1970s, manufacturing is no longer the sole province of a few highly industrialized nations and corporations. Instead, a new international division of labor has emerged, whereby geographical patterns of specialization are taking place, albeit on a global scale. The world's economy has seen the evolution of three principle trading zones including North America, Europe, and Southeast Asia. Seventy-seven percent of the world's exports are generated within these three regions. These three primary zones are both the source and beneficiary of FDI among the world's leading TNCs.[2]

INTERNATIONAL TELEVISION AND FILM DISTRIBUTION

The Economics of Program Supply

The study of international media trade cannot be considered without fully appreciating the larger dimensions of the economic system in which they operate. The business of international media trade is affected by many of the same economic forces that apply to other types of commercial enterprises. The sale and distribution of television and film products are first and foremost a business. According to Picard (1989):

> Media in the United States are for the most part capitalist ventures operated by private parties for the purpose of generating profit, and are thus subject to the operational principles of the market system. Even not for profit media—such as public broadcasting or organizational operated media—are influenced by the principles of the market system and are thus affected by its operations.[3]

There are two economic assumptions that characterize the foreign sale and distribution of television and film products. The first is that television and film products are examples of a public good. The cost of production is independent of the number of people who consume it. If a foreign viewer watches television, this action does not prevent others from watching.[4]

A second important assumption is that the costs of television and film production are fixed. Once the cost of production has been realized, the cost per viewer declines as the size of the audience increases. It costs much less to produce a single program for worldwide distribution than it does to produce separate programs for individual markets.[5] The objective, therefore, is to maximize audience reach and to favor those distribution media that can accomplish this.

Program producers try to maximize the sale of television and film products by carefully planning the selection of distribution windows and release times. Owen and Wildman (1992) refer to this as *windowing*; that is, the method by which television and film products are sold and distributed using "different distribution channels at different times."[6] The practice of windowing shapes the many competitive interactions between program producers and the various systems of delivery. The number of distribution windows has increased significantly since the early 1980s and now includes theatrical release, basic and pay cable television, videocassette rentals, DBS, multipoint multichannel distribution service (MMDS), and network television and syndication, both domestic and foreign. Table 3.1 considers some of the more typical release windows for U.S. films and their initial release time.

The practice of windowing allows television and film producers to price discriminate; that is, they have the ability to sell their products to individual buyers at different prices. This is especially important when it comes to international television trade and distribution. In principle, the producer can sell television and film products at a price that best reflects their value and affordability to individual buyers, rather than selling at a uniform price. The producer will sell programs at a price that the importing nation or broadcast service can afford to pay.[7] As a consequence, many countries often find it cheaper to buy U.S. and/or foreign programming than to produce locally made television. Sepstrup's (1990) research indicates that the supply of television hours and purchase price is determined by a number of related factors,

TABLE 3.1
Release Windows for U.S. Theatrical Films

Theaters	Months From Initial Release
Theaters	0–4+
Overseas theaters	4–18+
Home video	6–30+
Overseas home video	9–24+
First U.S. cable run	12–36+
U.S. broadcast network	36–60
Overseas broadcasters	48–60
Second U.S. cable run	66–72+
Syndication to U.S. television stations	72+

Note. Source: The Economist[8]

including the size of the home market, total economic resources available, language, per capita income, and the level of commercialization.[9]

The Nature of Program Demand

Television has become an important source of entertainment and information for much of the world's population. It has become the single most important influence in shaping today's popular culture. Television touches on all phases of human experience, including music, dress, food, sports, politics, and religion. Some critics have observed how the traditional arts have taken centuries to wield their cultural influence, whereas television's dramatic impact has occurred in less than three decades.

Television's international popularity has increased steadily since the mid-1960s. For an ever-increasing amount of the world's population, television has become the principal leisure activity. Table 3.2 illustrates the growth in international television set use among 25 select nations between the years 1967 and 1994.

The combination of worldwide privatization trends, coupled with advancements in new media technologies, has led to the gradual introduction of private commercial television stations throughout the world. Since the early 1980s, more and more countries are deregulating state-controlled television media in favor of privatization and competition. The trend is toward a dual system of broadcasting similar to the United Kingdom that allows private commercial television to coexist with state-owned television services. European counties such as the United Kingdom, France, Germany, Portugal, Spain, and Italy have all seen a gradual rise in private commercial television. Nor are such changes confined to Western Europe. The burgeoning democratic movements throughout Russia and the former Eastern bloc countries have begun the slow, arduous

TABLE 3.2
Growth in International Television Set Use: 25 Selected Nations: 1967–1994 (in Millions)[a]

Country	1967	1974	1981	1987	1994
Argentina	1.6	4.0	6.0	6.6	7.2
Australia	2.7	3.5	5.5	6.1	8.5
Brazil	5.5	8.7	15.0	22.0	59.0
Canada	5.7	9.1	10.0	12.1	19.4
Chile	0.1	1.0	1.3	1.5	4.8
China (Mainland)	0.1	2.7	3.8	11.8	150.0[b]
Denmark	1.1	1.6	1.8	2.0	2.7
France	7.2	14.8	19.0	25.0	32.0
Germany	12.5	17.1	24.9	25.3	42.2[c]
Greece	—	0.8	1.5	1.8	6.0
India	—	0.2	1.2	9.7	22.0
Iran	0.1	0.2	2.0	2.6	6.0
Italy	6.7	12.5	13.4	14.5	24.0
Japan	19.0	25.0	63.0	71.0	90.0
Korea (South)	0.1	1.1	5.3	7.3	9.3
Malaysia	0.1	0.7	1.1	1.6	2.6
Mexico	1.8	5.5	8.5	14.7	21.4
Nigeria	—	0.1	0.5	4.0	5.1
Norway	0.6	1.0	1.2	1.4	1.5
Poland	2.5	5.7	7.4	9.4	11.0
Romania	0.5	1.9	3.4	3.9	4.0
Saudi Arabia	—	0.3	0.3	1.5	3.8
Spain	2.1	5.6	9.6	12.6	15.2
United Kingdom	15.2	17.8	18.5	19.5	20.0
United States	70.3	84.6	121.0	155.8	195.0

[a]Most international research examining television set use differentiates between the number of television sets in circulation and television households (TV HH). This table identifies number of television sets in use. This becomes important when examining countries like Japan where TV HH is approximately 43 million, whereas, the number of television sets in use equals 90 million. No effort is made to distinguish between black-and-white and color sets.

[b]The information for this table was primarily obtained from the *Television and Cable Factbook* with additional information supplied by UNESCO and the *World Guide to Television & Video*. The data reported in this table are broad estimates. The accuracy of data varies somewhat from country to country. This is in part due to the quality of reporting by government ministry officials when filling out surveys. Some countries do not distinguish between (TV HH) and television sets in circulation. Some countries, as in the case of China, inflate their numbers or have no reliable way of reporting such information. There are also inconsistencies in the publications themselves such as the *Television and Cable Fact Book* where a country like Saudi Arabia is reported to have 300,000 television sets in use in 1981 and 1987.

[c]The former East Germany is now included in all reporting of German economic activity, including the sizable increase of television sets in use.

task of converting to a market economy. The Czech Republic, Slovakia, Poland, and Hungary are awarding greater concessions to commercial television and radio networks.[10]

Privatization is also taking place in different parts of Asia. The countries of Japan, Singapore, Hong Kong, South Korea, Thailand, Indonesia, and the Philippines are allowing new commercial program providers to enter those markets. This has been especially true for the cable television and Pan-Asian satellite television provider, Star TV. At the same time, media reform varies from one country to another. Many Asian countries have different rules concerning the reception of satellite television. For example, Malaysia prohibits the sale of satellite dishes to individual homes whereas Hong Kong is a strong proponent of it.

Although privatization has led to an increase in television and radio channels, few countries have the production capability to fill the sudden increased demand for programming. As a result, many domestic television broadcasters and cable networks will continue to rely on imported programming.

INTERNATIONAL TELEVISION EXPORTS

In past years, the U.S. television and film industries designed programs for the U.S. market with the expectation that good programming could be sold abroad. Television programs were produced for the U.S. market with little or no thought given to the suitability for a foreign market audience. In addition, the export of television and film products was highly profitable because no additional production costs were involved. The only real costs associated with the export of U.S. programming were related to distribution and language dubbing. For many nations, the purchase of U.S. television and film represented a less costly alternative than producing one's own programs.

Historically, the United States has led the way in providing much of the world's television and film entertainment. The sale of television and film products in overseas markets represents about half of all total sales for major U.S. producers. The foreign sale of film products generates a greater percentage of revenues outside the United States than it does domestically.[11] Varis' (1984) seminal work determined that imported television programming filled approximately one third of all broadcast hours in foreign countries.[12] The Motion Picture Association of America (MPAA) estimates that foreign countries spend up to $7.5 billion per year on U.S. television and film products.[13]

Although U.S.-made programming is still very attractive to foreign audiences, national governments have become increasingly concerned with the amount of U.S. media products that are routinely imported into local markets. In particular, U.S. television and films are presumed to be culturally laden with American images and artifacts. If given the choice, however, national and locally produced television and films are generally favored by a nation and its people over imported programming. As a consequence, many nations want to take firmer control over the import of foreign-made programming.

Regulatory Barriers to Entry

The same nations that, heretofore, imported U.S. programming have slowly begun to develop domestic media production that will lessen their dependency on U.S. and other foreign-made programming.[14] One way to accomplish this is through the imposition of regulatory barriers or program quotas. Canada, as an example, has long understood the potential benefits and difficulties of being geographically close to the United States. Although Canada may be a strong adherent to the North American Free Trade Agreement (NAFTA), this is the same country that has strict policies concerning the import of U.S.-made television.

It is not surprising, therefore, that several regulatory initiatives, most notably the European Television Without Frontiers Directive are designed to aggressively promote the development of indigenous television and film works. Ironically, as most countries seek to privatize and deregulate, there is a simultaneous effort to impose regulation in the area of television and film imports.

THE CASE OF EUROPEAN TELEVISION AND A SINGLE UNIFIED MARKET

In 1985, the EC heads of state agreed to a program comprising 300 separate pieces of legislation that would lead to a unified single market by 1992. The original timetable was designed to be front-loaded in order to allow sufficient time for EC nations to enact their own legislation that would bring them into compliance with future EC law. The result of this effort was the passage of the European Community Act, which provides the legal framework for future political and economic cooperation among member nations.[15] As already mentioned in chapter 2, revisions in telecommunications policy and planning now put the year 1998 as the target date for the full implementation of changes.

Two of the more prominent features of the European Act are the stated willingness to share scientific and artistic expertise among EC nations. Second, the European Act encourages the free movement of products and services across national boundaries. Nowhere are the proposed changes more profound than in the area of television and film production. On October 3, 1989, the EC, in a meeting of the 12 nation's foreign ministers, adopted by a 10 to 2 vote the Television Without Frontiers directive. Specifically, EC Directive 89/552 is intended to promote European television and film production. The plan calls for an open market for television broadcasting by reducing barriers and restrictions placed on cross-border transmissions. In addition, the EC

Directive is intended to promote business partnerships, provide tax breaks and reserve a majority of airtime for European works.

The Regulatory Challenge

As the EC moves toward unification, one of its most urgent needs is to unify the media laws among its 12 member nations. Otherwise, all newly proposed transborder television services are likely to face a maze of conflicting requirements among the various EC nations. The Council of Europe's passage of EC Directive 89/552 will affect EC member nations in three critical areas, including program quotas, increased advertising, and international partnerships and coproduction ventures.

Program Quotas

The EC is very concerned that the majority of broadcast airtime is filled with European programming. The Television Without Frontiers directive requires member states to insure "where practicable and by appropriate means" that broadcasters reserve for European works a majority proportion of their transmission time, excluding the time allocated for news, sports, games, advertising, and teletext services. The proportion is to be achieved progressively, with the European Commission (the executive branch of the EC) responsible for supervising its implementation.[16]

Present efforts to establish program quotas are an attempt to respond to both cultural and economic pressures. As Guback (1990) pointed out, European officials have long been concerned with the amount of U.S. programming that has culturally saturated European television in the past.[17] According to Mark Fisher, UK Labor Party Art & Media spokesperson, "What people are worried about is that [US programming] would become an unregulated flood and sweep away local drama and series, and its very important that we have a balance between international product and our own national culture and identity."[18]

Similarly, Carlo Freccero, Program Director for France's La Cinq Network, argues that Europe's broadcast practitioners are trying to find an accommodation between international television (of which U.S. films represent a standard model) and a "family TV that is tied to each country's national experience."[19] Jean Dondelinger, EC Commissioner for Media has tried to downplay the importance of the Television Without Frontiers directive by acknowledging that the United States has been and will continue to be the dominant supplier of television programs and films on the world market. At the same time, he has expressed the EC's desire to "regulate a European space" where the continent should at least have a 50% share of its own market. According to Dondelinger "You are certainly aware that Europeans are very far behind in film and television production. It is the responsibility of European governments to promote that sector—not to just subsidize production."[20]

European Advertising

Deregulation and privatization presents new opportunities for advertisers. In past years, many European and Scandinavian nations have placed restrictions on the amount and type of advertisements that could appear on domestic television. The countries of Denmark, Sweden, and Norway, for example, have historically disallowed any form of commercial advertising on their domestic television systems. Similarly, the countries of Germany, Switzerland, Belgium, and the Netherlands had imposed restrictions on the amount of time available for advertising. The United Kingdom was the only country in the EC that adhered to a dual system of broadcasting that allowed advertiser-supported television to coexist with its public system. All this is beginning to change with the development of advertiser-supported television.

As TNMCs gear up for the new Europe, they must determine whether their marketing and advertising plans are best achieved by producing local ads for each market, or by adopting a pan-European strategy that presumes a single, unified market approach. The distribution technologies of cable television and DDBS are affording TNMCs and advertisers increased opportunities for both regional and narrowcasted advertising.

International Barter Syndication

Dupagne (1991) reported that the U.S. commercial practice of barter and cost-plus-barter are beginning to appear in Western Europe. Barter is the practice of licensing and/or distributing a program at no cost in exchange for commercial airtime. The syndicator, in effect, retains some commercial spots for their own ads, providing the rest of the commercial minutes for the station to sell at its own discretion.[21] Some barter arrangements also include the payment of cash as well as advertising minutes.

International barter syndication holds strategic implications for the TNMC that either owns or works closely with Transnational Advertising Agencies (TNAAs). In addition to increased market share, the syndicator and TNAA realize certain synergies and economies of scale in the combining of programming and advertising. The close cooperative relationship allows for national and international advertising campaigns. The practice of international barter syndication is not without its critics. The availability of free programming is very appealing to those countries and their respective broadcast services that are severely underfinanced. However, many find the practice objectionable because the broadcast service (station) has relinquished editorial control.

Creating a New TV in Europe

The EC schedules an estimated 125,000 hours of television programming per year. Prior to 1992, only 20,000 hours were being produced locally. Great Britain, France, and Germany are the most successful at producing the majority of their own television programs. There are two explanations that account for the obvious shortage in television software production. The first has to do with financial constraints, a holdover from Europe's government-sponsored television past. For those countries that operated under a PT&T arrangement, state-supported television routinely found itself having to compete with other government agencies (i.e., education, health, and defense) for scarce financial resources.[22]

Second, there was not an established tradition for European based coproductions. The more established television broadcasters were reasonably self-sufficient. According to Bernard Miyet, France's Director General of Cultural Affairs:

> The broadcasting industry in Europe has been organized for decades on a national basis in the framework of public monopolies and with local regulations imposing production and broadcasting of local productions. As all of these public monopolies were financed through the license fee, there was no real problem of financing and broadcasting local productions at least for the main countries. [Italy, France, Spain, Germany and the UK.] The main countries could produce everything for themselves without buying or co-producing with other countries. That is the first thing. . . .
>
> Secondly, there were too many differences in terms of structure, language and recognition of the TV and movie stars to try and buy things from these other European countries. For decades and decades, the only foreign movies reaching every European country were the American movies.[23]

The EC hopes to encourage the progressive development of a European television industry. In order to accomplish this, the EC Directive places an important emphasis on European works. The said work should originate within the EC community or elsewhere in Europe. In addition, the work should be principally made by producers, writers, and actors living in Europe. In 1991, the EC approved a $ 250 million funding plan over 5 years called Media 92 that will help European TV and film producers and distributors to compete against U.S. and other foreign made programs.

As Europe becomes more fully privatized, the sudden increase in television channels will afford greater opportunities for European television and coproduction ventures. The main challenge that lies ahead in achieving successful European coproduction is the need to move beyond the equal sharing of responsibilities to a position where one nation or production company is able to assume responsibility for the production and financing of a given project. Their success will be in trying to produce television and films that have regional appeal rather than being targeted to one national audience. Two notable European coproduction ventures include a pay-TV service called Premiere that brings together Germany's Bertelsmann, France's Canal Plus (Europe's top pay TV service), and the Kirch group, a well-respected German production house. The Premiere service comprises feature films, sports, and live events.

The service began in the spring of 1991. A second major European coproduction entity is called Starcom; a three-way production venture between Germany's Kirch Group, Silvio Berlusconi Communications (Reteitalia) of Italy, and TFI of France.

Overcoming Regulatory Barriers to Entry: Program Quotas and GATT

For the TNMC and other television and film distributors a proposed European quota system could have a profound influence on the future export of television and film products. In past years, the export of U.S. television and film programming has been very successful in Europe. The MPAA estimates that the sale of U.S. television and film to Europe accounts for some $3 billion in annual revenues. This represents more than one third of all U.S. international television and film sales.

The U.S. television and film industries are especially concerned with the EC Directive on program quotas. During the General Agreement on Tariffs and Trade (GATT) talks in 1993, the United States took the position that television and film entertainment is a type of commercial product that should be allowed to compete in an internationally free marketplace. EC attempts to include cultural exemptions is viewed by the United States as a form of trade protectionism. According to MPAA President Jack Valenti:

> In an era when the phrase "surplus balance of trade" is seldom heard in our land, the U.S. visual entertainment industry is one of the U.S.A.'s glittering trade jewels. . . . Our movies and TV programs are hospitably received by citizens around the world. But if the U.S. signs a GATT agreement that submits to the isolation, the exemption or exile of American audio-visual material, we will have forfeited the future of one of the few U.S. products whose mastery in world markets is affirmed.[24]

Despite such assertions, the EC held firm to its position that anything having to do with culture be exempted from the final GATT trade agreement that was reached in December 1993. The issue of television and film quotas remains one of the few unresolved issues of the final GATT accord. The current status of the GATT agreement allows EC nations (as well as all nations) the flexibility to impose television and film import quotas at random. Specifically, the United States stands to lose the most if this exemption is codified into a final services agreement.

Research consultants Frost and Sullivan (1991) indicated that U.S. television and film distributors still control 69% of the international syndication market.[25] And although it can be argued that U.S. television producers have long dominated the international syndication market, there has in fact been a slow steady erosion of U.S. market share. Research performed by Carvath (1992) also indicates that U.S. market share has steadily declined. According to Carvath:

Where once the U.S. firms held international competitive advantage in the media industry, a number of developments—economic recession, global media mergers and acquisitions, legal and cultural import barriers in the European Community and Japan, and strategic miscalculations by U.S. media firms—have helped erode that competitive advantage.[26]

International Partnerships and Coproduction Ventures

As Europe begins to redefine its economic future, so too will the TNMC and U.S. entertainment industries. The result of the 1993 GATT negotiations is that the EC will continue to support program quota restrictions on foreign-made programming. As a result, the TNMCs and U.S. television and film distributors will be forced to readjust their business strategy accordingly. As a first measure, the United States, will continue to negotiate at the international level for a lessening of national quotas on television program imports. In addition, the United States is likely to seek a World Trade Organization (formerly GATT) resolution on international rules that apply to cultural issues.

The major buyers of U.S. television programs have traditionally been the leading industrialized nations. In order to offset the potential effects of program quotas, the TNMC and U.S. television and film distributors are likely to form international partnerships and/or engage in coproduction ventures. By becoming a European company or having a European affiliate, the TNMC and U.S. television and film distributors can exercise greater control over their international trade and export practices.

International partnerships and coproduction ventures have emerged as one of the most important programming trends of the 1990s. As a business strategy, they represent the most direct way of overcoming regulatory barriers to entry. In addition, the international partnership offers other strategic advantages as well, including the sharing in production costs, expanded market opportunities, operational and distribution efficiencies, and tax benefits and subsidies.

For the short term, the TNMC and other television and film distributors will continue to do well in those markets where new television services are coming on line. There will be a decided need to fill the programming void resulting from the start-up of so many cable and satellite-based services. The solution, in part, requires these media companies to produce and coproduce narrowcasted services and specialized language programming to the smaller, newly formed European channels. In short, the TNMC and its European counterparts will form Europroduction houses. Such productions will be designed exclusively for the European market. The early 1990s witnessed a number of U.S. coproduction deals including ABC's 49% interest in Tele-Munchen, a Munich-based TV production and distribution company; and German public broadcaster ZDF. Likewise, CBS and British commercial broadcaster Grenada Television have several coproduction agreements. NBC and Yorkshire TV have formed Tango Productions to coproduce for the international marketplace.

PROGRAM PACKAGING AND THE TECHNOLOGIES OF DISTRIBUTION

The development of new delivery systems and more affordable consumer electronics is enabling individuals to have access to a greater amount of programming than ever before. Whether it be video parlors in Pakistan or cable television in Argentina, present and future opportunities exist for media and telecommunication companies wishing to engage in program packaging and distribution. The three most notable technologies include cable television, DBS, and videocassette rentals. For the purpose of this discussion, we will consider cable television and DBS.

Cable Television

Cable television is a communications system that distributes broadcast and satellite-delivered programming by means of a closed wire network. The standard cable television system consists of three parts including the headend point, the distribution network, and the receiving equipment. The headend is the site of the receiving antenna and signal processing equipment. The cable company uses a combination of television antennas, satellite receiving dishes, and microwave receivers to gather in, downconvert, and process all incoming signals. Once the signals have been processed and assigned new frequencies, they are then transmitted via coaxial or fiber optic cable to the subscriber's home. The cable distribution network is patterned after a tree-and-branch architecture. In a typical cable system, the drop line coming into the subscriber's home connects to a converter box or directly to the user's television set.

Cable television got its start in the United States in the early 1950s. At that time, cable television was used primarily for improved television reception. Starting in the mid-1970s, the blending of satellite and cable communications created what Gershon (1990) described as the "satellite cable interface."[27] Prior to HBO, there was no precedent for the extensive use of satellite-delivered programming in the United States. HBO's 1975 decision to use satellite communications forever changed the broadcast and cable television industries. The satellite cable interface unlocked a floodgate of new cable programmers that were equally capable of leasing satellite time, including WTBS (1976), CNN (1980), Showtime (1978), ESPN (1979), USA (1980), and MTV (1981) to name only a few.[28]

Cable television's most enduring contribution is that it has given consumers greater choice in terms of program selection. The international development of cable television has been largely influenced by the U.S. experience. Cable television has become especially important in those parts of the world where governments are looking to downsize their role and involvement in television production. Table 3.3 provides a comparison of select countries according to

TABLE 3.3
International Cable Television Development (1995)

Country	Television Households (TV HH)	Cable Households (Cable HH)	Cable HH as a Percentage of TV HH
Argentina	9,050,000	4,900,000	54%
Austria	2,650,000	1,020,000	38%
Belgium	3,900,000	3,594,304	92%
Canada	10,286,000	7,994,800	78%
Chile	3,500,000	320,000	9%
China	280,000,000	30,000,000	11%
Czech Republic	3,815,000	450,000	12%
Denmark	2,338,868	1,173,000	50%
France	22,516,000	1,625,900	7%
Germany	37,400,000	14,647,000	39%
Israel	1,250,000	720,000	58%
Japan	43,100,000	8,340,000	19%
Mexico	15,100,000	2,000,000	13%
Netherlands	6,500,000	5,700,000	88%
Norway	1,500,000	610,000	41%
Slovakia	1,700,000	280,000	16%
Sweden	3,500,000	1,800,000	51%
Switzerland	2,559,534	2,235,900	87%
United Kingdom	21,600,000	908,018	4%
United States	94,930,000	58,800,000	62%

Note. Data from USA National Cable Television Association.

television households (TV HH), cable households (Cable HH), and Cable HH as a percentage of television households.

Much of the programming available on today's worldwide cable systems is distributed by several of the more well established cable program services in the United States. Perhaps the best known U.S.-based cable service is Ted Turner's Cable News Network, which is received in more than 210 countries around the world via 12 satellites. CNN has become the world's most widely viewed television news service. CNN is routinely watched by world leaders and citizens alike and has had a major impact on international news coverage.

> Among the most avid watchers of CNN, although they don't always like to admit it, are other journalists. In almost every major U.S. newsroom and in many elsewhere in the world, the channel is perpetually on and someone is watching, or at least glancing over frequently. Once upon a time, newspapers broke the

news to the public. Then TV took over that role, and ever since, newspapers have tried to redefine themselves by becoming more analytical. Now, even most TV reporters try and pride themselves on doing a story analytically and in depth; it is a foregone conclusion that CNN will do the story first.[29]

Although CNN has had the most dramatic impact on international television and cable television distribution, there are many U.S. based cable services that are now beginning to emerge worldwide. According to CNN's founder, Ted Turner:

The really big development that will occur in the 90s is that the rest of the world will be catching up with the multitude of formats that are occurring here in the United States—and that's already happening. Cable is going into Israel and direct satellite in Europe and Japan and so forth. And there will be cable or DBS in Hong Kong. So the people will be getting more choices in other parts of the world and that always in creases total television viewing.[30]

Table 3.4 provides a listing of of some of the more notable U.S.-based cable services and the regions or countries of the world that they currently serve.

Direct Broadcast Satellites

The communication satellite has long captivated the imagination of development planners and business entrepreneurs. For many countries, the communication satellite has become an integral part of the development process. The communication satellite, in essence, is a microwave relay operating 22,300 miles above the earth's equator. It receives microwave signals in a given frequency and retransmits them at a different frequency. The communication satellite makes it possible to reach isolated places on the earth and is considerably less expensive than terrestrial links for purposes of broadcasting and thin route communication.

The satellite footprint or area of coverage permits multiple earth stations to simultaneously receive the same signal. When considering any distance greater than a few hundred miles, the cost of broadcasting via satellite is significantly less expensive than landline transmission because only one relay station is involved. The satellite allows for certain efficiencies by overcoming both distance and terrain factors. An economy of scale is realized because there is no additional cost involved in the uplinking and downlinking of a signal. In short, cost bears no relationship to the distance involved and/or to the number of users.

Today's generation of satellites have become more sophisticated in design. They are larger in size and have an amplifying capability that is 200 times more powerful than their predecessors in the 1970s. Conversely, earth stations have become smaller and less expensive. DBS represents a new generation of high-powered satellites capable of transmitting signals to small, inexpensive earth stations.

3. THE GLOBALIZATION OF TELEVISION

TABLE 3.4
Select Guide to U.S. Interests in Cable Programming and Distribution

Name of Company	Program Format	Areas Served
Black Entertainment Television	Features Black artists and entertainers—presents news, talk shows, and music	South Africa, Europe, and the Caribbean
Bravo	U.S. and international films and art works	Canada
Country Music Television	Video network—featuring U.S. and international country music artists	Europe and Asia
Discovery Channel	Nonfiction programming in science and technology, history, and human adventure	Latin America, Asia, and Europe
ESPN International (ESPN Latin America, ESPN Asia, Eurosport, Supersport)	Provides live and taped coverage of international sports competition and exhibitions	Europe, Latin America, South America, Asia, Pacific Rim, Middle East, Africa, and sub-Saharan Africa
Fox Latin America (Canal Fox)	Features off-network series, films, specials, and children's programming	Central America, South America, and the Caribbean
Home Box Office (HBO Hungary, HBO Czech, HBO Ole/Cinemax, HBO Brazil HBO Asia)	Feature films, specials, comedy and sports without commercial interruption	Eastern Europe, Latin America, South America, and Asia
MTV Networks	Features music videos, including both rock and contemporary music	Europe, Asia, and South America
Prime International	Provides live and taped coverage of international sports competition and exhibitions	Europe, Pacific Rim, Asia, Latin America, South America, and Middle East
Turner International (CNN International, TNT Latin America, Cartoon Network)	International news, general and children's entertainment	Europe, Africa, Middle East, Latin America, South America, Asia, and Pacific Rim

Note. Sources: Company reports and International Cable

THE CASE OF DBS IN JAPAN[31]

Government/Business Partnerships

In Japan, the partnership between government and business is considered essential to the proper planning and design of infrastructure. Japan is unique among nations in its ability to establish economic priorities and to coordinate a unified plan for industrial development. The main value of government/business partnerships is the development of an orderly, smooth plan in which business participants make decisions that are consistent with the overall strategic plan, still allowing for a certain degree of autonomy.[32]

The development of DBS was first conceived as an integral part of Japan's overall space development program. Discussions concerning a future DBS program first began in 1968, with the formation of the Space Activities Commission. The future decision to launch a DBS system demonstrated a national commitment to advance the cause of a highly sophisticated technology. DBS was clearly a high-profile project that would invite both national and international attention. Designing the world's first DBS system would establish Japan as an international leader in telecommunications. The successful partnership of government and business sponsored under the auspices of Japan's MPT would provide additional proof that such planning arrangements can work and are indeed the way of the future.

NHK is Japan's premiere public broadcasting system. For more than six decades, NHK has served the country with its programming and technological advances. Starting in 1972, then NHK Chairman, Yoshinori Maeda, became very interested in developing a DBS system. His successor, Keiji Shima, also became very interested in DBS policy formulation. Shima believed that DBS would enable NHK to become a world leader in broadcast communication. Part of this strategy included NHK becoming a major program producer as well as the next CNN in terms of international news reporting.[33]

The heart of Shima's restructuring plan was to develop a dual network concept that offered DBS subscribers both noncommercial and commercial entertainment, the latter being financed with direct viewer subscriptions. The two DBS channels were expected to generate new sources of revenues that would subsidize NHK's overall program operations. The privatization of NHK under Shima posed a serious challenge to Japan's commercial broadcasters who saw the new NHK as an unregulated government monopoly. In the beginning, Japan's commercial broadcasters were adamantly opposed to a national DBS program. Their concerns were based on two principle fears, namely, a growing sense that NHK was becoming too commercial-like in its operations, and a fear that DBS could bypass the existing system of commercial broadcasting due to inherent efficiencies that a proposed DBS system would offer.[34]

In the end, Japan's commercial broadcasters had very little choice. The MPT was determined to move ahead with or without their support. There was too much at stake politically and financially. The MPT had moved well beyond its role as a government partner (or consensus builder) and was now mandating a course of action. For its part, Japan's commercial broadcasters reasoned that it was better to participate in the planning process rather than simply be a victim to its effects. On September 30, 1983, 14 commercial broadcasters were given preliminary approval to begin developing a joint business plan for DBS service. Japan Satellite Broadcasting (JSB) would be licensed and controlled by the MPT.

Today, there are approximately 43 million television households in Japan. An estimated 5 to 6 million households (or 15%) watch the Broadcast Satellite (BS) DBS service. NHK offers subscribers two channels of service per month. Approximately 96% of NHK's DBS revenues are derived from viewer subscription fees. The remaining 4% are made possible through other commercial activities and government subsidies. The NHK channels include world news, sports, music entertainment, and movies.[35] The remaining 1 to 1.5 million households subscribe to the WOWOW channel, which is priced separately and is operated by JSB. The WOWOW channel began operation in April 1991 and offers a similar set of program offerings.

Simultaneous to the development of BS satellites, Japan has maintained a separate set of low-powered satellites, henceforth referred to as communication satellites (CS) for the purpose of delivering traditional telecommunication services, including voice, data, and video services. The CS generation of satellites have followed a more traditional common carrier approach to the delivery of services. Starting in 1992, the CS generation of satellites are being used to deliver an altogether separate set of DBS television services. In all, there are six CS-DBS services that are offered to the public on a subscription basis. They are priced separately and provide a full range of news, entertainment, and sports programming.[36] It should be noted that the BS and CS-DBS services require separate satellite receiving equipment.

Successful industrial planning presumes the ability on the part of government to target high-growth industries for the future. The assumption is that a master plan will naturally emerge from close, cooperative consultations between government and the private sector. The expectation is that all participants, both public and private, have agreed in principle to operate by the same script. The problem occurs when government (in this case the MPT) steps out of its role as facilitator and mandates a plan of action that may be fundamentally flawed.

What Japan's MPT did not foresee were the unintended consequences that resulted from planning a new system of broadcast communication that involved balancing the unique requirements of NHK's nonprofit organizational status with Japan's five commercial broadcasters. The MPT became so preoccupied with the cause of DBS that they chose to ignore the very real concerns of Japan's commercial broadcasters. The nation's commercial broadcasters were concerned about NHK's quasi-commercial status and their ability to unfairly dominate DBS in Japan. The problem was compounded by the sudden addition of six new DBS entrants under the guise of open competition. By favoring NHK and promoting open DBS competition, the MPT did so at the risk of destabilizing Japan's system of commercial broadcasting. In the final analysis, the MPT was unable to achieve the proper balance between government-supported DBS and the desire to promote a truly privatized business climate. They were incompatible policy objectives.[37]

The status of Japan's DBS program was also complicated by a national recession. The decision to move ahead with a DBS program came at a time when Japan's economy was booming. By the early 1990s however, Japan was experiencing a recession that has strained national resources. Today, the economy is slowly recovering and the prospects for DBS are looking much better. Japan's commercial broadcasters are slowly adjusting to the changes.

NEWS CORPORATION LTD.

British Sky Broadcasting

News Corporation holds a 40% interest in British Sky Broadcasting (BSkyB), which operates the leading pay television service in the United Kingdom and the Republic of Ireland. BSkyB has 4 million subscribers. BSkyB first began operating in 1983 as the Sky Channel. The company used satellite communications as way to circumvent the United Kingdom's four-channel system by delivering alternative programming to subscribers equipped with earth stations. The Sky Channel also delivered programming to the United Kingdom's infant cable television industry. The Sky Channel venture was an abysmal failure during its early years of development, having sustained $1.6 billion in losses.[38] By 1990, the combined losses of Sky Channel and Fox Television appeared out of control, leaving many analysts to speculate whether both projects would eventually imperil the entire News Corporation operation. Rupert Murdoch's solution to the Sky Channel dilemma was to merge his operation with rival DBS player British Satellite Broadcasting to form British Sky Broadcasting. The merger enabled both companies to reduce costs and expand programming. By March 1992, BSkyB showed the first signs of profitability.

Today, BSkyB consists of nine wholly owned television channels, including five premium channels and four advertiser-supported basic channels. In addition, BSkyB markets the Sky-distributed channels; that is, 12 direct-to-home channels that are owned and operated by third-party distributors. The BSkyB group derives its revenues from subscription fees, payments from cable operators, and the sale of advertising on the Sky basic channels. News Corp. has invested heavily in programming, evidenced by its $456 million investment in Premiere Soccer that began broadcasting in 1992. Premiere Soccer has been a major reason that BSkyB has achieved record profits.[39]

BSkyB plans to offer digitally compressed signals starting in 1996. The plan is to increase the number of signals from its present 22 channels to 200. Much of that programming will include near video-on-demand movies that will start every 15 minutes. BSkyB also plans to expand its service to the European continent.[40] The delivery of BSkyB programming will pose some unique privacy problems as DBS footprints are constantly crossing national boundary lines. Still to be determined is whether EC member nations are fully open to the satellite feeds from BSkyB and other program distributors.

Star Television

In July 1993, News Corporation Ltd. acquired a 63.6% interest in Star Television Ltd. Murdoch paid $525 million for the Pan-Asian satellite network. The original Star TV network was launched in 1991 by Hong Kong business magnate Li Ka-Shing and his company, Hutchison Whampoa. At the time of the purchase agreement, Star TV claimed an estimated viewership of 65 million people in 15 million homes.[41]

Today, Star TV provides DBS programming to China, India, and some 50 other nations. The Star TV footprint can be seen from Israel to Japan, and from Turkey to Indonesia. Star TV provides two satellite beams including a southern feed that covers Turkey, across the Middle East, through India, and down to Indonesia. Programming on the southern feed consists of six advertiser-supported television services including BBC World Service Television (news and public affairs), Prime Sports, Channel V (Asian and international music videos), Star Plus (family entertainment), Zee TV (Hindi television), and a combination of the Chinese Channel (variety and entertainment in Mandarin) and El TV (original programming in Hindi).

Star TV's northern feed reaches China, Japan, Korea, Taiwan, Hong Kong, and the Philippines. Programming on the northern feed consists of four advertiser-supported television services, including Prime Sports, Channel V, Star Plus, and the Chinese Channel. Starting in April 1994, Star TV launched a premium movie service on its northern feed called STAR Movies, which is broadcast in Mandarin, with the remaining programs in English with Mandarin subtitles.[42]

Star TV plans to offer digitally compressed signals starting in 1996. The plan is to customize its programming to meet different geographic and programmatic markets. Much of that programming will include special language channels to meet the needs of its highly diverse Middle Eastern and Asian audience. One of the important markets for the future is the People's Republic of China. News Corp., by virtue of its U.S. and British programming, is on a collision course with Chinese officials who are concerned about cultural trespass and undue political interference. Chinese officials, like their Malaysian counterparts, have thus far been very resistant to Star TV. They have placed restrictions on the sale and ownership of satellite receivers on the mainland.

DISCUSSION

Government-supported broadcasting is now giving way to the private sector. The high cost of television production has caused many of the world's leading PT&Ts and regional coalitions (the EC) to reassess the amount of money they are willing to spend on television production. For government policymakers, the continued privatization of television is not only attractive, but inevitable. The result will be an explosive growth in new commercial ventures.

Privatization will affect the international television and film market in three ways. The first is the large-scale increase in the volume of programs purchased from commercial sources. In Europe, Asia, and Latin America, the demand for new sources of programming is likely to increase, given the rapid expansion in television channels due to new media technologies. Equally important is that Latin America and Asia are both becoming important suppliers of television and film programming as well. It should be noted that television and film production companies in Brazil, Venezuela, and Argentina are becoming important regional suppliers of television programming and are exporting their program software to such countries as Spain, Portugal, and Hispanic broadcast stations and cable services located in the United States. Similarly, television and film production companies located in India, Japan, and Hong Kong are the preeminent suppliers of programming to Asia and will continue to be so throughout the rest of the decade.

The second effect of privatization will be significant competition for software products among potential program buyers. State-controlled broadcasters have traditionally been able to behave as monopsonists in their purchase of programming.[43] By contrast, the newly emerging broadcast, cable, and DBS services will soon outnumber those channels that are government supported. The likely result is that state broadcasters will have to bid against commercial broadcasters for many of the same programs. The competition for program software will bid up the price for television and film products.[44]

The third result of privatization is that much of the program software is likely to be produced by well-established TNMCs. They are well-positioned to take on the demands of international financing, resource allocation, production, and distribution. In order to overcome regulatory barriers to entry and improve production and distribution efficiencies, the number of coproduction ventures are likely to increase as well.

The concept of global television is fast becoming a reality in terms of news, sports, and music entertainment. The geopolitical and cultural walls that once separated the nations of the earth are becoming increasingly difficult to maintain. The world of global television, albeit CNN, Olympic sports coverage, MTV, and Disney feature films, are quickly eroding the barriers. At the same time, there is not likely to become a single, unified market for television entertainment. Differences in culture, including language, shared common experience, and social values, will preclude that possibility.

Tomorrow's television programmers are likely to program toward several countries at once. More and more, programs will be produced for regions of the world where there is a commonality of language and experience. The importance of the TNMC and coproduction ventures are going to foster a programming philosophy based on the assumption that the world can be broken down according to cultural zones. With the increase in channel capacity, it is expected that the next generation of television viewers are likely to be people who can simultaneously appreciate World MTV and still have a decided preference for the locally originated dramatic series or sporting event. As a social force, television and films (in combination with communication technology in general) will continue to homogenize culture. As a countermeasure, the preservation of culture will take on increasing importance in the years to come.

NOTES

[1] Peter Dicken, *Global Shift*, (New York: Guilford), pp. 16–17.
[2] Ibid., p. 45.
[3] Robert G. Picard, *Media Economics*, (Newbury Park, CA: Sage), p. 14.
[4] Ibid., p. 66.
[5] Bruce M. Owen & Steven S. Wildman, *Video Economics*, (Cambridge, MA: Harvard University Press), pp. 49–52.
[6] Ibid., pp. 26–27.
[7] "A Survey of the Entertainment Industry," *The Economist*, 23 December, 1989, p. 5.
[8] Tapio Varis, "The International Flow of Television Programs," *Journal of Communication*, 34(1) 1984, pp. 143–152.
[9] Governments that underwrite the cost of production must balance priorities between television production costs and other development expenditures (i.e., hospitals, schools, military, roads, etc). Sepstrup further noted the importance of shared language between television producer and importing nation as being an important determinant in the amount of programming that will be imported. See Preben Sepstrup, *Transnationalization of Television in Western Europe*, Academic Research Monograph # 5. (London: John Libbey & Co., 1990), pp. 24–55.
[10] National Telecommunications & Information Administration, *Globalization of the Mass Media*, (U.S. Department of Commerce, NTIA Special Publication: 93–290, 1993), pp. 42–45.
[11] J. L. Renaud and Barry R. Litman, "Changing Dynamics of the Overseas Market for TV Programming," *Telecommunications Policy*, August, 1985. pp. 245–261. See also Muriel G. Cantor and Joel M. Cantor, American Television in the International Marketplace, *Communication Research* 13(3), 1986, pp. 513–519.
[12] Varis, pp. 143–152.
[13] The MPAA obtains its data from from its member companies, which include 10 major production companies as well as independent production companies that comprise the American Film Marketing Association.
[14] David Waterman, "World Television Trade: The Economic Effects of Privatization and New Technology," *Telecommunications Policy*, June, 1988, pp. 141–146.
[15] Anton Lensen, *Concentration in the Media Industry: The European Community and Mass Media Regulation*, (Washington, DC: Annenberg Washington Program, 1992), pp. 17–24.
[16] Fred H. Cate, "The European Broadcasting Directive," Communications Committee Monograph Series, (Washington, DC: American Bar Association, 1990), pp. 1–10.
[17] Thomas Guback, "What the Quota Really Means," *Television Quarterly*, 24(3), 1990, pp. 81–89.
[18] "Europe and America Prepare for 1992," *Broadcasting*, 17 April, 1989, p. 38.
[19] "Creating a New TV in Europe," *Electronic Media*, 22 October, 1990, p. 18.
[20] "Europe to Expand Film-TV Copyright Protection," *Broadcasting*, 5 May, 1990, p. 58.
[21] Michel Dupagne, "International Syndication: Trends and Strategies in the 1990s," A paper presented to the Broadcast Education Association Conference, Las Vegas, NV, April, 1991, p. 17.
[22] For many countries, the privatization of television represents an opportunity to redirect those same government resources toward other projects.

[23] "French Official Works for European Unity," *Electronic Media*, 22 October, 1990, p. 26.
[24] Jack Valenti, President of the Motion Picture Association of America, Presentation given to The Los Angeles World Affairs Council, Los Angeles: November 7, 1990.
[25] "MPAA's Latest Salvo Against European Quotas," *Broadcasting*, 18 February, 1991, p. 89.
[26] Rod Carvath, "The Reconstruction of the Global Media Marketplace," *Communication Research*, 19(6), 1992, p. 705.
[27] Richard A. Gershon, "Pay Cable Television: A Regulatory History," *Communications and the Law*, 12(2), 1990, pp. 20–22.
[28] Richard A. Gershon and Michael Wirth, "Home Box Office," *The Cable Networks Handbook*, (Ed.) Robert Picard, (Riverside, CA: Carpelan Press, 1993), pp. 115–116.
[29] "CNN's Ted Turner: Man of the Year," *Time*, 6 January, 1992, p. 25.
[30] Marc Doyle, *The Future of Television*, (Chicago: NTC Business Books, 1992), p. 21.
[31] Portions of this material first appeared in Richard A. Gershon and Tsutomu Kanayama, Direct Broadcast Satellites in Japan: A case study in government business partnerships, *Telecommunications Policy*, 19(3), 1995, pp. 217–231. The author wishes to thank Mr. Kanayama for his assistance in the development of this material. Special thanks to *Telecommunications Policy* for allowing us to use select portions of this material.
[32] Richard A. Gershon and Tsutomu Kanayama, "Direct Broadcast Satellites in Japan," *Telecommunications Policy*, 19(3), 1995, pp. 217–219.
[33] Ise, Akifumi *NHK no 21 Seiki Senryaku [NHK's Strategy for the 21st Century]*, Soyo Sha, Tokyo, 1991, pp. 32–58.
[34] Gershon and Kanayama, pp. 221–223.
[35] NHK Corporate Communications, "NHK's Future Vision: Outlook for the 21st Century," (Tokyo: NHK, 1993), pp. 14–17.
[36] "Yen," *Yomiuri Shimbun*, 23 November, 1992, p. 12.
[37] Gershon and Kanayama, pp. 229–231.
[38] "Murdoch's British Satellite-TV Venture, Long a Loser, Posts Huge Jump in Profit," *Wall Street Journal*, 4 February, 1994, p. A4.
[39] Murdoch's Satellite Network Aims to Fly as a Public Company," *Wall Street Journal*, 7 October, 1994, p. B1.
[40] "Man Buys World," *Business Week*, 29 May, 1995, pp. 26–29.
[41] "Murdoch Star deal Transforms Asia," *Broadcasting & Cable*, 2 August, 1993, pp. 34–35.
[42] The News Corporation Ltd., Filings Before the U.S. Securities and Exchange Commission (Form 20–F), June 30, 1994, pp. 17–18.
[43] In Australia, for example, a monopsony condition was created through regulation. Although competitive broadcasting is allowed, only the Australian Broadcasting Commission is permitted to purchase foreign programming. They, in turn, resell it with a mark-up to Australian broadcasters. See Colin Hoskins, Rolf Mirus, and William Rozeboom, "US Television Programs in the International Market: Unfair Pricing?" *Journal of Communication*, 39(2), 1989, pp. 58–61.
[44] Steven S. Wildman and Steven E. Siwek, "The Privatization of European Television: Effects on International Markets for Programs," *Columbia Journal of World Business*, Fall 1987, pp. 71–73.

4

The Transnational Advertising Agency: Global Messages and Free Market Competition

Heidi H. Holwerda
Richard A. Gershon

Marshall McLuhan's vision of the global village has materialized, bringing with it new business, technological, and cultural changes. The decade of the 1980s witnessed a significant increase in the worldwide consolidation of TNCs. Consolidation and expansion trends in the mass media and other industries have triggered a similar growth in transnational advertising.[1] The expansion of transnational advertising agencies (TNAAs) is the result of worldwide privatization trends coupled with advancements in telecommunications technology, including satellite communication and cable television. Such technologies have allowed for greater efficiency in the targeting and distribution of advertising messages.

The TNAA thrives on a free enterprise system grounded in competition; a system that requires aggressive marketing and advertising strategies to create consumer demand and increase market share. Major advertisers no longer limit themselves to domestic markets. Examples of global advertisers include Coca-Cola, Ford, Shell, AT&T, General Foods, Exxon, Colgate-Palmolive, Procter and Gamble, Unilever, and Nestle.[2] As large corporations become increasingly transnational in scope, they are faced with the need to create a unified marketing strategy in order to efficiently develop consumer bases across national boundaries.[3]

The field of advertising is dominated by a few TNAAs that are primarily headquartered in the United States. This is in part due to the fact that advertising has its roots in the U.S. free-market economy and privatized media.[4] TNAAs are profit driven and as such are a subject of concern for many countries because of the discrepancies that may exist between the marketing goals of the TNAA and the clients they represent and the development goals of host nations. Transnational advertising poses a particular problem because the content of promotional messages are sometimes culturally laden and can have a significant influence on the values, economics, and politics of host nations. Anderson (1984) wrote:

> In effect, the TNAAs do far more than provide mere advertising services. They also transmit consumerism and other values, communicate information, influence behavior both of individuals and of institutions and affect development policies and plans.[5]

Proponents of transnational advertising argue that it brings industrialization and development to developing countries. This chapter examines the modern-day TNAA and considers the reasons for their formation and the consequences resulting from worldwide privatization trends. Special attention is given to the challenges that TNAAs pose to the national sovereignty and cultural integrity of developing nations.

THE RISE OF THE TRANSNATIONAL ADVERTISING AGENCY

The concept of advertising is a uniquely American phenomenon. This is due primarily to the atypical media infrastructure of the United States, which has historically relied on the private sector for financing as opposed to being government funded. Although today's TNAAs thrive on the openness of borders and the free flow of information, advertising first began as a strictly domestic enterprise to support national and regional clients. During the decades of the 1960s and 1970s, the skills, knowledge, and technologies associated with advertising placed U.S. agencies at a distinct advantage as companies began to do business beyond their own national borders. Today, 20 of the 50 largest advertising agencies in the world are headquartered in the United States.[6]

The field of advertising grew substantially in the United States in the years following World War II. This was largely due to the increase in manufacturing levels and the technological development of television, which provided corporations with a cost-effective means for reaching large potential audiences. At the same time, agencies began to develop additional services for clients such as market research and consumer demographic information. As large companies expanded their markets abroad, they were forced to use several agencies simultaneously. This relationship proved inadequate due to inefficiencies and lack of standards in such areas as billing, commissions, demographic/market information, and creative quality. Advertising agencies recognized these inefficiencies and seized the opportunity for growth.

International expansion exploded in the 1960s, as agencies established foreign offices in various countries in order to meet the needs of their internationally expanding client base. Such growth was facilitated by advancements in broadcast and satellite technology. The newly emerging international environment prompted advertisers to develop a unified marketing strategy for a global market. Such globalized plans required homogeneity in consumption patterns, and television provided the ideal vehicle for this strategy. There was a corresponding change in the design of advertising messages from product information to persuasion-oriented campaigns that appealed to the emotions and psychological needs of the audience.[7]

TNCs were not alone in their desire to utilize the services of Western TNAAs. Clients in other nations also wanted to take advantage of the expertise and media technology of U.S. advertising agencies.[8] As a result, the predominantly U.S.-based advertising agencies gradually expanded into international markets. The soon-to-be TNAA wielded considerable influence by writing the early rules of advertising in terms of strategy and application. The TNAAs capitalized on this influence and developed additional marketing skills and services. The TNAAs could now offer a globally oriented marketing campaign. According to Janus (1981):

> What the agencies offer their transnational clients is now a total communication package, including product design, packaging, testing, and positioning in the market. This "total communication package" represents the marketing experience gathered by the agency on a global basis over the past decade.[9]

Starting in the mid-1980s, the field of advertising has experienced increased consolidation similar to other TNMCs. Some of America's leading agencies are merging with European groups and are also purchasing smaller U.S. agencies. A key example of concentration can be found in the Interpublic Group of Companies (IPG), the second largest TNAA in the world. IPG is parent company to such notable U.S.-based agencies as McCann Erickson, Lintas, and the Lowe Group. Similarly, the Omnicom Group is the third largest TNAA in the world and boasts BBDO Worldwide and DDB Needham Worldwide, the fifth and eighth largest U.S.-based agencies.[10]

The TNCs and TNAAs have become business partners and are increasingly financially interlinked. The trends of TNAA expansion and consolidation will most likely continue, especially given worldwide privatization trends and the fall of communism. Anderson states that "transnational advertising agencies have become profitable global communication enterprises that are powerful when compared to indigenous agencies."[11] The combination of sheer market power and technological and creative expertise, have established TNAAs as the undisputed leaders in the field. Table 4.1 provides a detailed examination of BBDO Worldwide, including a representative sample of nine important TNCs and the more than 40 BBDO foreign offices used to service those clients. Table 4.2 identifies the world's leading TNAAs according to ranking and equity gross income for the years 1991 and 1993.

TABLE 4.1
BBDO Worldwide Operations Select Clients and Agency Offices[a] (1995)

	Apple Computer	Campbell Soup	Delta Airlines	Federal Express	General Electric	Gillette	Pepsi Cola	Sony	Visa
The Americas									
Argentina				X			X		
Brazil	X			X		X	X		X
Canada	X	X	X	X	X	X			
Chile						X	X	X	X
Colombia						X	X	X	X
Costa Rica				X		X	X		
Dom. Rep.				X			X		
Ecuador					X	X	X		
El Salvador				X		X	X		X
Guatemala				X		X	X		X
Honduras				X		X	X		
Mexico		X	X	X		X	X		
Nicaragua				X			X		
Panama				X			X		X
Peru							X		X
Puerto Rico		X	X	X		X			X
U.S.	X	X	X	X	X	X	X		X
Uruguay							X		
Venezuela				X			X		X

(continued)

TABLE 4.1 (continued)

	Apple Computer	Campbell Soup	Delta Airlines	Federal Express	General Electric	Gillette	Pepsi Cola	Sony	Visa
Europe									
Austria	X		X			X	X		
Belgium	X		X	X		X	X		
Bulgaria	X						X		
Croatia	X						X		
Cyprus	X				X				
Czech Rep.	X		X			X	X		
Denmark	X		X			X	X		
Finland	X		X			X	X		
France	X	X	X	X		X	X		
Germany	X		X			X	X	X	
Greece			X			X	X	X	
Hungary			X				X		
Italy	X		X			X	X		
Netherlands	X		X	X		X	X		
Norway	X		X			X	X		
Poland			X				X		
Portugal			X			X	X		
Romania	X		X				X		
Russia			X		X		X		

	Apple Computer	Campbell Soup	Delta Airlines	Federal Express	General Electric	Gillette	Pepsi Cola	Sony	Visa
Slovakia									
Spain	X		X			X	X		
Sweden	X		X			X	X	X	
Switzerland	X		X			X	X		
Turkey			X				X		
U.K.	X		X			X	X	X	
Middle East									
Egypt						X	X		
Kuwait				X			X		
Lebanon				X			X		
Saudi Arabia				X			X		
United Arab Emirates				X			X		
Asia/Pacific									
Australia	X	X			X	X	X		
China					X				
Hong Kong			X	X	X				
India			X	X	X		X		
Indonesia	X								
Japan		X	X	X			X		

(continued)

TABLE 4.1 (continued)

	Apple Computer	Campbell Soup	Delta Airlines	Federal Express	General Electric	Gillette	Pepsi Cola	Sony	Visa
Malaysia				X					
New Zealand	X	X				X	X		
Pakistan	X			X		X			
Philippines									
Singapore				X				X	
South Korea		X				X			
Taiwan	X		X	X	X				
Thailand					X				
Vietnam									

Note. Data from BBDO Worldwide.

[a] Many TNCs employ more than one TNAA (or agency) to handle their account(s). The choice of TNAA (or agency) is a function of product line and geographical location. This table illustrates BBDO's worldwide operations, including companies and product lines that they share with other agencies.

TABLE 4.2
10 Leading Transnational Advertising Agencies Ranked by Equity Gross Income

Rank		Transnational Advertising Agency	Worldwide Income (in millions)		
1994	1993	1991		1994	1993	1991
1	1	1	WPP Group, London	2,768.2	2627.5	2,661.8
2	2	2	Interpublic Group of New York	2,211.0	2,125.2	1,798.9
3	3	4	Omnicom Group, New York	2,052.6	1,909.1	1,471.2
4	4	5	Dentsu, Tokyo	1,641.7	1,403.2	1,451.0
5	5	3	Cordiant/Saatchi & Saatchi Co., New York/London	1,431.5	1,355.1	1,705.5
6	6	6	Young & Rubicam, New York	1,059.7	1,008.9	1,057.1
7	7	7	Euro RSCG, Paris	813.3	864.8	1,016.3
8	8	8	Grey Advertising, New York	808.7	765.7	659.3
9	9	9	Hakuhodo, Tokyo	774.2	727.9	655.6
10	10	10	Leo Burnett Co./Foote, Cone & Belding, Chicago	677.5	622.4	616.0

Note. Data from *Advertising Age.*

TRANSNATIONAL ADVERTISING: BUSINESS CHALLENGES

The TNAA, like its TNMC counterparts, continue to expand and reshape its holdings through international acquisitions. There is a clear recognition among advertising's top leaders that in the years to come, a highly select group of TNAAs will dominate the field, committed to the goals of expansion, financial strength and the building of synergies.[12] As the world becomes more fully privatized, the next generation of TNAAs are faced with three principal business challenges, that include overestimation of synergies, financial solvency, and client conflicts.[13]

Overestimation of Synergies

Vertical integration and the prospect of improved synergies has long been a driving force, prompting mergers and acquisitions in business. The presumption is that a merger will provide the corporate family with additional resources that can be tapped for a variety of projects in support of agency clients. Synergies would be realized in such areas as promotion, direct mail, and public relations. Additional synergies could be expected in media buying, where clients can obtain volume discounts due to the purchasing power of consolidated media buying units.[14] Additional efficiencies would be realized in such nonproprietary areas as data processing, market research, and lease management. The intention is to centralize these services and thereby eliminate redundancies across divisions.

Although such synergies look good on paper, they often prove elusive in practice, largely due to the human element. Anticipated collaboration in many areas is often curtailed, largely due to their proprietary nature. Issues of ego and turf also enter into the equation, as advertising executives are reluctant to relinquish creative and strategic concepts lest they are needed for future clients. Similarly, centralization efforts for many other departments are often aborted due to a lack of support by managers and employees.[15]

The most frequently cited anticipated synergy is that of pooled media buying, which has also proved elusive. In principle, such consolidation would ensure entry into other countries where media time is scarce and often designated for those media companies with the largest size and strength.[16] Although the intention is to maximize buying leverage by creating increased buying power through consolidation of client lists, the structure of media industries and client concerns over conflicts have thwarted the realization of such synergies.

Over time, TNAAs discovered that the structure of the broadcast and print industries enabled pooled media buying to work in only a few countries. France, Spain, and Belgium are among those countries where media ownership also is concentrated and businesses are accustomed to engaging in *bonification*, the practice of providing extra discounts on volume. Most media organizations, however, are not open to rate negotiations based on volume.[17]

In addition, many clients are concerned about combining their advertising dollars with competitors in order to increase buying levels. Although joint buying strategies would benefit the TNAA, little advantage is perceived by clients. This is especially true for larger clients who do not see the value of combining their buying power with that of a competitor in order to achieve increased buying leverage on behalf of the TNAA. More specifically, such clients feel that their special needs will get lost in the shuffle in deference to another account. The vision of potential synergies and economies of scale remains a goal of TNAAs. However, most agencies have yet to translate that vision into reality once acquisitions and expansion have taken place.

Financial Solvency

A second issue faced by TNAAs is that of debt load. The Omnicom Group and Saatchi & Saatchi Co. sparked the trend of agency consolidation in 1986. The formation of these mega-agencies and others was facilitated by the easy financing available during the 1980s. At the time of its formation, Omnicom undertook a debt load of $275 million and WPP and Saatchi & Saatchi Co. both assumed debt loads estimated at more than $400 million each.[18] These and other megamergers occurred at a time when advertising expenditures grew in double-digit figures each year. The assumed debt was supposed to be paid off with an expected cash flow that has yet to materialize for some companies. Although the assumption of a high debt load was considered an acceptable business practice for the 1980s, it became especially problematic during the early 1990s. At that time, the world's economy underwent a major recession that translated into a significant decrease in advertising revenues.[19] In addition, the challenge to stay solvent was intensified as agency commission percentages would sometimes drop from the standard 15% to between 11 and 13%.[20]

Client Conflicts

The predominant issue that TNAAs will face in the future is how to service competing clients while still expanding. How many acquisitions can a TNAA absorb before client fallout surpasses account and positioning gains? How large can an agency become before it meets itself coming and going? The issue of client conflicts is rather unique to the advertising field. Increasingly, the largest advertising groups are having to decide which clients will be kept and which clients will be divested. An examination of the Omnicom Group, for example, reveals a rash of client fallout due to Omnicom's common association with competitive clients serviced by their BBDO Worldwide and DDB Needham Worldwide divisions, respectively.[21]

Client conflicts are a major problem that only intensifies as the account lists for each division deepen. Locating new clients to pitch is difficult due to potential conflicts with existing accounts. TNAAs must be discerning about future acquisitions and recognize the point of diminishing returns. The alternative will be massive client fallout or the need to divest much of the conflicting divisions that come with the acquisition. At issue is the fact that such divisions are often sold for less than their true value, thus compromising the value and purpose of the acquisition itself.

TRANSNATIONAL ADVERTISING AND HOST NATIONS

The combination of privatization and advanced communication technology will be a major catalyst in promoting the expansion of transnational advertising. As government-owned broadcast facilities become more fully privatized, there will be a corresponding need to promote advertising as a way to underwrite the cost of programming.[22] FDI, in all likelihood, will be sought by those nations looking to reap the short-term benefits of jobs, technology, and tax revenues. Such FDI, however, is not without its social costs.[23] Technology also brings with it some unint ended consequences.

In the years to come, advancements in satellite and cable communications will contribute to a worldwide increase in television channel capacity. In the process, some countries will find themselves the unwilling recipients of satellite-fed programming and advertising that cuts across national borders.[24] The problem will only intensify with the continuing development in DBS, which are capable of transmitting both programming and advertising across national borders to viewers equipped with small earth stations.

Host nations are rightfully concerned about the direct sell messages of advertising whose purpose is to target consumers and influence their buying patterns. This influence is present in countries around the world, but the effects are decidedly real when one examines the dissemination of advertising messages into developing countries. In general, there are three primary concerns about the influence of transnational advertising on host nations. They include cultural trespass and the homogenization of culture, the influence on national economic priorities, and the dissemination of inappropriate products.

Cultural Trespass and the Homogenization of Culture

TNAAs achieve marketing efficiencies for their transnational clients by disseminating messages across national borders in the form of global advertising campaigns. Designing a global advertising message enables the TNAA to maximize audience reach among different peoples with diverse cultures. The problem is that homogenized or broad appeal messages often fail to consider the impact on local cultures.[25] Transnational advertising promotes consumer demand for Western products and lifestyles, regardless of the real-life needs and wants of local culture. The issue becomes especially problematic when the product being advertised is hazardous or inappropriate for local consumption.

The term *media imperialism* is closely associated with homogenization of culture. Traditional discussions concerning media imperialism are usually related to one country's ability to export and influence another country through its media products and services. The terms *media* and *cultural imperialism* that were once so popular in the 1970s have given way to a more revised thinking about the role of Western media exports. The United States and Western media are no longer the primary targets for such criticism.[26] Instead, the TNMC—and specifically the TNAA—have become the subject of much research and investigation. Transnational advertising is perceived to be a threat to developing countries because it is culturally laden and has the potential to influence social values and economic priorities.

Critics argue that such advertising increases dependency on the West for luxury and consumer goods that often stand in marked contrast to the development goals of the host nation.[27] Evidence of dependency can be found in Sub-Saharan Africa, where the proliferation of advertising has created consumption patterns inconsistent with the values and lifestyles of developed nations. Transnational products typically showcase products such as soap, cosmetics, tobacco, processed foods, and drinks—items far removed from the basic and unfilled needs for clothing, housing, and food.[28] This, in turn, creates a dependency on the West because many of those same products cannot be produced locally. In the end, such products and services provide revenue to the TNC without providing substantial benefit to the host nation and its local citizenry.

Influence on National Economic Priorities

All governments exercise the right to national sovereignty. The concept of national sovereignty requires the ability to create laws that regulate the economic activity within national boundaries. These regulations include taxes, tariffs on imports, privacy laws product quality, and so forth. At issue is the host governments' ability to maintain control over the activities of the TNAA when it is felt that the TNAA is promoting products and services that are contrary to the best interest of a country and its citizens.[29]

One area for concern is that of the demonstration effect, also referred to as the *theory of rising frustrations*. Subtle exposure to Western programming and advertising is thought to create desires in individuals and ethnic groups. Western advertising conveys images of material prosperity that increase the expectations on the part of viewers. They, in turn, begin to demand more and more of government and its limited national resources in order to attain their desired lifestyle. Because the government or economy is unable to meet these demands, ethnic groups or individuals become frustrated, leading to domestic violence and lack of cooperation with government. In essence, advertising and mass media stimulate the consumption of luxury items among those who can afford them and induce frustration among those who cannot.

In the country of Brazil, for example, most advertised products are targeted for the higher socioeconomic strata that represents approximately 15% of the entire population. They have little to do with the basic needs of the remaining 85% of the country's population. Television is the preferred medium for transnational advertising despite the fact that newspapers and magazines are the media most highly correlated with education and income. As a result, television advertisements that are intended for the higher economic strata of the population are in fact seen by all. Critics argue that TNCs are promoting values and consumption habits for luxury goods as opposed to the basic essentials that most Brazilians need to survive.[30]

Oliveira's (1991) research revealed that exposure to advertising and mass media stimulates the desire for luxury goods and items. The problem, however, is that ordinary citizens have no corresponding means for acting on their aroused desires. In short, those with the highest desire to consume often have the least potential to realize their aspirations. It is interesting to note that Brazil has implemented one of the world's most highly sophisticated satellite television systems, which has only intensified the role of advertising. As a result, the media has sharpened the disparity between existing social groups, thus aggravating social differences.[31]

Dissemination of Inappropriate Products

A third area of concern is the advertising of products that are inappropriate for the host country and its citizens. The combination of limited education and illiteracy often contributes to a lack of discernment skills on the part of consumers. Of particular concern are health-related products such as food staples and pharmaceuticals, which are often used incorrectly by citizens of developing nations.

Howard and Mayo (1988) revealed that many TNCs use product commercialization techniques that include an effective advertising campaign, free samples, and point-of-purchase displays.[32] Baudot (1991) expressed concern about such techniques utilized in the advertising of pharmaceuticals because many citizens in Third World countries lack the ability to choose the best product and to understand the differences between name-brand and generic alternatives. Pharmaceutical advertising is criticized for encouraging the use of chemical dependence as a basis for health over the use of traditional remedies that work as effectively without draining the limited financial resources of consumers. The advertising of synthetic foods and remedies as replacements for natural staples has also been criticized because it often results in poor health and economic hardship. Perhaps the most infamous example of this concern is illustrated by the marketing of infant formula by Nestle and other corporations in the 1970s. The advertising of these products discouraged breast feeding and resulted in a misuse of products that in turn caused the deaths of thousands of infants.[33]

The advertising and sale of tobacco products to developing nations has become an issue of growing concern. In the face of increased regulation and consumer awareness, tobacco use in the West has declined. In order to offset lost revenue, developing countries have been singled out as new target markets.[34] Critics point to the obvious health risks associated with smoking and that citizens of developing countries are particularly susceptible to the claims made by advertisers. In short, they have not yet fully developed the discernment skills necessary to distinguish fact from fiction. In such circumstances, the input and sensitivity that might be employed by indigenous, local agencies is sorely missed.[35] Although many countries are beginning to pass legislation to protect citizens against such advertising practices, the political inefficiencies present in many developing countries make enforcement difficult.[36]

DISCUSSION

The combination of worldwide privatization trends coupled with advancements in new media technologies have spawned the era of the TNAA. The exponential increase in transnational advertising has raised awareness on the part of host nations about advertising's potential side effects. This is especially true for those countries that have not had a long history of advertising as part of their domestic media infrastructure.

Critics raise legitimate concerns about cultural trespass and promoting new forms of dependency. Proponents support the enforcement of artificial barriers to protect the culture and autonomy of host nations. This protectionist sentiment was best illustrated by UNESCO's 1976 MacBride Commission report that recommended that special preference be given to noncommercial forms of communication. The report further recommended that restrictions be imposed on transnational advertising, including ". . . a tax on advertising; guidelines for advertising content, and greater state control over the activities of transnational companies."[37] Those most adamant about cultural trespass and dependency issues argue that developing countries should adopt a more centralized approach to media planning, and eliminate advertising altogether.[38]

Transnational Advertising and Host Nations

The TNAA engages in FDI in order to expand business into new markets. To that end, the TNAA is no different than any other type of business. The TNAA likewise engages in FDI in order to more successfully service its local and regional clients. The real question is whether host nations should treat TNAAs differently from other types of businesses? Herein lies the problem of opposing philosophical perspectives about advertising and its relationship to society. What is often overlooked in such discussions are the potential advantages that transnational advertising stands to offer the host nation.

As the world becomes increasingly privatized, no country can afford to operate independently from other nations. A return to centralized media planning and artificially imposed regulatory barriers to entry would preclude a country's full participation in a 21st-century global economy. Transnational advertising is part of the information currency that drives international trade. The TNAA represents a source of jobs, professional training, and capital investment.[39] At a time when governmental resources are limited, advertising underwrites the cost of media infrastructure development. Advertising benefits the host nation by allowing it to redeploy scarce financial resources to support other, albeit more essential, development projects, including housing, food, and education.

When are the times that a host nation should monitor the practices of TNAAs and exercise appropriate regulatory constraints? Host nations have a responsibility to support laws that would protect their citizens from false and misleading advertising, similar to legislation that currently exists in most industrialized countries. If indeed we are to treat media and advertising as commercial products, they must be subject to the same kinds of laws that apply to commercial manufacturing. Host nations regularly impose restrictions on the sale and distribution of hazardous products. To that end, host nations have a responsibility to impose similar restrictions on advertising that would promote the sale and use of hazardous products. In short, advertising must be considered within the context of product safety law.

Host nations, likewise, have a responsibility to protect environmental and cultural resources through the proper establishment of zoning laws. The traditional application of zoning laws applies to the separation of commercial and residential property. A similar case can be made for zoning laws that would protect national wildlife parks from billboard displays, as well as restrictions on commercial advertising during religious programming. Zoning laws that would apply to advertising are not meant to restrict the free flow of ideas and information. Rather, the intention is to allocate advertising a proper time and place when such information collides with the maintenance of a host nation's cultural and environmental resources.

Equally important to the discussion is self-regulation on the part of TNAAs that need to recognize that cultural sensitivity in advertising also demonstrates good business sense. In the final analysis, self-regulation measures adopted by agencies and marketers will promote better understanding and support from host governments. A climate of true international cooperation will provide long-term benefit for expanding TNAAs. A good track record will help sustain current business relationships and provide opportunities for future partnerships.

NOTES

[1] Ben H. Bagdikian, "The Lords of the Global Village," *The Nation*, 12, June, 1989, p. 816.
[2] Michael H. Anderson, *Madison Avenue in Asia: Politics and Transnational Advertising*, (Rutherford, NJ: Fairleigh Dickinson University Press, 1984), p. 89.
[3] Richard A. Gershon, "International Deregulation and the Rise of Transnational Media Corporations," *Journal of Media Economics*, 6(2), 1993, pp. 3–4.
[4] Anderson, *Madison Avenue in Asia*, p. 26.
[5] Ibid., pp. 66–67.
[6] "World's Top 50 Advertising Organizations," *Advertising Age*, 13 April, 1994, p. 12.
[7] Noreene Z. Janus, "Advertising and the Mass Media in the Era of Global Corporation," *Communication and Social Structure*, (Eds.) Emile McAnany, Jorge Schnitman, and Noreene Janus (New York: Praeger, 1981), pp. 290–303.
[8] Richard J. Barnet and Ronald E. Muller, *Global Reach: The Power of Multinational Corporations*, (New York: Simon & Schuster, 1974), p. 143.
[9] Janus, "Advertising and the Mass Media," p. 306.
[10] "Worlds Top 50 Advertising Organizations," *Advertising Age*, 13 April, 1992, p. S24.
[11] Anderson, *Madison Avenue in Asia*, p. 102.
[12] Patrick Reilly, "Media's Big Bang: Three Years After Omnicom, Media Industry Braces for Mergers," *Advertising Age*, 20 March, 1989, p. 1.
[13] Peter Dicken, *Global Shift*, (London: Guilford, 1992), pp. 148–187.
[14] Anthony Ramirez, "Do Your Ads Need a Superagency?," *Fortune*, 27 April, 1987, pp. 81–85.
[15] "Most of the Vision Died in Issues of Ego, Turf," *Advertising Age*, 30 September, 1991, pp. S17–S22.
[16] Steve Ellwanger, "Ogilvy, Omnicom Jointly Dialing for Media Euro Bucks," *Adweek*, 6 February, 1989, p. 59.
[17] "Casting a Media Shadow," *Marketing and Media Decisions*, September, 1988, pp. 49–53.
[18] "Advertising's Big Bang is Making Noise at Last," *Business Week*, 1 April, 1991, pp. 62–63.
[19] "Mad as in Madison Avenue: The Advertising Business is Roiled by Tumult and Change," *Barron's*, 3 December, 1990, pp. 12–39.
[20] Ramirez, "Do Your Ads Need a Superagency?", pp. 81–85.
[21] "Exiting Omnicom? Buyouts Hinted for Ingalls Waring," *Advertising Age*, 28 November, 1988, p. 2., and "Life After Omnicom: Spinoff Shops Face a Friendlier World," *Adweek*, 1 January, 1990, pp. 1,44.
[22] Ira W. Lieberman, "Privatization: The Theme of the 90's," *Columbia Journal of World Business*, 28(1), 1993, pp. 11–14.
[23] Karl P. Sauvant, "Sociocultural Emancipation," *National Sovereignty and International Communication*, (Eds.) Kaarle Nordenstreng and Herbert I. Schiller, (Norwood, NJ: Ablex, 1979), p. 13.
[24] William H. Melody, "The Information Society: The Transnational Economic Context and Its Implications," *Transnational Communications: Wiring the Third World*, (Eds.) Gerald Sussman and John A. Lent, (Newbury Park, CA: Sage, 1991), p. 35.
[25] Anderson, "Madison Avenue in Asia," p. 66.
[26] John Tomlinson, *Cultural Imperialism: A Critical Introduction*, (Baltimore, MD: Johns Hopkins University Press, 1991), pp. 35–36.
[27] William H. Meyer, *Transnational Media and Third World Development*, (New York: Greenwood Press, 1988), p. 70.
[28] S. T. Kwame Boafo, "Communication Technology and Dependent Development in Sub-Saharan Africa," In *Transnational Communications: Wiring the Third World*, (Eds.) Gerald Sussman and John A. Lent, (Newbury Park, CA: Sage, 1991), pp. 117–118.
[29] Gershon, "International Deregulation and the Rise of Transnational Media Corporations," p. 6.

[30] Omar Souki Oliveira, "Mass Media, Culture, and Communication in Brazil: The Heritage of Dependency," In *Transnational Communications: Wiring the Third World*, (Eds.) Gerald Sussman and John A. Lent, (Newbury Park, CA: Sage, 1991), pp. 201–212.

[31] Ibid.

[32] Donald G. Howard and Michael A. Mayo, "Developing a Defensive Product Management Philosophy for Third World Markets," *International Marketing Review*, 5(1), 1988, pp. 31–40.

[33] Barbara Baudot, "International Issues in the Advertising of Health Related Products," *European Journal of Marketing*, 25(6), 1991, pp. 24–25; see also S. Prakash Sethi, *Multinational Corporations and the Impact of Public Advocacy on Corporate Strategy: Nestle and the Infant Formula Controversy*, (Hingham, MA: Kluwer, 1994).

[34] "Smoking 'Em Out," *Economist (UK)*, September, 1990, pp. 83–84.

[35] American advertising experienced a significant change in approach during the late 1960s, when the focus of advertising shifted from providing information about the product to persuasion–oriented campaigns that appealed to the emotions and psychological needs of the audience. As the composition of advertising changed, U.S. viewers became more discerning in their ability to separate fact from fiction.

[36] Baudot, "International Issues in the Advertising of Health–Related Products," pp. 24–25.

[37] Anderson, *Madison Avenue in Asia*, p. 59.

[38] Meyer, *Transnational Media and Third World Development*, p. 71.

[39] The highly successful TNAAs recognize the importance of local partnerships and contacts. Such contacts can be mutually beneficial because the citizens of host nations have a unique understanding of local market conditions. In turn, these citizens have the opportunity to learn skills that can one day contribute to the establishment of autonomous, local businesses. This is perhaps best illustrated in India, where indigenous agencies are flourishing after a period of development and training under the auspices of Western-based agencies.

ACKNOWLEDGMENT

Heidi H. Holwerda is an Advertising Media Buyer for Horizon Group Inc. in Muskegon, Michigan. Ms. Holwerda received her MA in the Department of Communication at Western Michigan University.

5

Telecommunications and Intelligent Networks: Managing the Transnational Corporation

As internal communication within a TNC becomes technically easier, it has redefined both strategic decision making as well as the division of labor, production, and manufacturing. The TNC is no longer limited by physical geography. The TNC can engage in FDI and/or locate foreign operations wherever they can achieve a comparative advantage. The TNC has undergone an evolutionary process of decentralization whereby an increasing amount of critical decision making and operations are being performed on site. The combination of telecommunications and distributed data processing have virtually eliminated the distance barriers that once separated a company's strategic center from its affiliate sites. Telecommunications enables the TNC to communicate in real and asynchronous time with its affiliate sites and thereby makes possible a company that truly operates in a global environment.

Transnational Communication and Decentralization

Since the late 1940s, there has been a slow, paradigmatic shift away from top-heavy, centralized decision making toward decentralization where greater responsibility has been given to the regional manager for routine decisions. Implicit in this trend is a growing realization that the regional manager has a closer and perhaps more pragmatic understanding of local market conditions. Equally important was the increased use of foreign staffing, labor, and improved manufacturing techniques that allowed products to be produced at significantly lower cost. Early information technology, in the form of telephone and telex communication, enabled senior management to have direct ties with the company's foreign locations and managers. As Roche (1992) pointed out, the technology that supports today's TNC evolved slowly and was required to "overlay the pre-existing structures and traditions of the corporation."[1] The telecommunications and data solutions adopted by the TNC had to be incorporated into the existing methods for doing business on a worldwide basis. The solutions were seldom neat or complete because the multinational was often combining paper-and-pencil accounting systems with highly automated technical solutions. The result was a patchwork quilt of both efficient and inefficient business practices.

The current generation of telecommunications technology, including telephone, video conferencing, facsimile, and electronic mail has had a major effect on the spatial reorganization of activity within the global organization. Communication is instantaneous and thereby allows for more immediate decision making, as well as the worldwide coordination of production, manufacturing, and marketing of goods and services.

THE INTELLIGENT NETWORK

At the heart of any telecommunications system is the intelligent network. The intelligent network can be likened to the internal nervous system of an organization. It provides the basis for the seamless integration of information and communication, both internal and external to an organization.[2] For the transnational organization, the intelligent network is responsible for ensuring the steady stream of communication on a worldwide basis. The intelligent network performs the proper switching and routing of electronic communication between a set of global users that might include senior management, project managers, research and design teams, finance and accounting, general administration, marketing and sales, operations, and purchasing.

The intelligent network is a dynamic information resource designed to support both strategic decision making and routine operations. Network intelligence is a direct function of the amount of permeability built into the system. The intelligent network must have the ability to adhere to a rigid set of system instructions while having the capacity to grow and develop. What gives the network its unique intelligence are the people and users of the system and the value-added technology they bring to the system via critical gateway or (access) points. By providing such added value and efficiency, the intelligent network makes it possible for an organization to operate on a worldwide basis. In short, the intelligent network provides the communication links that make global communication possible.

Intelligent Networks and Transnational Applications

The TNC, by its very nature, has to think globally in terms of strategic planning and operations. If we assume that two primary goals of TNC are to be profitable and cost effective, then strategic planning and operations presupposes that the organization will engage in FDI in those markets that offer some form of comparative advantage. In chapter 1, I identified five reasons why a TNC engages in FDI, including proprietary assets and natural resources, foreign market penetration, production and distribution efficiencies, overcoming regulatory barriers to entry, and empire building.

Telecommunications does not obviate the need for the kinds of strategic and routine information that managers still require, regardless of organizational size. Financial reporting and sales figure updates will continue to be the information lifeblood that managers require in order to strategically plan and make decisions. What distinguishes the TNC from other types of companies is that the information being assembled is being coordinated and routed from different parts of the world. It is usually the same information, but only on a larger scale. At the same time, the size and complexity of an organization will impose greater demands on the manager who must synthesize the sheer volume of that information. What the new telecommunications offers transnational managers are two strategic advantages:

1. Improved methods of communication among managers, division heads and other corporate staff. This, in turn, translates into more immediate access and cost savings that are built into the very communication itself.
2. The ability to access powerful information databases and/or to run software programs that can synthesize data for purposes of strategic decision making and direct marketing.[3]

Both sets of tools provide what is referred to as decision support systems that enable the organization to make faster and more precise decisions, as well as improve efficiency. Organizational efficiency can be defined as those systems and processes that contribute to the overall improvement of the organization.

This chapter considers intelligent networks and the primary technologies that allow companies to become more transnational in their design and operations. In addition, I examine four areas where intelligent networks are used to enhance the business operations of the TNC. They include financial networks, electronic messaging networks, global manufacturing networks, and research and online database networks.

It should be pointed out that the network strategies described in this chapter are not unique to the TNC. Rather, it is the combination of networks and the applied strategies within that make it possible for the TNC to be truly global in its business operations. The specific design and configuration of intelligent networks are tied directly to the unique business requirements of the organization.

FINANCIAL NETWORKS

The world's financial markets have been revolutionized by the application of computer and telecommunications to the banking process. International banking offers both business and private users the ability to deposit funds in those locations where specific banks offer the comparative advantage of better interest rates, privacy, security, and a safe haven from taxes. The primary method for the international deposit and withdrawal of funds is Electronic Funds Transfer (EFT).

EFT operates as information (or the promise of actual funds) and not as physical currency. The real impact of EFT on organizations and the public is greater convenience (time and cost savings) by not having to physically handle money during routine transactions. In general, EFT has permeated financial transactions at four levels in the world of business and personal finance. They include:

1. The national and international transfer of money between banks and other financial institutions.
2. The transfer of money from the accounts of an organization or business into the direct accounts of banks and other financial institutions. This can include direct deposit payments on behalf of an organization's employees.
3. Public use of terminals and automated teller machines (ATMs) that can deposit and withdraw funds via electronic access. Funds can also be transferred from one account to another.
4. Public use of direct debit cards now used in supermarkets, gas stations, and convenience stores that transfer funds from the buyer's account directly into the seller's account.[4]

In the United States, the Federal Reserve Board and the National Automated Clearing Houses Association operate extensive nationwide telecommunications networks that establish the procedures for the authorization of payment and EFT between different U.S. banks and/or financial institutions. At the international level, the financial network known as S.W.I.F.T. is responsible for millions of EFT transactions daily between banks and financial institutions around the world. S.W.I.F.T. has established the most highly developed financial network for the international transfer of funds between domestic banks and their overseas counterparts.

The TNC and Financial Networks

The intelligent financial network, at the most basic level, enables the TNC to engage in EFT between the company's multiple sites in order to support operational expenses, salaries, equipment purchases, and so forth. The intelligent financial network also plays an important role by providing the TNC with immediate access to the world's financial markets for purposes of investment. The TNC is able to strengthen its financial position through the electronic surveillance of national changes in currency and interest rates. What makes the surveillance of foreign exchange so important is the speed at which the market can change. Such changes are the result of minute shifts in political events and central bank activities. The resulting changes can translate into billions of dollars in won-and-lost market opportunities on a daily basis. The three major international stock exchanges—London, New York, and To-

TABLE 5.1
A Comparison of the Share Value Traded Daily: 1989 and 1992

Stock Exchange	1989	1992
London	$187 billion	$303 billion
New York	$129 billion	$192 billion
Tokyo	$115 billion	$128 billion

Note. Data from the Bank of International Settlement.

kyo—saw a dramatic increase in the number of shares traded daily between the years 1989 and 1992. This can be seen in Table 5.1.

Computers and telecommunications have transformed the foreign exchange industry by providing instant access to the world's financial markets. A number of foreign exchanges have seen the value of automation, particularly in extending trading hours to capitalize on worldwide market activity. According to Childs (1994), "Computers and telecommunications not only react to world markets, they have created a new international monetary system based on instantaneous reaction to world events."[5] The resulting speed and volatility can significantly impact changes in currency and the value of stock.

In the United States, NASDAQ and the Chicago Mercantile Exchange are considered pioneers in the development of automated trading. The National Association of Securities Dealers (NASD) is the organization that regulates over-the-counter trading in the United States. Prior to the 1970s, the NASD provided trading opportunities for lesser known or poor performing stocks. The major trading floors were the New York Stock and Chicago Mercantile Exchange centers. In 1971, the NASD launched a computer-based trading system called NASDAQ (National Association of Securities Dealers Automated Quotations). A large centralized computer provided up-to-the minute stock quotations that were electronically available to financial traders all across the United States. According to Chorafas and Steinman (1990), the result was dramatic:

> Within a dozen years, share volumes rose more than 16-fold and the number of display screens grew from a few thousand in 1972 to more than 120,000 in 1985. By 1985, share volume had reached 16 billion shares with a value of some $200 billion. This made the networked NASDAQ the third largest stock exchange in the world, smaller only than New York and Tokyo.... Today, the NASDAQ computerized system is still the second largest U.S. stock exchange, but it is also an integral part of an ongoing effort by major exchanges towards 24 hour global trading.[6]

Elsewhere in the world, major innovators include Marche a Terme Internationale de France (MATIF), the London International Financial Futures Exchange (LIFFE), Singapore (SIMEX), the Sydney Futures Exchange (SFE), the Swiss Options and Financial Futures Exchange, and the New Zealand Exchange.

In the world of financial services, international financial investment or global custody has developed out of the belief that corporate investors should be able to access any financial market in the world on an equal basis. The intersection of information, multicurrencies and worldwide privatization trends has hastened the move toward the globalization of financial services. In 1979, Walter Wriston, former CEO of Citicorp, declared that the future of worldwide banking was tied directly to the proper organization and delivery of information. This assertion is evidenced by the number of automated financial systems that rely on the electronic handling and transfer of information, including checking accounts, credit cards, and ATM cards. In addition, financial services, including the listing, purchase, and sale of securities, account for more than 50% of all online database information.[7]

In past years, international banking systems were no more than domestic banks with a financial accounting system that could translate foreign currency into U.S. dollars. However, the demands of FDI and international privatization trends have forced banks to develop sophisticated financial networks and software approaches to match the objectives of global custody or financial management. Banks wishing to offer their clients a global custody service must provide them with three important features: securities management and control (SMAC) capability that tracks the financial transaction settlement; global securities accounting (GSA), which maintains accurate records of a customer's account; and international currency-to-currency conversions.[8] A global custody system should provide the user with an integrated foreign and domestic financial report in multiple languages. The future of global custody banking will also require that customers have online, real-time access to information.[9]

ELECTRONIC MESSAGING NETWORKS

In past years, the traditional corporation was characterized by two important features, including centralization and concentration. The principle of centralization can trace its origins to the age of industrialization and the formation of the auto and steel industries. According to Toffler (1980), centralization presumes that maximum efficiency can be achieved by concentrating a large number of people together in one central facility. It further presupposes that senior management is the central organizer of work activity and that strategic decision making is performed in a hierarchical (or top-down) fashion.[10]

Intelligent networking is the complete antithesis of centralization. As companies become increasingly global in their operations, most forms of centralization are difficult to maintain. Centralized organizational structures often require company managers to fly in for routine meetings in order to exchange information and coordinate strategy. In today's transnational environment, routine meetings and decisions are accomplished electronically via a combination of telephone, videoconferencing, electronic mail, and/or facsimile. The value to the organization is that information is both timely and cost effective. One indirect consequence is that intelligent networking tends to flatten organizational hierarchies by allowing direct communication and access between organizational players.

What are the technologies that extend the reach and hasten the speed at which organizations can communicate? Table 5.2 identifies the primary electronic messaging technologies used by transnational organizations. They are divided into three general classifications of use, including voice, data, and video communication.

Telecommunications and Organizational Planning

The number of new and enhanced electronic message delivery (EMD) systems have increased significantly since the early 1980s. Telecommunication managers and information specialists understand that the purpose of new communication technology is to create greater efficiencies in the workplace. At the same time, the introduction of new technologies does not replace the need for older technologies. As an example, the increased use of facsimile does not replace the need for physical mail delivery.

For the TNC, choice of information tools becomes an essential requirement in order to accommodate the organization's diverse needs. The selection of communication technology is based on how much information content (or depth of information) the sender wishes the receiver to have. The selection process is often tempered by such practical considerations as cost and the need for message security. To that end, the telecommunications manager (or information specialist) must routinely ask three questions:

1. What are the important considerations for selecting one information technology over another?
2. What are the information objectives (IOs) of the sender and/or project teams?
3. What are the intended and unintended consequences that result from the implementation of such technologies on the organization as a whole? Such effects can be measured in terms of:
    1. Organizational efficiency.
    2. Equipment costs (i.e., the cost of communicating).
    3. Staffing and personnel changes.

Researchers in the past have attempted to explain the process of media and technology selection. One of the best known models of media selection was first proposed by Daft and Lengel in 1984. The media richness model suggests that the selection of media and communication channels differ significantly in their ability to convey information. Daft and Lengel argue that organizational communication tasks vary in their level of ambiguity. Ambiguity refers to the level of conflicting and multiple interpretations of a message. Accordingly, the

TABLE 5.2
Telecommunications and Data Message Delivery Systems Used in International Business and Commerce

Category of Service	Description & Principal Advantages
Voice Communication	
Traditional Telephones	Traditional telephone service is the science of converting speech sounds into electrical signals that can be transmitted via a combination of wire, microwave, and satellite communications. The telephone network is the most ubiquitous of communication networks. Plain old telephone service (POTS) provides voice communication between two or more persons. The information can operate in real time or can be stored on voice mail.
Cellular Telephones	Cellular telephony provides over-the-air telephone service to cars and to hand-held portable phones. Cellular systems are designed to interface with the local telephone system that enables users to make local or long-distance telephone calls. A cellular system is designed to service customers within a specified geographical area, known as a cellular geographic service area (CGSA). The CGSA usually corresponds to a metropolitan area including a central city, its suburbs and some portion of its rural fringe. The CGSA divides an area to be served into hexagonal zones or cell sites. Each cell is approximately 5 to 8 miles in radius. The current trend is toward making cells smaller in size. Each cell has its own low-power transmitter. The low-power transmitter is part of a Mobile Radio Base Station, which is located at the three alternate corners of each hexagonal cell. As cars pass from one cell to another they are automatically assigned a dedicated frequency that allows the cellular user to interface with the local telephone system.
Data Message Delivery Communication	
E-mail	Electronic mail is a message delivery system that can link multiple workstations for purposes of exchanging text information. The value to the organization is that information exchange does not have to operate in real time. The information is stored by a host computer and can be readily accessed by the individual or terminal for whom the message was sent. E-mail has become a primary message transport system for TNCs and organizations that are engaged in large-scale collaborative research and design projects.
Facsimile	Facsimile is a method used to replicate and transmit documents long distance using the public telephone network. During a facsimile transmission, the characters of the original document are scanned and converted into analog or digital signals The signals are transmitted to their destination via the public telephone system and are then reconverted and printed into hard text.
Pagers	Pagers are small portable receivers that can be worn on belts or carried in breast pockets. Paging systems rely on over-the-air radio communication as the basis for transmitting a one-way signal from the sender's point of origin to the person who is operating within a specified area of coverage. The area of coverage will range in size from 1 to 15 miles. The signal format can include an electronic message, telephone number, or a simple beep indicating that the person must call in for the full message. Paging systems are ideally suited for people who are constantly mobile within a closed building or setting (i.e., physicians, engineers working on a shop floor, maintenance staff, etc.).

Video Communication

Video conferencing Video conferencing provides an electronic meeting format using video images and audio sound. People are linked together at two or more locations. The rationale is that video conferencing is the next best thing to a face-to-face meeting. The videoconference operates in real time and benefits the organization by reducing travel costs and the amount of time required to get people together for meetings, especially when it involves multiple worldwide location sites. There are two types of video conferencing options. The first is full-motion videoconferencing, which changes pictures 33 times per second and thus creates a lifelike image or moving picture. This represents the most expensive video conferencing option and is most often used in situations where a company is making a formal presentation to its employees and/or introducing a new product. The second type of video conference is slow-scan or freeze-frame television. Slow-scan is an appropriate communications tool when there is little visual movement such as a conversation among executives or the visual display of a document. Slow-scan video conferencing is less expensive than its full-motion counterpart because it does not have the same bandwidth requirements. It is an easier video conference to organize because it can be accessed on a dial-up basis using regular telephone lines. In years to come, the need to conserve bandwidth will become less of a factor given technical improvements in satellite and fiber optic deployment as well as bandwidth compression techniques.

Desktop video Desktop video permits the full integration of voice, data, and video communications from a desktop terminal. Desktop video provides many of the same features as a standard video conference, except that it allows for person-to-person communication.

Videocassette tapes The videocassette recorder (VCR) is a playback device that records and plays magnetic tape providing simultaneous audio and video pictures. The VCR goes one step beyond a telephone call or e-mail message. The VCR allows the additional benefit of video communication, which enables the sender or creator of the message to package the information for the simultaneous and uniform viewing experience of the receiver.

VCR tapes are ideally suited for those organizations that want a uniform presentation format as the basis for training and instruction for new employees. Likewise, VCR tapes are well-suited for a public relations presentation that can be seen by the general public. It allows for consistent video display and explanation.

Cable television and institutional networks Cable television is a broadband medium that is capable of transmitting multiple signals via a closed wired system of coaxial and/or fiber optic cable. An institutional network is a private cable network that utilizes the inherent advantages of cable television for applied internal use. Institutional cable networks can provide internal video communication for purposes of linking a local school district, a local business to its employees, etc.

telecommunications manager (or information specialist) should select a message delivery system that corresponds to the ambiguity of the task.[11]

The Business Communication Model

The media richness model only goes so far in helping to explain the selection process. There are other considerations that can factor into the selection process, including the social and cultural environment of the organization as well as the pragmatics of cost and message security. The Business Communication Model is a logical extension of the media richness model, whereby the telecommunications manager (or user) should select the technology to meet the complexity of the task. However, in a business setting, especially one that is transnational in scope, there needs to be a greater specificity in defining media richness. Table 5.3 identifies six criteria that should be considered when selecting and designing an EMD system.

The six criteria making up the business communication model are highly interdependent. The challenge for the telecommunications manager (or user) is to select an EMD system that allows for both acceptable and optimum levels of communication. The determining factors are application and use. At the same time, the system(s) must be available to the organization at a reasonable cost. For example, the telephone usage pattern of a securities trading company is going to be very different than that of a university. The securities firm would be willing to pay more because their business is largely dependent on the telephone and customer access. As a consequence, the information specialist (or user) must routinely balance the competing requirements in selecting one EMD technology over another.

EMD systems provide the many electronic highways that connect a company's internal and external communication. Such technologies enable the TNC to be truly global in its operations. The EMD systems, when configured as part of a wide area network, contribute to what Rheingold described as a "virtual community of workers."[12] Virtual communication, however, has its price. Electronic communication, no matter how clear and well-constructed, is no substitute for face-to-face meetings. All EMD systems have their social and technical limitations. Video conferencing, for example, is an excellent medium for the routine exchange of information. It is rarely used for strategic decision making. The EMD system imposes its own special brand of communication etiquette that requires users to know how to optimally use the medium.

The organization that depends on a worldwide system of virtual communication must ensure that the communication is reliable and secure. It is the responsibility of the telecommunications manager to ensure signal integrity. This becomes especially important for companies engaging in electronic funds transfer or the routine delivery of precision documents. EMD systems are built with varying levels of redundancy in order to ensure that the signal sent is the signal received. EMD systems can also require secure channels of communication, depending on the application. Companies that engage in proprietary research are

TABLE 5.3
The Business Communication Model

1. The information objective	What is the nature of the message being sent and who are the intended recipients? The information objective (IO) is a prerequisite to selecting the proper technology to meet the task. Cellular telephony is the proper technology for users who require communication in a mobile setting.
2. Speed	How fast the message is sent. Does the message need to arrive right away or can it arrive later? This can have a direct impact on the cost of transmission. For example, 2-day mail delivery as opposed to overnight.
3. The message receiver site or (geographical location)	Designing a message that is point-to-point is very different than a message that is point-to-multipoint. For example, a satellite point-to-multipoint videoconference allows a product announcement to be shared by all employees of a company on a worldwide basis.
4. Real time vs. asynchronous communication capability	Strategic decision making usually requires face to face communication or telephone communication at the very least. Alternatively, transnational corporations that use project teams routinely communicate in asynchronous mode; that is, the ability to communicate between two or more points regardless of time of day. One of the primary benefits of electronic mail is the ability to engage in asynchronous communication.
5. Message security	The selection of technology (and related services) may also require that the message being sent is fully encrypted depending on the nature of the information being sent. Corporations routinely encrypt a videoconference if the information being discussed is highly proprietary in nature.
6. Cost effectiveness	The selection of technology (and related services) is largely dependent on one's operating budget and the ability to cost justify the expenditure. For example, a point-to-multipoint satellite videoconference is an expensive proposition but may be a cost justified expenditure for a new product announcement. However, the same approach to videoconferencing may be too costly for a routine sales meeting between three locations. The alternative may be a slow scan videoconference using a dial-up, point-to-point telephone link.

Note. Based on the Business Communication Model, Richard A. Gershon.

understandably concerned that they can send and receive information over secure channels. In the end, the successful use of an EMD system is dependent on the user's perception that the system is consistent, reliable, and secure.

GLOBAL MANUFACTURING NETWORKS

Most companies have access to excellent hardware and software capabilities in today's international business environment. The distinguishing factor often centers on speed and turnaround time. Time-based competitiveness reduces the manufacturing process to its bare essentials in order to process a customer order in the shortest amount of time. The seamless integration of information technologies and manufacturing is bringing about the formation of quick-response organizations. Faster product cycles and the ability to train and produce worldwide production teams have transnationalized the manufacturing process. It is the ability of the TNC to apply time-based competitive strategies at the global level that enables such companies to manage inventories across borders. According to Goldhar and Lei (1991):

> We are now in a global competitive environment in which flexibility, responsiveness and low cost/low volume manufacturing skills will determine the sustainability of competitive advantage. The strategic picture is clear. . . . [Today's manufacturers] must also manage that most precious of all resources: time. . . .
>
> Fast response, global manufacturing demands nothing less than a complete break with yesterday's operating procedures, organizational methods and attitudes to survive. Time has become the paramount competitive resource as today's innovations become tomorrow's commodities seemingly overnight.[13]

At the heart of time-based competitiveness is quick-response manufacturing, which allows a company to meet an order in the least amount of time. The philosophy of quick response was born out of a need to improve customer service by lowering operating costs through reduced inventories. Quick Response was developed through the efforts of Robert Milliken, Chairman and CEO of Milliken and Company, a major manufacturer of textiles.[14] Since 1989, when it was first introduced, it has gained the full support of the Voluntary Interindustry Communications Standards (VICS) Committee, a U.S. organization of retailers, textile, apparel, and general merchandise manufacturers committed to the idea of improving the time it takes to get a product to market.

In designing a quick-response strategy, there are two essential parts, including reducing the manufacturing cycle to its essentials and creating internal efficiencies in materials supply, manufacturing, distribution, and transportation.[15] To accomplish this, quick-response requires several important elements.

The Use of Universal Product Codes (or Bar Codes). The use of Universal Product Codes (UPCs, or bar codes) enables a manufacturer to track the status of a product throughout the distribution cycle. It relies on optical scanning technology that reads the bars and lines (or characters) that are printed on special labels affixed to the product. The value of bar codes is that they provide the manufacturer with automatic data collection that allows information to flow in all directions. Such information can be used to determine shipping status, inventory levels, and/or consumer buying patterns. UPCs are used with such products as music CDs, personal computers, overnight mail delivery, and so forth.

Global Inventory Management. An electronic inventory management system uses bar code scanning at the point-of-sale, or checkout. This provides the retailer with critical information pertaining to inventory levels. The result is that the manufacturer and retailer keep inventory levels at an appropriate level and ensures that oversupplies do not accumulate. Global inventory management refers to a method for tracking inventory on a worldwide basis. The TNC is able to make manufacturing decisions based on separate information coming in from various distribution sites. Such information is especially important when it comes to the manufacture of large-scale products.

Implementing Bar Code Scanning at the Point of Sale (or Checkout) for Purposes of Database Marketing. Database marketing relies on a new generation of computers that are able to consolidate multiple information streams into a coherent database. The information is used to develop consumer profiles based on an analysis of customer purchases. The same information can also be cross-indexed in order to assist in new product development and for direct marketing purposes.[16] Bar code scanning at the point of sale (or checkout) provides an important stream of information that can be used for database marketing. In addition to bar code scanning, other sources of information including 1-800 telemarketing inquiries, responses to coupon and sweepstakes entries, and the purchase of name lists provide central databases with continual information about customer behavior. The information can be sorted according to such consumer variables as brand loyalty, volume use, purchasing power, and credit history. Once the information is gathered and factor analyzed, it can be used to support new product development and direct marketing. In the area of marketing, such information is used for mailings to narrowly defined segments of the population, informing potential customers of the new product availability, planning local promotional mailings, and designing promotional displays and layouts.

Implementing Electronic Data Interchange Links Between Manufacturing and Distribution Outlets. The size and complexity of global manufacturing can have a downward negative effect when different segments in the production process work separately. The lack of coordination or teamwork can result in the serious delay of manufactured goods. The problems become exacerbated when the communication difficulties are crosscultural. Quick response presupposes that all steps in the manufacturing process need to be clearly defined. In order to accomplish this, different participants in the manufacturing process including raw material suppliers, manufacturers, and distributors have to work together toward the common goal of meeting customer needs in the least amount of time. One way to reduce time is through the use of electronic data interchange between manufacturing and distribution outlets. Electronic data interchange provides real-time information links between the various partners that make up the manufacturing process, so that everyone knows the current status of a product throughout the entire manufacturing and distribution cycle.

Implementing Flexible and Just-in-Time Manufacturing. Flexible manufacturing strategies allow for the manufacture of multiple product designs and small-batch orders. At the heart of flexible manufacturing is computer-integrated manufacturing, which combines computerized inventory control with smart, multidimensional tools into one integrated platform. Just-in-time manufacturing allows a company to produce enough quantity of a select product to meet customers' needs without building up an unnecessary inventory of product. Such companies are able to stock shelves with much less waste, because it is based on actual buying patterns. In the field of publishing, the equivalent trend is in just-in-time publishing, which allows for the production of enough product to meet the requirements of the purchase order. Just-in-time publishing is often used for the production of college textbooks.

RESEARCH AND ONLINE DATABASE NETWORKS

Nowhere has the information revolution been more pronounced than in the field of library science. There was a time when the value of a library was measured by the volume and quantity of its holdings. Libraries of the future are being measured against an altogether different standard. Electronic access to online database networks has become the new standard for measuring a library's real information power. It is not surprising, therefore, that the term *information science* more aptly describes what a library does. The library of the future will provide access to regional, national, and international databases. The very methods for conducting research and gathering information have been transformed by the power of electronic access to worldwide database networks. In describing this trend, de Sola Poole wrote:

> The Harvard University Library and the New York Public library have made American publishers rather unhappy by taking the lead in forming a cooperative arrangement for the division of labor, specialized collecting and sharing of resources, partly by telecommunications. Those great libraries have recognized that they are reaching the inflection point at which exponential growth of collections of books and documents must slow. Increasingly, they will have to find ways of providing access to knowledge by telecommunications between the users wherever they are, and the medium storing that knowledge, wherever it happens to be located, rather than by depositing copies of all documents in each library.
>
> All of this implies the end of primary depositories and the retention of much data in its normal place of origination. There is a limit to what can be prepared for library deposit. For those who want the data more quickly, or want detailed data that has not been compiled, the ultimate means in the future for collecting

data will be to get on line (with permission) to the operating data of the source organization.[17]

As online information retrieval grows and takes over many of the present functions of traditional libraries and reference publications, it is worth considering how electronic access has changed the very conduct of research itself. To what extent does such online access make research and collaboration efforts more transnational in scope? Several of the world's leading TNCs in such diverse fields as electronics, pharmaceuticals, automobiles, and telecommunications routinely engage in collaborative research and development projects between affiliate sites. The networking of information is made possible via the messaging technologies discussed earlier in this chapter. Those same messaging technologies in combination with electronic access to international database networks enable companies to perform research anywhere within the organizational structure.

Information Providers versus Database Marketers

There is an obvious distinction between those who create data for publication and those who market and package it for public use. People who create data tend to be narrow specialists. They are the researchers and writers who create narrowly focused information in such topical areas as medicine, law, and telecommunications, to name only a few. Within these topical areas are the subspecialties, including neuroanatomy, contract law, and satellite communications. The journals, trade magazines, and related book publications that comprise these fields are often supported and administered by well-respected leaders in the field.

The print and electronic publishers have a different professional focus. They are more concerned with designing a commercially viable product that can be sold to both professional users and the general public. They understand the need to make such information accessible and cost effective. In the case of online database networks, the electronic publisher performs three important functions:

1. They organize the information and provide users with a guide to what information is available.
2. They design a search procedure (user-data protocol) that allows users access to the system.
3. They perform the billing function in order to ensure that the information providers are paid for the information services that have been provided.

Electronic publishers are responsible for creating and maintaining an online database service that has a sizable central processor and storage capability that can expand depending on the number of users. Creating and storing the information accounts for the largest part of the expense in designing an online database service. The data network must have a suitable interface that can accommodate multiple users, including the ability to handle peak loads. In order to achieve the highest level of use, the trend is toward global expansion by making the data available to the largest number of users.

Online Database Networks

It is beyond the scope of this book to consider the many thousands of online database networks that are used to support highly specialized areas of research. Such database networks as Lexus, Nexus, Dow Jones News Retrieval, and Wilson are just a few of the better-known database networks that support law, general news information, business, and finance, respectively. The value of such database networks is that they provide both comprehensive and immediate access to information. The information can be downloaded onto one's computer or workstation. The same information can then be printed, electronically mailed, or faxed according to the information requirements of the project team.

Multipurpose Online Database Services

At the first level, there are three multipurpose online database networks that are offered to the general public. They include Compuserve, Prodigy, and America Online. A brief description is given in Table 5.4.

TABLE 5.4
Three Multipurpose Online Database Services

Compuserve	Compuserve is the oldest and most comprehensive of the three major database services. It offers a variety of services, including stock quotations, news, an airline reservation system, and tickets to sports events and concerts. In addition, it provides access to the world's leading libraries, which enables users to download a variety of documents from multiple libraries worldwide. Compuserve also provides Internet access.
Prodigy	Prodigy began as a joint venture of Sears Roebuck & Co. and IBM. It is a midlevel service offering and is perhaps best known for its combination of online news information and home shopping capability. Prodigy is also noted for its graphic displays. In addition, Prodigy provides basic Internet features like browsing, e-mail, and Usenet groups.
America Online	America Online (AOL) is the best known (and newest) of the three major mulitpurpose database services. AOL offers a wide variety of original content as well as basic Internet features like browsing, e-mail, and Usenet groups. AOL is a favorite among Internet users, given AOL's easy-to-learn interface.

Note. Source: Company reports.

The Internet

The Internet is the world's largest computer network. It would be more accurate to say that the Internet is an international network of networks that link together tens of thousands of government, corporate, and commercial networks. The Internet reaches an estimated 35 million computers worldwide.[18] The Internet evolved from a computer system built in the late 1960s by the U.S. Department of Defense. The original Arpanet system was first conceived as a computer network that would allow academic, private industry, and military researchers to collaborate on U.S. government-sponsored projects. The three sets of players share in the cost of maintaining the system.[19] As the network expanded, researchers and other users soon discovered that the network could be used for sending electronic mail as well as providing a method for posting news and information. Over the years, millions of people have gained access to the Internet system.

There are three primary applications that are available via the Internet, including electronic mail, Usenet groups, and network search. Usenet groups (or news groups) are a collection of electronic bulletin boards that allow users to post news and information about a variety of topics. The Usenet groups are organized according to subject matter and cover the full spectrum of the arts, sciences, entertainment, and leisure. The quality and sophistication of the Usenet groups vary from one Usenet group to another. As the Internet has evolved, more than 5000 Usenet groups have been added to the system. The Internet is primarily accessed via university and private business accounts. Compuserve, Prodigy, and America Online do provide e-mail capability and access to the Internet system.

For those engaged in research, network search provides important communication links to a variety of worldwide database networks. Until recently, accessing the many thousands of database networks required some degree of computing skill. To offset some of these problems, Internet user groups developed a concept called the World Wide Web, which uses a hypertext approach. The Web's hypertext markup language (HTML) has emerged as the universal standard for Internet access. Clicking on a highlighted word or phrase on the screen takes the user to a related article of interest. Several browser programs, most notably Netscape and Microsoft Explorer, make the navigation process a lot easier.

IntraNets

Several of the world's leading TNCs in such diverse fields as pharmaceuticals, automobiles, and telecommunications routinely engage in collaborative research and development projects between affiliate sites. The increased use of the Internet has transformed both internal and external communications for international business. The most highly visible side of Internet use is for external communications and marketing. However, the Internet's infrastructure and standards are also being used to create IntraNets; that is, private, internal networks that utilize the standards and protocols of the Internet for the purpose of internal communication and collaborative research.

Relational Database Networks

The real power of computing is the ability to factor like variables together in order to spot emerging trends. Unlike hierarchial databases, where the users must define how information is to be sorted ahead of time, relational database networks allow the user to sort the information according to features or characteristics that are important to the user. One important research database, First Search, allows users of the system to access hundreds of databases according to a general set of classifications. Depending on the user, the information can be sorted according to title, author, subject, key words or phrases, time frame, or any combination. The information is then sorted according to the features that are important to the user. For example, an inquiry about DBS from the major communication and business publications might yield some 1,500 citations on the subject in the past 5 years. A further inquiry into DBS in Japan, tying together the two key words "Direct Broadcast Satellites" and "Japan" will refine that inquiry to some 200 citations. The resulting information is more highly selective, based on the unique set of information requirements of the user.

Database networks provide an important method for gathering and sharing information between project teams. Primary access to information is no longer determined by physical location. Instead, electronic access becomes the great equalizer by ensuring that all members of a project team are able to get the information that they require. The combination of shared database networks and messaging technologies allows critical information to be shared across functional departments and national borders. This, in turn, has had the effect of flattening traditional organizational structures in terms of product development. As futurist Alvin Toffler (1994) noted:

> The key word in the future is configured. We are moving from monolithic, pyramidal organizational structures toward highly transient, temporary configurations of production units of people. We'll assemble the appropriate information talents and producers, irrespective of where in the world they happen to be.
>
> We're going to have good automatic translation. It won't be perfect, but you're going to be able to carry out most work conversations. That means you're going to be able to put together a team from India, from Silicon Valley, from Peru and from Fiji, for that matter. People, wherever they happen to be, are going to be able put their heads together to solve a problem, and languages will ultimately become transparent.[20]

DISCUSSION

In the early 1980s, the personal computer was truly a revolutionary device. The introduction of the first Mac and IBM personal computers gave users a stand-alone capability to perform a variety of information-processing tasks. Now, 15 years later, the personal computer has been subsumed by the desktop workstation. What distinguishes the workstation from the personal computer is its versatility. The desktop workstation can perform all of the routine functions of a stand-alone personal computer. What gives the desktop workstation real power and definition is its ability to access intelligent networks. The future growth in transnational communication is not to be found in people talking to people, but rather, workstations talking to workstations via a sophisticated intelligent network.[21]

The intelligent network has become the internal nervous system of the transnational organization. It is redefining work patterns, staffing requirements, and spatial relationships. As organizations become more transnational and decentralized, their information requirements become increasingly more complex. Managing the modern organization presupposes an understanding of the role of telecommunications and intelligent networking. The effective use of such technology is fundamental to both decision making and operations.

Information has become a vital resource that needs to be shared by multiple users. At the most basic level, the intelligent network allows information to be shared across diverse groups and departments. The level of ease and access has eroded many of the traditional barriers that once separated functional departments. New systems and processes have eliminated management layers and allow for direct communication between users.[22] The power of intelligent networking allows research and development teams to work together on projects, regardless of time and distance factors. Similarly, quick-response manufacturing and global inventory management networks enable companies to be more flexible and responsive to a worldwide customer base. The result has been a dramatic improvement in the time it takes to bring a product to market.

All this points to a change that is taking place in the way business is being conducted across borders. More and more, time has become the critical element in allowing companies to be fully competitive in a global business environment. The use of telecommunications and intelligent networking has streamlined both internal and external communication. By providing such added value and efficiency, the intelligent network makes it possible for an organization to operate on a worldwide basis.

NOTES

[1] Edward M. Roche, *Managing Information Technology in Multinational Corporations*, (New York: Macmillan, 1992), pp 24–25.

[2] Robin Mansell, *The New Telecommunication: A Political Economy of Network Evolution*, (London: Sage, 1994), pp. 1–7.

[3] Frederick Williams, *The New Telecommunications*, (New York: The Free Press, 1991), pp. 24–37.

[4] James Martin, *Telecommunications and the Computer*, (Englewood Cliffs, NJ: Prentice-Hall, 1990), p. 17.

[5] Julian B. Childs, "The Impact of Technology on Foreign Exchange," *The Bankers Magazine*, May/June, 1994, p. 31.

[6] Dimitris N. Chorafas and Heinrich Steinman, *Intelligent Networks: Telecommunications for the 1990s*, (Boca Raton, FL: CRC Press, 1990), p. 81.

[7] Andre Lussi, "Economics and Ecumeme: The Globalization of the Securities Industry," *The Banker*, October, 1990, pp. 74–75.

[8] Alan Radding, "Beyond Multicurrency," *Bank Management*, October 1991, pp. 31–34.

[9] Ralph Carlyle, "Financial Systems that Bust Borders," *Datamation*, 15 November, 1990, p. 82.

[10] Toffler, Alvin, *The Third Wave*, (New York: Bantam, 1980), pp. 46–61.

[11] R. L. Daft and R. H. Lengel, "Information Richness: A New Approach to Managerial Information Processing and Organizational Design." In B. Straw and L. L. Cummins (Eds.), *Research in Organizational Behavior* (Vol. 6. Greenwich, CT: JAI Press, 1984), pp. 191–233. See also R. L. Daft, R. H. Lengel, and L. K. Trevino, "Message Equivocality and Media Selection: Implications for Information Systems," *MIS Quarterly*, 11, 1987, pp. 355–366.

[12] Howard Rheingold, *The Virtual Community: Homesteading on the Electronic Frontier*, (Menlo Park, CA: Addison-Wesley, 1994).

[13] Joel D. Goldhar and David Lei, "The Shape of Twenty-First Century Global Manufacturing," *The Journal of Business Strategy*, March/April, 1991, p. 38.

[14] "Quick Response," *Industry Week*, 19 August, 1991, pp. A4–A5.

[15] "Integrated Manufacturing: Compressing Time-to-Market," *Industry Week*, 4 May, 1992, pp. IM 4–5.

[16] "Data Base Marketing," *Business Week*, 5 September, 1994, pp. 56–57.

[17] Ithiel de Sola Poole, *Technologies Without Boundaries*, (Cambridge, MA: Harvard University Press, 1990), p. 95.

[18] Philip Elmer-Dewitt, "Battle for the Soul of the Internet," *Time*, 25 July, 1994, pp. 50–56.

[19] Rheingold, *The Virtual Community*, pp. 70–89.

[20] "An Interview With Alvin Toffler," *Communications Week*, 3 January, 1994, p. 53.

[21] Paul Saffo, "Looking Ahead to the Next Decade," *Communications Week*, 3 January, 1994, p. 52.

[22] "The Information Revolution: The New Face of Business," *Business Week*, Special Issue, 1994, pp. 100–104.

6

Expanded Cable and Open Video Systems: Establishing a Blueprint for Broadband Residential Services

Historically, the world's leading PT&T companies have enjoyed a unique monopoly position as the providers of traditional telephone service. Among developed nations, telephone communications touches virtually all phases of business activity. On January 1, 1984, the divestiture of AT&T in the United States caused an economic rippling effect felt around the world. The breakup of AT&T heralded an irreversible change that was about to take place in the field of international telecommunications. Private and government-supported telephone monopolies would no longer be assured protection from outside competition.

The result has been a communications revolution in Europe, Asia, and South America. Starting with British Telecom and later Japan's NTT, many of the world's leading PT&Ts have begun the process of deregulation and privatization. They have begun examining a number of unregulated business activities including cellular telephone, business paging services, electronic publishing, and cable television. Cable television potentially represents one of the best ways for telephone companies to enter into an unregulated business. It offers high rates of return and is compatible with the core telephone business of wire communications to the home. Cable television provides an excellent means for delivering broadband (or multichannel) services to residential subscribers.

Several of the major transnational telecommunication companies and newly privatized PT&Ts are now building large-capacity fiber cables, digital switches, and high-speed satellite links to accommodate business and residential customers. The information highways that are being built represent a new phase in national planning and community development. In proposing a U.S. information superhighway concept, the Clinton/Gore administration wrote:

> Accelerating the introduction of an efficient high-speed communications system can have the same effect on the U.S. economy and social development as public investment in railroads had in the 19th century. It would provide a critical tool around which many new business opportunities could develop.[1]

6. EXPANDED CABLE AND OPEN VIDEO SYSTEMS

The new architects of tomorrow's cities are the telecommunications and data communication specialists. Their designs will include such things as smart buildings, teleports, geographic information systems, cellular telephone systems, integrated community networks, and broadband residential networks.

This chapter considers the delivery of broadband residential services and what it means for community development and enhanced quality of life. It further considers the role of the transnational media and telecommunications corporation as a primary player in the planning and design process. Special attention is given to future design characteristics and format features for both expanded cable television and open video systems (OVS). The future integration of voice, data, and video services will give new meaning to the term *programming*.

EXPANDED CABLE AND OPEN VIDEO SYSTEMS: ESTABLISHING A BLUEPRINT FOR RESIDENTIAL SERVICES

Designing a broadband residential network represents a core component in the development of any proposed information superhighway concept. Good policy formulation requires that we ask who are the rightful owners of a future broadband network to the home? Is the broadband network the property of the telephone carrier, the local cable operator or is it a community resource? Implied in this question are three related questions:

1. Are there natural monopoly requirements of wired communication that preclude the possibility of two or more video services from successfully competing in the same marketplace?
2. How would expanded cable television or a proposed OVS be organized according to design, format, and rate structure?
3. How do communities ensure that such services are made available to all members of the community at a reasonable cost?

The provision of broadband residential services cannot be fully realized until such time as cable television undergoes a redefinition as to its true purpose and the economies that support it.[2] The future design and development of a broadband residential network has to be understood in the broader context that it is providing an electronic gateway for a whole host of entertainment, utility, and value added services. The proposed solutions will have a long-term effect on all aspects of telecommunication services to the home, including:

- Education.
- Governmental and public utility services.
- Television entertainment.
- Energy management.

- Shopping.
- Emergency communication and medical services.
- Online database services.

Community Planning Issues

In the 21st century, the provision of expanded cable or an OVS type service will become a necessity for a society that is dependent on timely news, entertainment, and information. That decision, however, raises some important policy considerations for community planners and utility regulators alike, including:

1. The feasibility of competitive services.
2. Consumer demand and the cost of service.
3. Selection of appropriate technology and service.

The Feasibility of Competitive Services

A primary consideration for any community is whether it can support two or more broadband communication services to the home.[3] A proposed OVS service (like its cable television counterpart), may exhibit natural monopolylike features. The cost characteristics of a broadband residential service, including the deployment of optical fiber, switching and routing equipment, decoder boxes, customer billing, and possible franchise fees could make competition difficult to sustain in small- to medium-sized communities. In short, the duplication of two wired services to the home could seriously undermine both businesses from successfully competing.[4]

One solution for the future is to create one information delivery system or gateway containing competitive services. Researchers like Egan (1994) argued that cable and telephony should join forces to build one fiber network to homes and not compete for the wire. Instead, the competition should be in the provision of program software and services. John Malone, CEO of TCI, concurs and says that in many cases, one wire makes the best sense. It would be more cost effective and would result in a lower break even point for both companies.[5] Alternatively, there are those who would argue that advancements in digital ATM technology and software development are driving the cost of switching and routing of programming down to a point where competition will become viable even among the smallest of systems.

Consumer Demand and the Cost of Service

Another important consideration is whether there is sufficient demand for new and enhanced information services. Community planners will have to consider how the development of such projects is going to be organized and financed. Specifically, they will need to consider whether community residents are prepared to share in the cost of delivery.[6] According to one analysis performed by Bellcore research, the estimated cost of a broadband fiber-to-the-curb residential network will range between $1,400 and $1,600 per household.[7]

Several of America's state Public Utility Commissions (PUCs) have begun to examine whether broadband residential networks should be properly included in the rate base. The principal test used by state PUCs is whether the property is used and useful in the provision of service. A select number of PUCs have permitted the inclusion of property acquired for future use as part of the rate base.[8] An alternative solution is to require local exchange carriers (LECs) to pay franchise fees similar to cable systems for the right to operate. Under the terms of the 1996 Telecommunications Act, all telephone companies that elect to operate as cable television operators would be obligated to pay franchise fees under the same terms and conditions as their cable television counterparts.[9]

Selection of Appropriate Technology and Service

A third planning consideration pertains to the selection of appropriate technologies and services. Community planners need to be aware of the opportunities, as well as the risks, involved in selecting the right kinds of technologies and services.[10] It is not the responsibility of the community planner to actually design the delivery or gateway system. Instead, community planners should be involved in the proper selection of vendors and prioritization of telecommunication services. A strong effort must be made to prioritize those services that are critical to a community's future, as compared to those services that are not immediately practical. Decision making in this regard should involve representatives from all parts of the community including business, public safety, health care, education, and the public citizenry. Such discussions will help to determine priorities and ensure that services are made available to all members of the community.

SYSTEM DESIGN AND PLANNING

Integrated Community Planning

Planning a broadband residential network represents a core requirement for tomorrow's "smart cities." The implementation of a broadband residential network is likely to be incorporated into a larger master plan that will provide access to a variety of community-based applications including local government, public safety, health care, education, and business. The heart of any community-based telecommunications master plan is the integrated community network, which interconnects all metropolitan users of the system.

SYSTEM DESIGN AND PLANNING

Singapore is perhaps the best example of implementaion of a comprehensive, national strategy for improving telecommunications at the community level. As early as 1984, Singapore announced its intentions to implement a national information technology plan. The country fostered the use of information technology on different levels, including the construction of a highly sophisticated fiber-based Metropolitan Area Network. The plan went into effect in 1986. By 1989, Singapore was the first country to have nationwide integrated services digital network (ISDN) capability at one seventh the cost of conventional telephone service. By 1994, the national and international telephone network was fully digitized.[11]

Interactive Customer-Based Networks

The concept of an interactive television network is not a new idea. In 1972, Ralph Lee Smith wrote in *The Wired Nation*:

> A second area of great promise was made vivid by an exhibit at the second annual convention of the National Cable Television Association. It displayed a home communications center in which the user, through appropriate switching circuits, could enter into two way exchanges with local stores, could dial-a-play, could have at his fingertips the full information in vast libraries. This is no dream. The cable industry could carry it all and the technology is in existence or soon will be.[12]

The technology is referred to as two-way interactive cable television, and has captivated the imagination of cable television entrepreneurs since the late 1960s. A cable television system is capable of not only transmitting audio, video, and data signals from the headend point to the subscriber's home, but can likewise send those same signals in a reverse direction. A typical subscriber is equipped with a hand-held keypad that allows the user to send information upstream to the cable headend or transmission center.[13]

It has taken several years and many failed commercial attempts before the technology has finally begun to succeed. The first applications were educational in nature and involved the production of local community and school events. Early supporters of interactive television realized that two-way capability would allow a cable system to offer programming on a pay-per-view (PPV) basis; that is, the ability to charge a customer by the program rather than by the channel or monthly service fee. Premium sporting events such as boxing and first-run feature films were excellent programming vehicles that could be offered using a PPV approach. Moreover, it was felt that the technology of interactive television would eventually spur the development of other types of home information services, including home shopping, security, and banking.[14]

In 1978, Warner Amex Communication introduced Qube, America's first operational interactive cable system, into Columbus, Ohio. At the high point of its development, the Qube system offered subscribers 30 channels of entertainment, information, and education, plus the capability for two-way interactive communications. Qube also offered its subscribers a number of PPV options, including professional boxing and Ohio State football. In the end, the combination of high operational costs coupled with the lack of good programming proved to be the biggest challenge facing the Warner Amex Corporation.[15] The Qube system, however, demonstrated the viability of an interactive network and the ability of a host computer to track program purchases and to perform automatic billing functions. The introduction of the Home Shopping Network (HSN) in the mid-1980s has proven to be the first successful application of interactive television.

In 1995, Time Warner took an altogether different approach to the problem of interactive communications. Time Warner has been at the forefront in developing a prototype broadband residential network. Starting in January 1993, Time Warner began construction of its Full Service Network in Orlando, Florida. The network features broadband switching, fiber/coaxial cable architecture, and digital compression technology. The Full Service Network will provide subscribers with voice and data transmission, cable television, personal communication services, and PPV film libraries.

The Deployment of Fiber Optic Cable

Planning for a broadband communication system to the home presupposes the deployment of fiber optic cable. It is the optimum carriage medium for integrated community networks (ICNs) and future broadband residential services to the home. Fiber optic cables are thin strands of glass capable of transmitting large quantities of information over long distances with little signal loss. Fiber optic cable offers greater potential bandwidth than other types of transmission media.[16] When bundled together in a duct or passageway, the combined bandwidth of a fiber optic cable provides more than sufficient capacity for most voice, data, and video applications. Moreover, it allows for expanded growth as information needs change.[17] Fiber optic cable is not susceptible to electromagnetic interference and can be used in select locations where corrosive chemicals or high degrees of noise are present. Its light weight and flexibility makes it ideally suited for placement below ground.[18]

Advancements in fiber optic technology have seen a corresponding decrease in cost. The price for fiber optic cable has steadily declined since 1982, and is expected to decrease by an average of 5% per year until 1998, whereas the price for copper cable is expected to increase by 6%. As the cost of fiber continues to decrease, it is being used for a variety of telecommunications requirements, including local area networks (LANs) for data distribution, and cable communication for video distribution.[19] Thus fiber optic technology has become the transmission medium of choice for both the telephone and cable industries.

Telephone and Cable Delivery of Broadband Residential Service

Telephone carriers and cable operators are both capable of delivering broadband residential services, albeit in different ways. The LEC understands the business of switching and routing of electronic messages. Under the terms of the 1996 Telecommunications Act, the telephone company could provide video services to the home in one of four ways, including:

1. Wireless service (MMDS, DBS, etc.).
2. Common carrier.
3. Open video systems (OVS).
4. Cable television.

As a common carrier, the telephone company would be obligated to provide the primary conduit to the home as well as to lease channel capacity to all would-be programmers without discrimination. In principle, the consumer would be given greater control in the selection of voice, data, and video services. In addition, the LEC is tied into a national and international telecommunications infrastructure that allows for the delivery of enhanced telecommunications service to the home, including videotelephony and online database services.

Under an OVS scenario, a telephone company must make channels available to nonaffiliated programmers without discrimination. If demand exceeds capacity, the telephone company cannot control more than a third of the available channel capacity. In addition, the OVS service provider is obligated to pay the local community a 5% operator's fee. The OVS service provider, however, is not subject to other federal cable regulations and need not obtain a local franchise.

Telephone companies can also elect to become cable operators. In this regard, the telephone company functions no differently than a traditional cable operator having to adhere to the same terms and conditions. Several leading U.S. RBOCs are actively pursuing cable television. The value of building and operating one's own cable television system is that all programming and pricing decisions are left to the cable operator. Moreover, cable television is a known quantity and will prove to be the most attractive short-term solution for those telephone companies wishing to engage in video delivery. As telephone companies become more familiar with the medium, there will be a natural progression to combine voice and video services together as part of a complete package.

Cable operators understand the business of television programing and marketing. In the United States, cable television is currently available in 64% of all homes. The cable industry's commitment to a future multichannel television system would involve a more gradual transition since it requires the logical expansion of their current set of offerings. The cable industry is also looking to expand beyond its news and entertainment base. One important strategy for the future is to provide competitive local telephone service.

Under the terms of the new Telecommunications Act, cable operators will now be able to provide telephone communication within their own service area. Specifically, local telephone companies will be required to negotiate with cable operators (and new telephone entrants) in terms of:

1. Interconnection.
2. Number portability.
3. Dialing parity.
4. Access to rights of way.
5. Reciprocal compensation.

A study performed by Arthur D. Little Consulting indicated that the cable industry is well positioned to provide local telephone service and may prove to be the overall winner in terms of evolving markets. Their reasoning is that the telephone market is five times larger than the existing cable market. By gaining even a small portion of it, the cable industry could increase its revenues substantially. Time Warner, for example, plans to invest $5 billion to rebuild its cable systems.[20] In May 1994, the company won approval to offer local telephone service in Rochester, New York in direct competition with Rochester Telephone. Starting January 1, 1995, Rochester became the first U.S. city with locally competitive telephone service. Cable television is also well positioned to take advantage of its existing broadband cable to the home by offering data customers high-speed cable modems for the transmission and receipt of online information.

Media Software and Technology Partnerships

The clear lines and historic boundaries that once separated broadcasting, cable, media entertainment, and telephony are becoming less distinct. A natural convergence of industries and information technologies are blurring those distinctions. Today, the level of economic restructuring and partnerships is unprecedented in the history of telecommunications. Nowhere was this more evident than in the July 1995 announcement that the Walt Disney Company would spend $19 billion to purchase Capital Cities/ABC. The merger was the second largest in corporate history and has made Disney one of the largest entertainment companies in the world.[21]

U.S. telephone carriers have not been traditional players in the field of television programming. It is for this reason that several RBOCs and long-distance carriers are pursuing joint ventures in media entertainment and programming. They are positioning themselves for the new world of telephone-delivered news and entertainment. In March 1996, US West announced plans to purchase Continental Cablevision for $10.8 billion. Similarly, US West spent $2.5 billion in May 1993 for a 25% interest in Time

Warner Entertainment, which includes the company's film studios, cable systems, and Home Box Office, Inc. In 1995, MCI Corporation invested $2 billion in News Corporation Ltd. In 1994, NYNEX spent $1.2 billion for preferred stock in Viacom Corporation's bid to purchase Paramount Studios.[22]

The motivation behind such strategic partnerships of this kind is a realization that the future delivery of broadband residential services will require considerable financing as well as complimentary planning and operational strengths. Table 6.1 identifies some of the proposed and completed mergers and acquisitions among North American media and telecommunication companies.

Expanding Program Choice

Between 1952 and 1977, the three major U.S. television networks (CBS, NBC, and ABC) were responsible for approximately 92% of all television viewing. That figure has since declined to 67%. The emergence of cable television has given consumers greater choice and made television viewing far more specialized.[23] One indication is the successful emergence of such cable program services as CNN, HBO, ESPN, and MTV. The cable industry, like the magazine industry, has moved toward highly specialized (or narrowcasted) programming. The trend is irreversible.

Poole (1990) suggests that the mass media revolution is undergoing a reversal; that is, "instead of identical messages being disseminated to millions of people, electronic technology permits the adaptation of electronic messaging to the specialized or unique needs of individuals."[24] Expanded cable and OVS represent a logical progression in narrowcasted services and specialization. The real value of a broadband residential service is the ability to provide consumers with entertainment and information services on demand. It is the consummate form of PPV or use, depending on the application.

Convergence of Modes and Multimedia

Pool (1984) characterized the joining of two altogether different technologies to create a third technology as a "convergence of modes."[25] Research and development in home entertainment and information systems is undergoing such a transformation. The trend is toward multimedia or modularity of design, whereby components can be easily interfaced to create entirely new forms of media use and application. One example of this is the large-screen video monitor, which is currently designed to service multiple video applications, including cable television, VCRs, Compact Disc Interactive, and video games. The design trend is likely to continue and will eventually include videotelephone service, medical infomatics, public safety, electronic shopping, and banking. Audio speakers are likewise undergoing a similar transformation and are currently designed to service CD and audiocassette music, television,

TABLE 6.1
Mergers and Acquisitions: Media and Telecommunication Companies North America (1993–1996)

North American Investment Plans	Description	Price	Time/Status
Bell Atlantic & NYNEX	Both RBOCs will merge together in the form of stock swap valued at $25 billion.	$25 billion	April 1996 Pending
SBC (formerly Southwestern Bell) & Pacific Telesis	SBC will acquire PacTel in the form of a stock swap valued at $17 billion.	$17 billion	April 1996 Pending
US West & Continental	US West will purchase Continental Cablevision for $10.8 billion. The merger will give cable partner Time Warner 16.2 million subscribers.	$10.8 billion	March 1996 Pending
Time Warner & Turner Broadcasting	Time Warner purchased Turner Broadcasting in the form of a stock swap valued at $8 billion.	$8 billion	September 1995 Pending
The Walt Disney Company & Capital Cities/ABC	Disney purchased Capital Cities/ABC for $19 billion. The merger will provide Disney with greater direct access to U.S. television homes.	$19 billion	July 1995 Completed
Westinghouse & CBS	Westinghouse purchased CBS for $5 billion. The purchase included all CBS owned and operated stations.	$5 billion	July 1995 Completed
MCI & News Corporation	MCI spent $2 billion for a 10% interest in News Corp The plan is to market interactive services.	$2 billion	April 1995 Completed
Viacom & Paramount/Blockbuster	Viacom spent about $10 billion to purchase both Paramount Communications and Blockbuster Entertainment.	$10 billion	September 1994 Completed
NYNEX & Viacom	NYNEX obtains preferred equity stake in Viacom's purchase of Paramount Communications & Blockbuster.	$1.2 billion	October 1993 Completed
Bell Canada Enterprises (BCE) & Jones Intercable	Bell Canada purchased a 30% interest in Jones Intercable with the understanding that BCE could buy the rest of the company in 8 years.	$400 million	June 1994 Completed
US West & Time Warner Entertainment	US West spent $2.5 billion for a 25% interest in Time Warner Entertainment.	$2.5 billion	May 1993 Completed

Note. Source: *BusinessWeek, Newsweek,* and company reports.

and computer applications. One likely scenario for the future is to use audio speakers to service telephone communication as well.

Digitalization

The main driving force behind convergence is the digitalization of all media and information technology. According to Ray Smith, CEO of Bell Atlantic, "The relevant fact is this: the cable, telephone, broadcast, wireless and information industries are converging. We are increasingly all in the bit business."[26] Digital technology improves the quality and efficiency of switching, routing, and storing information. It increases the potential for manipulation and transformation of data.

The primary platform for all future cable and telephone-switched services to the home is the digital video client server. The video client server is a large storage device that uses computer hard drives under the control of one or more computer processors. It can access stored video, time code, and associated program elements. One of the most attractive features of a video server technology is its ability to provide multiple outputs. In principle, a video server network allows for the simultaneous delivery of voice, data, and video signals to the home. For example, a cable system using a video server can play the same film or PPV event at different times to multiple subscribers.

OVS AND EXPANDED CABLE

Broadband Residential Services: Select Features

Organizing a multichannel universe will require the vendor to provide a user-friendly navigation guide to available services on the system. In a future common carrier or OVS scenario, one channel would be allocated for video telephone service. Basic telephone service would presumably originate in audio mode and then provide optional video capability. Channels 2 and 3 would be designated as an electronic directory and would provide a listing of all entertainment, information, and dedicated channels. The directory would include a series of menus that would guide the user through the more specialized application phases, such as PPV or home shopping. The selection process would be accompanied by the use of a remote control keypad. The remote control keypad would consist of numbers and icons (i.e., a sports or business icon) that could automatically switch the user to either the main directory, a program service category, or a specific channel.[27]

Table 6.2 provides one possible scenario for a multichannel television service to the home. This model provides the basic architectural framework in organizing a multichannel universe of one-way and two-way programmatic services to the home. It calls for all information, entertainment, and hybrid media service channels to be organized into 12 program service categories.

TABLE 6.2
Future Scenario Expanded Cable and OVS Service Menu

Channel 1	Telephone and picturephone service
Channels 2–3	Program guide and listings directory
Channels 4–49	Broadcast and cable networks
	Broadcast networks (CBS, ABC, NBC, Fox), cable networks, (CNN, MTV, ESPN, TNT, etc.), independent and public broadcast stations, Superstations (WOR, WGN, WTBS, etc.)
Channels 50–70	Pay television services
	HBO, Disney, Showtime, The Movie Channel, etc.
Channels 71–90	Foreign language channels
Channels 91–100	Public safety and medical emergency
	Dedicated online emergency communication to local police, fire, and hospital services; also includes public safety and medical emergency premium services (channels 91–95)
Channels 101–110	Educational channels
	Includes distance learning channels, local continuing education, videoconferences
Channels 111–130	Local community and business channels
	Includes cable access, local government channels (televising community town meetings), utility metered services
Channels 131–159	Home shopping channels
	Home Shopping Network, also includes video catalogs (L.L. Bean, Lands End, Penney's, etc.) and online shopping capability
Channels 160–180	PPV: Special events
	Includes professional sports (professional boxing, baseball, regional sports action, etc.) and concerts (Chicago Philharmonic Orchestra etc.)
Channels 181–200	Online information services
	Provides access to a variety of information and entertainment services that can be downloaded to the home, including Internet, America Online, video games, etc.
Channels 201–500	PPV: Film entertainment
	Includes a virtual library of current and past films that can be downloaded on request

Note. Based on Gershon Model of "Broadband Residential Service Menu."[28]

Expanded cable and OVS will make possible a whole host of utility and value-added services. The joining together of television and applied utility services will fundamentally change the way people regard the business of cable television and telephony. It is for these reasons that both media and telecommunication companies are working with community planners to design a system of television distribution that can accommodate these changes. The concluding section of this chapter considers several important program services that are likely to transform the nature of television at home. They include:

1. Medical infomatics and telemedicine.
2. Education and distance learning.
3. Video home shopping.
4. Public safety and medical emergency (PSME).
5. PPV television (video on demand).

Medical Infomatics and Telemedicine

Health care around the world is under increasing pressure to become more cost effective. Present efforts to reduce the cost of health care services have proven ineffective. Between 1980 and 1992, the cost of health care in the United States has quadrupled. The trend in more recent years is to shorten hospital stays and to provide select medical services in an outpatient setting. Medical infomatics and, more specifically, telemedicine applications represent an important step toward achieving greater cost effectiveness without compromising health care treatment.

The field of medical infomatics serves to link both medical professionals and patients via local, regional, and international telecommunication networks. Medical infomatics allows both physicians and allied health care professionals to consult with regional and national specialists, regardless of distance and location. Such communication networks are used for medical consultation, obtaining medical research information, and continuing education. The basic premise behind medical infomatics is that the timely and coordinated sharing of a patient's medical history will enable the attending physician to design a better medical treatment plan.

At the heart of any medical infomatics strategy is the use of a comprehensive patient healthcare database (PHDB). In past years, the lack of a coordinated patient medical database could result in lost time and redundant costs when:

1. A medical record, including a patient history, is not available during patient visits.
2. Laboratory tests are reordered because earlier test results are either unavailable or have been lost.
3. Diagnosis and support information are not recorded.
4. A patient has moved to a new community and/or is traveling and suddenly requires emergency medical attention.

The successful development of a PHDB will promote better health care by providing medical professionals with more accessible information for purposes of medical diagnosis and decision making. When medical infomatics is combined with cable television, it enables the physician to engage in remote medical consultation and monitoring of the patient at home. This ensures that the patient is being regularly monitored, reducing hospital stays. In addition, medical information can be downloaded to the patient's home for personal viewing as part of a larger effort toward patient education.

One important feature of any telemedicine system is the use of a medical emergency response system (MERS). A dedicated communication link is established with the hospital via a cable or telephone channel. In the event of an emergency, an alarm is activated by pressing a keypad. A signal is sent upstream to a central switching facility that will route the signal to the proper public safety destination and/or medical facility.

Education and Distance Learning

Distance learning refers to new and innovative ways to educate students and working professionals through the use of audio and video communication. The distance learning classroom links two or more physically separate classrooms together by means of a television monitor and electronic blackboard. A television camera focuses on the instructor and electronic blackboard. The distance learning classroom is further supported by enhanced information equipment, including personal computers, facsimile machines, and electronic overhead viewers. Distance learning, in combination with cable television, also provides opportunities for local schools to design learning channels that work to support ongoing classroom instruction.

Distance learning is most often associated with rural areas, where an educational district lacks the in-house expertise and/or where individual schools have too few students to justify a fully developed curriculum. This is especially true in select areas of mathematics, science, and foreign languages. A distance learning classroom provides access to recognized experts in the field, as well as transmitting video demonstrations of scientific processes and cultural events that would otherwise be unavailable.

Distance learning at home provides opportunities for local schools to design learning channels that work to support ongoing classroom instruction. Several communities have introduced a strategy called *homework hotline* that extends the formal classroom via cable television for purposes of information review, special presentation, and exam preparation. The same learning channels are also used for nonformal education goals. Such programs are designed to provide information and increase awareness about important social issues that directly affect students and their community.

Distance learning is also used by business and professional organizations for the purpose of training and development. The demands for a more highly educated workforce require periodic upgrading in professional skills and knowledge. Distance learning in combination with cable television makes it possible for students and working professionals to pursue portions of their education selectively and in the privacy of their own home.[29] The level of instruction can range from formal classrooms for course credit to highly specialized presentations. Gallagher and Hatfield (1989) note that the convergence of such technology offers greater flexibility over one's work and leisure time by providing access to a variety of remote educational centers and information databases.[30] Table 6.3 provides an overview of priority learning applications that would be made available via a system of distance learning and cable television to the home.

Video Home Shopping

The successful launching of the Home Shopping Network (HSN) in the mid-1980s demonstrated the market potential for interactive shopping. During its early start-up, HSN mostly sold high-volume, low-budget catalog products. HSN became enormously successful and was soon followed by a host of imitators that resulted in a major market shakeout. By the late 1980s, HSN and Cable Value Network (CVN) became the two most profitable home shopping services. Both HSN and CVN are carried to people's homes via their local cable operator and use an 800 telephone number as the principal method for ordering merchandise. In exchange for cable carriage, HSN and CVN pay the cable operator a 5% commission based on sales in each operator's franchise area.[31]

Since 1987, industry-wide home shopping revenues have seen a sixfold increase, to a current estimate of $2.2 billion per year.[32] The natural progres-

TABLE 6.3
Education and Distance Learning Priority Applications

<u>Extended school day</u>
Homework hotline
Communication with homebound students
Specialty speakers
Foreign language instruction
<u>Professional training and development</u>
Health care
Business
Government
Formal classroom instruction
<u>Distance education</u>
Formal classroom instruction
Specialized presentations
<u>Citizen education</u>
Public safety
Health
K–12 school–parent partnerships

sion in home shopping is to become more upscale and specialized. This form of home shopping appeals to working professionals who have little time to shop and/or prefer the convenience. QVC is perhaps the best known cable channel for upscale home shopping. QVC has attracted an impressive list of retail merchants including Saks, Bloomingdales, and Nordstrom. Eventually, the major catalog companies, including Lands End, L.L. Bean, Sears, and J.C. Penney will become prime candidates for home shopping services. The combination of video display and convenience will make shopping at home very commonplace.

Pay Per View Television (Video on Demand)

Pay-Per-View (PPV) involves charging the customer by the program rather than by the service or channel. Premium sporting events such as professional boxing and first-run feature films are made available on a PPV basis. The rationale has always been that the consumer only wants to pay for the specific programs viewed. PPV is not a new idea. The strategy has been tried many times since the early 1960s. The basic limiting factor was the lack of addressable technology capable of ordering up programming on demand.

PPV represents the consummate form of interactive television. The organization of Pay-per-view would be divided into three service categories: (a) special event programs, (b) PPV Movies, and (c) online database services.

Starting in the mid-1980s, PPV began to fulfill its long overdue promise with new sources of programming, including sports, films, and concerts. The economies that support special event programming have made it the most successful of PPV options. Research conducted by Kagen & Associates (1990) confirmed that boxing and wrestling were responsible for 89% of PPV's gross revenues in the calendar year 1990.

Given the revenue potential and rising costs of sports franchises, many professional teams have begun examining PPV as an important new source of revenue. Most U.S. professional sports teams televise a select percentage of their home games on a pay channel and/or PPV basis. PPV will take on increasing importance in the future delivery of sports programming.

Video on demand represents an emerging category of PPV services capable of downloading feature films and concerts on request. Near video on demand allows for a start-time every 15 minutes. Video on demand may prove to be the most important strategy that cable system operators have in competing against the highly dominant VCR tape rental industry.

The future success of PPV films and concerts will be largely dependent on designing an interactive system that is capable of downloading a virtual library of film and music products. Modularity of design and convergence of modes is important to this discussion because it is a key marketing element in promoting the increased use of PPV. Concert performances, in particular, will greatly benefit from the combination of HDTV and digital audio technology.

Similarly, high-resolution graphics and expanded audio capability will promote the increased use of online information services and games.

DISCUSSION

In a multichannel universe, the origins of entertainment, information, and utility-based services will become indistinguishable. They will be transparent to the user. The main challenge for telephone managers and cable operators will be to organize the selection of program services in ways that are least disruptive to well-established industry structures and practices.

The Telecommunications Act of 1996 has already taken some of those issues into account. The following are just a few examples:

1. Network nonduplication.
2. Syndication exclusivity.
3. Must-carry and retransmission consent.
4. Commitment to universal service.

Planning for a broadband residential network requires some new definitions as to the purpose of the network and who are its rightful owners. Community planners will have to resolve such topical issues as information access, life-line services, rights of way, and possible franchise fees. Their deliberations will have a direct impact on local community development, including business, education arts and entertainment, health care, and public safety. It is therefore incumbent on community planners to become involved in the planning process because the design, format, and cost structures of broadband residential network will have a long-term effect on a community's economic future and quality of life.

NOTES

[1] William Clinton and Albert Gore, *Technology for America's Economic Growth: A New Direction to Build Economic Strength*, (Washington, DC: Government Printing Office, 1993), p. 16.

[2] Richard A. Gershon, "Video dialtone: A Study in Policy Alternatives," *Telecommunications Policy*, March, 1992, pp. 114–115.

[3] The term *broadband* refers to any method of delivery that is capable of transmitting multiple channels of service.

[4] The argument that cable television should be regulated as a type of public utility is not without its critics. Economists and policy analysts such as Hazlett (1986), Noam (1982), Posner (1969), and Demsetz (1965) argued that public utility regulation is wrong in principle and ineffectual in practice.

[5] Bruce Egan, "Building Value Through Telecommunications: Regulatory Roadblocks on the Information Superhighway," *Telecommunications Policy*, 18(8) 1994, p. 578.

[6] Bruce Egan and Douglas A. Conn, "Capital Budgeting Alternatives for Residential Broadband Networks," *Telephone Company and Cable Television Competition*, (Ed.) Stuart Brotman, (Boston: Artech House, 1990), pp. 136–137.

[7] "US West Maps Broadband Strategy," *The Cable-Telco Report*, January, 1993, p. 8.

[8] In past years, the used and useful standard referred to that property that was actually used for regular operations, maintenance, and repairs. Materials for new construction, extensions, and future service were not allowed in the rate base. This is now beginning to change. See Karl Lessker, Michael McGregor, and Michael Dupagne, "Economic, Political and Regulatory Constraints on the Deployment of Fiber to the Home," *Telecommunications Policy*, January/February, 1993, pp. 66–69.

[9] The Telecommunications Act of 1996, Section 653B.

[10] David Gibbs, "Telematics and Urban Economic Development Policies," *Telecommunications Policy*, May/June, 1993, pp. 253–255.

[11] *Corporate Networks, International Telecommunications and Interdependence*, (Ed.) Henry Bakis, (London: Belhaven, 1993), pp. 49–55.

[12] Ralph Lee Smith, *The Wired Nation*, (New York: Harper & Row, 1972), p. 9.

[13] Thomas F. Baldwin and D. Stevens McVoy, *Cable Communication*, (Englewood Cliffs, NJ: Prentice-Hall, 1988), pp. 147–157.

[14] In the United States, some of the earliest experiments included the Tocom Corporation in Woodlands, Texas and the Coaxial Scientific Corporation in Columbus, Ohio. See Richard A. Gershon, *Pay Cable Television: A Regulatory History & Selected Case Studies*, (Athens, OH: Ph.D. Thesis, 1986), pp. 75–77.

[15] "Warner Cable's Qube Exploring the Outer Reaches of Two Way TV," *Broadcasting*, 31 July, 1978, p. 27.

[16] Fiber optics uses light as a method for multiplexing its signal. A standard optical-fiber link consists of a light source, typically a Light-emitting diode (LED) or laser and optical fiber as a transmission medium and detector. A standard 3-inch thick telephone cable contains 1,200 pairs of copper cable that can transmit 14,400 telephone conversations. By comparison, a half-inch thick fiber optic cable contains 72 pairs of optical cable that can carry 3.5 million telephone conversations (either voice or data). See Corning Inc., *Just the Facts: A Basic Optical Fiber Overview*, (Corning, NY: Corning Inc., 1989), p. 8.

[17] Henry Geller, *Fiber Optics: An Opportunity for a New Policy*, A Report of the Annenberg Washington Program, (Washington, DC: Annenberg Washington Program, 1991), pp. 143–145.

[18] The primary motivation for optical fiber use in cable television is channel capacity and system outage reduction. In a standard cable television supertrunk there may be as many as 30 or 40 amplifiers. When one fails, all downstream amplifiers become inoperable as well. In addition, the more amplifiers to the system, the greater likelihood of increased noise and distortion. The use of single-mode optical fiber in supertrunks and distribution trunks (e.g., network backbones) can reduce the number of amplifiers between signal origination points and subscriber homes to as few as three.

[19] Corning Glass, Inc., "Fiber Gets Ready for Cable TV Industry," *Guidelines* 5(2), 1990, pp. 1–2.

[20] "Study: Telco, Cable May Trade Revenues," *Telephony*, 25 July, 1994, p. 9; and "Telco-cable Giants Converge," *Broadcasting & Cable*, 24 May, 1994, p. 6.

[21] "Walt Disney Acquiring ABC in Deal Worth $19 Billion; Entertainment Giant Born," *New York Times*, 1 August, 1995, p. 1

[22] "Deal Mania on the Infobahn," *Business Week*, 20 June, 1994, pp. 38–39.

[23] Richard A. Gershon, "Pay Cable Television: A Regulatory History," *Communication and the Law*, 12(2), June, 1990, pp. 22–26.

[24] Ithiel de Sola Poole, *Technologies Without Boundaries*, (Cambridge, MA: Harvard, 1990), p. 8.

[25] Ithiel de Sola Poole, *Technologies of Freedom*, (Cambridge, MA: Belknap Press, 1983), pp. 27–42.

[26] "On line with Ray Smith. The Ambitious and Iconoclastic Leader of Bell Atlantic Talks About Life After TCI," *Educom Review*, July/August, 1994, pp. 12–15.

[27] In December 1992, Discovery Communications Inc. announced a prototype design of a remote control keypad and ordering system called Yourchoice. The system is intended to be used in conjunction with digital compression terminals and will support interactive programming.

[28] Gershon, "Video dialtone: Is it the Future of Telephone Programming," p. 22.

[29] For many years, satellite communications has played a significant role in higher education, business, engineering, and law. Universities across the nation offer undergraduate and graduate courses by satellite that extend beyond their physical campuses. National Technological University and the American Management Association are among the more notable programs that offer professional education courses via satellite.

[30] Lynn Gallagher and Dale Hatfield, *Distance Opportunities in Telecommunications Policy and Technology*, A Report of the Annenberg Washington Program, (Washington, DC: Annenberg Washington Program, 1989), pp. 8–22.

[31] Raymond L. Carroll and Donald M. Davis, *Electronic Media Programming*, (New York: McGraw-Hill, 1993), p. 466.

[32] QVC reaches an estimated 47 million U.S. homes. Annual revenues have risen from $13.28 in 1987 to $23.37 in 1991. See Ken Auletta, "Barry Diller's Search for the Future," *The New Yorker*, 22 February, 1993, and "Highbrow Goes Lowbrow," *Newsweek*, 5 April, 1993, pp. 48–49.

7

The Transnational Media Corporation: Cultural Trespass and Challenges to National Sovereignty

The world has become a series of economic centers consisting of both nation states and TNCs. Today, a new international division of labor exists, made possible through the complex organization and command technology of the TNC. The TNC has emerged as one of the world's important power brokers. It is able to generate capital and commit technical resources at a rate that is faster and more efficient than many developed nations.

In a transnational economy, strategic decision making and allocation of resources are predicated on economic goals and efficiencies with little regard to national boundaries.[1] As the world's economy becomes more fully privatized, the goals of nation states and the goals of the TNC will increasingly find themselves on a collision course. For it is the purpose of nation states to strengthen the cause of political and economic sovereignty whereas the goal of the TNC is profitability.

The TNC stands to offer the host country significant opportunities for economic development in terms of potential jobs, allocation of resources, and tax revenues. As so often happens, the establishment of an overseas facility by a TNC can have some far-reaching consequences. The precise nature of these consequences and the extent to which they cause greater good or harm is sometimes difficult to assess. It is not surprising, therefore, that the TNC is both courted and feared by host governments because it represents such a large assemblage of management, technology, and resources.

Nowhere is the problem of divergent goals more apparent than in the area of media products and telecommunication services. What distinguishes the TNMC from other types of TNCs is the fact that the principle commodity being sold is information and entertainment. And yet, the financial imperatives that drive the TNMC are not always compatible with the goals and objectives of the host nation. At issue is the potential loss of privacy, cultural integrity, and technological/product dependency. This chapter considers some of the direct consequences that are likely to result from the TNMC that operates beyond national borders. It further considers the obligations and rights of the host nation.

CHALLENGES TO NATIONAL SOVEREIGNTY

All governments exercise the right to national sovereignty. The concept of national sovereignty requires the ability to create laws that regulate economic activity within national boundaries. These regulations include taxes, tariffs on imports, privacy laws, regulations on working conditions, product quality, and more. At issue is the host government's ability to maintain control over the activities of the TNC when it is felt that the TNC is engaged in practices that are contrary to the best interest of the host nation. Such practices are well documented, including the ability to introduce inappropriate products and values, exert inordinate influence on host governments, and distort the economies of host governments.

THE DISSEMINATION OF CULTURAL VALUES

The extraordinary growth of TNMCs in the latter part of the 1980s had a profound influence over the international marketplace of ideas. As Mowlana (1975) observed, the [TNMC] "has become one of the chief organizers and manufacturers of the international flow of communication."[2] Similarly, Bagdikian (1991) wrote:

> Together, they exert a homogenizing power over ideas, culture and commerce that affects populations larger than any in history. Neither Ceaser, nor Hitler, Franklin Roosevelt nor any Pope, has commanded as much power to shape the information on which so many people depend to make decisions about everything from whom to vote for—to what to eat.[3]

The TNMC is capable of promoting and distributing a set of messages that effectively bypasses traditional channels of communication including family, church, and schools. The messages of advertising, television, and music are often culturally laden and can sometimes promote political attitudes and social beliefs that are contrary to the values of the host nation and its domestic culture.

Media Imperialism

The term *media imperialism* is used to describe the one way flow of media products and services from a few highly industrialized nations to Third World developing countries. Traditional discussions concerning media imperialism are usually related to one country's ability to export and influence another country through its media products. In essence, the media products being exported are more than just mere entertainment and information. They often demonstrate differences in social and economic values that have direct and indirect consequences. Research into the potential effects of media imperialism are well documented. Several studies, including Nordenstreng and Varis (1974), Boyd-Barett (1977), Tunstall (1977), Beltran and de Cardona (1977), Lee (1980), and Varis (1983), identify the problems associated with the one-way flow of media products between Western developed countries and Third World developing nations.[4] According to Nordenstreng and Varis, there exists a one way flow of television programs from the big exporting countries to the rest of the world. Furthermore, these programs are primarily entertainment in nature and the majority of them originate in the United States.

Early research into the effects of media imperialism can be traced to the post-World War II period, when social researchers became interested in U.S. entertainment industries and the role of media trade with developing nations. Several research studies began to link the importance of media exports as way to explain the cultural domination by Western developed nations on the more fragile political and economic life of Third World nations.[5] Much of this investigation centered on the TNMC whose operations are primarily motivated by financial considerations. Schiller (1979), for one, argued that such media exports are done with a preconceived ideological or economic agenda in mind. Accordingly, transnational media exports are part of a larger economic system used to reinforce Western material values:

> The transnational media are inseparable elements in a worldwide system of resource allocation generally regarded as capitalistic. They function as private profitmaking enterprises seeking markets, which they term "audiences." They provide in their imagery and messagery the beliefs and perspectives that create and reinforce their audiences' attachment to the way things are in the system overall.[6]

The term *media imperialism* that was once so popular in the 1970s has given way to a more revised thinking about the role of Western media exports. The United States and Western media are no longer the primary target for such research and investigation. Instead, the TNMC has become more of the focus on issues of political hegemony and cultural influence.[7] The TNMC has become the dominant force in the production, sale and distribution of international media products. Schiller wrote:

> One important change in the world scene demands attention. No longer is the global arena dominated by US power, as it once was in the early post World War II years. Though the American presence in the message and image remains strong, a powerful expansive transnational corporate order is the main engine of current worldwide cultural and economic activity.[8]

Critics point to the fact that the TNMC is motivated by whether the product can sell rather than if it is appropriate for a foreign culture. As was mentioned in chapter 2, the TNMC has become content or software neutral. Consideration for such things as media violence, obscenity, and indecency has given way to the overriding objective of increased sales. By allowing marketplace solutions to guide media decision making, the TNMC has abandoned both its civic and moral responsibility.

The preoccupation with profitability can also factor into the creative process itself and directly affect the finished product. The result is popular, mass appeal programming that has little to do with the host country and its people.[9] A further consequence is that TNMCs become highly resistant to supporting less profitable, narrowly focused media enterprises. The field of publishing is highly illustrative of these changes. Seven major book publishing TNMCs now dominate what was once a highly diverse field. The large publishers have eliminated many of the smaller imprints, thus reducing both the quality and diversity of publishing outlets. According to one *Newsweek* account:

> In their zeal for profits and efficiency, big publishers have drummed most of the fun out of what was once a collegial, if somewhat haphazardly run business. . . . Recently, big companies have shuttered many small imprints, fired editors and whittled down the number of books published. As publishing loses the diversity that comes from many editorial tastes, the public has less to choose from and the culture suffers from a blander diet.[10]

Transnational Advertising

The TNAA is based on a free enterprise system that is rooted in competition. It is a system that requires aggressive marketing and advertising as a way to promote consumer demand and increase market share. As large corporations become increasingly transnational in scope, they establish global identities and design media products that cut across national boundaries. Janus (1981) examined the importance of transnational advertising as a way to penetrate markets and establish demand for consumer products. According to Janus, "Today's advertising campaigns tend to stress images and references that have global appeal with heavy use of jingles, visual images, and trademarks."[11]

The issue of media influence is particularly evident in transnational advertising. The major questions in such discussions focus on whether the use of transnational advertising disrupts the economy of foreign nations. Inclusive of this idea is the added problem of promoting goods and services that may be contrary to the values and norms of the recipient nation. This is especially true for developing countries. The content of promotional messages is oftentimes culturally laden and can have a significant influence. The values being communicated can influence not only individuals but the larger institutions that must establish appropriate policies and plans.[12]

The unintended consequences of such messages can lead to what Lerner referred to as the principle of rising frustrations. According to Lerner, the messages of material prosperity promote consumer desire. The lack of financial resources—and/or domestic governments' inability to provide such material goods and services—can lead to dissatisfaction with one's government and/or living conditions.[13] This, in turn, can cause political and social instability. Such patterns of instability can be seen in the former Soviet Union and East Germany.

A Theory of Dependency

A strong corollary to the principle of media imperialism is dependency theory. The developing nation is said to depend on Western nations for capital investment, technology, and manufactured goods. The same dependency can also include a willingness to absorb cultural values as well. Several researchers, including De Cardona (1976), Cardoso and Faletto (1979), and Salinas and Paldan (1979) argued that Western lifestyle portrayed through the export of mass media is said to create desires on the part of consumers to emulate Western culture.[14] The result leads to increased importation of Western commodities and increased dependency by less developed countries.

Dependency can, and often does, distort material values. In his research on the country of Brazil, Oliveira (1991) pointed to the disparities between rich and poor generated by the country's mass media. After the 1964 military coup, the Brazilian government invested heavily in the development of its telecommunications infrastructure and used television as one method for securing its political control. The combination of mass media (i.e., television, radio, magazines, and newspapers) is more or less centralized in Sao Paulo and Rio de Janeiro. Much of the nation's advertising is directed toward the 15% of the population consisting of the wealthy and upper middle class, while virtually ignoring the remaining 85%. According to Oliveira, two worlds live side by side in Brazil; the one that revels in the advertising images of good food and extravagant vacations versus the 7 million abandoned children who wander the downtown streets of Brazil's overpopulated cities. Thus Oliveira concluded that the combination of modernization coupled with the mass media has tended to sharpen Brazil's social differences.[15]

TRANSBORDER DATA FLOW

Transborder data flow (TBDF) generally refers to the flow of international voice, data, and video communications across national borders. The TNC, whether it be an international banking institution or news organization, is regularly involved in the sending and receiving of information to affiliate sites worldwide. Such information is made possible via a sophisticated network of computer and telecommunications technology. The high-speed voice, data, and video links have all but eliminated the physical borders and time differences that once separated TNCs from their affiliate locations.

Since the mid-1970s, several nations have become increasingly concerned with the enormous power of these networks to facilitate the storage, retrieval, and manipulation of data across national borders. The instantaneous flow of information poses a continuing challenge to national sovereignty. In general, a host nation is likely to impose three types of TBDF restrictions. They include restrictions pertaining to scientific and technical data, transaction data, and privacy data.

Scientific and Technical Data

The free flow of information may put the host country at an economic disadvantage. A country may not wish to have classified information pertaining to new product development flowing out without having some restrictions placed. The unrestricted flow of scientific and technical data or databases may compromise trade secrets. This is especially important for countries trying to promote a competitive advantage in highly specialized areas of technology or service. Some countries are understandably concerned that sensitive technical data should not be made available to the wrong countries. This is especially true when it comes to matters of defense and national security. The development of weapons systems and installations is a prime example.

Financial Transaction Data

Financial transaction data refers to the electronic transfer of money that form the basis of direct deposits and debits across national boundaries. Electronic funds transfer goes to support a wide variety of organizational needs including salaries, purchasing of equipment, administrative costs, raising capital, financial investments, and the return of profits to the company's corporate center. The TNC and its affiliate locations are routinely engaged in the electronic transfer of funds.

Financial transaction data has become an issue of growing concern to host nations. Private corporate networks that allow for the sudden transfer of money can directly impact currency reserves of the host nation. The routine transfer of funds becomes especially problematic when it comes to the paying of taxes. Information pertaining to a TNC's level of profitability is one of the most closely guarded secrets within a transnational organization. The TNC will engage in variety of accounting practices that best serve the interests of the organization. Host governments, for their part, want to assess the proper taxes on the TNC as part of the cost of doing business. Obtaining accurate information is difficult to achieve because there is no reliable way to monitor financial transaction data without being highly intrusive. Moreover, the host nation lacks the power to enforce the release of such information beyond its own borders.

The result is a clash of interests between the TNC and host nation. As Irwin and Merenda (1989) pointed out:

> Networks generate instantaneous data transfer. It is the velocity of information flow that permits the firm to circumvent government disincentives whether embodied as taxes, rules, interest payment or capital restrictions. Given their transparency, telecommunication networks enable multinationals to elude the reach of state control.[16]

Privacy Data

Rapid advances in computer and telecommunications technology have taken individual records and papers out of the control of the individual. The record keeping explosion of the information age has enabled the government and the private sector to keep previously unimagined amounts of data pertaining to the individual. One major by-product of computers and instantaneous communication is the loss of individual privacy.[17]

The TNC with strong centralized data networks are able to internally transfer data in a series of cross-checks. This cross-checking, for example, allows a magazine's circulation files to be linked with marketing and sales in order to develop a more complete demographic profile on prospective customers. This information can be used by the TNC and/or sold to outside companies that have a direct marketing interest. Although the sale of circulation lists is quite commonplace, the ability to do instantaneous cross-checks raises questions related to privacy abuse. The potential for abuse creates a fine line between improved marketing efficiencies and infringement on personal liberty.[18]

The issue of privacy abuse becomes more problematic at the international level. Privacy laws are not uniform among nations and virtually nonexistent among developing nations. The TNC maintains large data files on prospective customers and uses this information in its international marketing and sales efforts. There is a real concern among host nations that the unrestricted flow of information can potentially compromise the privacy of a nation by making its citizens the target of sophisticated international marketing efforts. As a result, several industrialized countries have enacted data protection or privacy laws. The purpose of these laws is to avoid the misuse of personal data files by foreign governments and/or TNCs.

THE TNC AND GOVERNMENT RELATIONS

The decision to engage in FDI can be a risky proposition for a TNC because it must adhere to the laws and regulations of the host nation. A sudden change in political leadership can have a direct impact on the TNC and its ability to continue doing business in the host nation. The result can be disastrous for the

TNC whose foreign direct investment is potentially at risk. A new political regime may decide to promote a change in economic policy that can include the usurpation of a TNC's resources and research. Historic examples include the countries of Chile, Iran, and Cuba, which under new political or religious administrations simply nationalized (took) resources that previously belonged to foreign-owned companies. Alternatively, a change in political leadership may result in the introduction of new rules and requirements of the TNC that may be costly and inefficient.

As a foreign-owned company, the TNC is obligated to respect the political and economic sovereignty of the host nation. The United Nations charter for multinational corporations requires that companies wishing to engage in FDI shall (a) respect the sovereignty of the host nation and are subject to its laws, (b) operate in conformity with the development policies set out by host governments, and shall work seriously in contributing to these goals.[19]

The principles set forth in the U.N. charter are designed to protect the political and economic sovereignty of the host nation. But equally important to the discussion is whether the TNC is entitled to certain business rights and protection when operating in a foreign country.

Nations That Engage in Unethical Business Practices

All too often, the host nation participates in or condones unethical business practices. The general public seldom understands the political and economic cross-currents that the TNC must face when operating in a foreign country. As can sometimes happen, the TNC finds itself unable to separate its daily business operations from the ongoing political, social, and economic policies of the host nation. This can include everything from the former apartheid practices of South Africa to the exploitation of prison workers in the People's Republic of China. Despite public outcries against such practices, the TNC is bound by the U.N. charter not take any steps with the intention of trying to correct the situation. To do otherwise would be perceived as trying to promote instability and interfering with the sovereignty of an independent nation.

Buying Influence

One of the more commonplace examples is buying influence. There is no internationally accepted guideline concerning the practice of buying influence whether it is bribing a local customs official or buying expensive lobby representation in a nation's capital. In many countries, bribery is not only seen as an accepted way of doing things, but is regarded as the way to get things done, especially when it comes to government bureaucracies.[20] In Germany, the paying of bribes is typically written off as a tax-deductible expense, reflecting a pragmatic attitude that bribery is part of the cost of doing business in some cultures.[21] According to a U.S. intelligence report, Siemens Corporation was allegedly responsible for offering bribes in connection with bids on

11 contracts from 1984 to 1994. Siemens was successful in winning seven of those contracts.[22]

The hiring of a public relations firm and/or political lobby can be an effective way to purchase influence in a foreign country. In the United States, one way to promote favorable legislation is to hire a political lobby and to make use of political action money. Both the countries of Japan and Saudi Arabia, through their auto and oil industries respectively, have long understood the importance of political action money as a way for a foreign company to get things done in the United States. In some cases, nation states will even become directly involved in the negotiation process as a way to leverage a deal on behalf of a domestic company. In 1993, France warned an African government that it would withdraw government guarantees on outstanding loans if Alcatel did not win a $20-million telecom switching contract. Similarly, in order to win a $30-million supercomputer order from Brazil, the Bank of Japan said it would credit the purchase against Brazil's existing debt to Japan.[23]

In the case of transnational media, buying influence takes the form of complimentary (or supportive) media coverage. Political leaders have long understood the power of the news media to help shape political opinion.

Political leaders are highly sensitive to media coverage. They recognize the power of the news media to help shape public opinion. As can sometimes happen, political leaders grant business favors in exchange for favorable news coverage. Transnational media owners Rupert Murdoch and Silvo Berlusconi are often cited as men who have used their considerable media holdings as a way to extract business favors from political leaders. Both men have a long history of using their respective media holdings as a platform to support preferred political candidates.[24]

In the case of Murdoch, his News Corp. Ltd. was highly supportive of former U.K. Prime Minister Margaret Thatcher and U.S. President Ronald Reagan. Murdoch's extensive newspaper and television holdings gave both political leaders favorable treatment during their administrations. In Britain, Murdoch was able to obtain the influential *London Times* that would have otherwise been difficult to purchase due to the country's monopolies commission. In addition, he was able to win approval to launch Britain's first DBS service. In the United States, Murdoch was able to circumvent FCC rules governing both broadcast and newspaper cross-ownership and syndication financial interest rules with the start-up of the Fox television network. Similarly, Silvio Belusconi, Italy's largest transnational media owner, used his friendship with former Italian Prime Minister Craxi as a way to leverage the start-up of Italy's first commercial television network. Italian law had previously forbidden the formation of commercial television networks.[25]

Intellectual Property and Copyright

Another business right that is subject to violation is the failure to protect intellectual property and copyright. Some countries demonstrate a complete disregard for the rights of international business when they fail to enforce regulations governing patent protection and copyrights. Lax standards of enforcement can translate into an incalculable loss of revenue. The latter issue is of particular importance to companies engaged in the business of international media trade, where the pirating of illegal television film and computer software is a daily occurrence.

The rapid expansion of information and entertainment, including television, film, computer software, music CDs, and tapes, brings with it new opportunities for international export. At the same time, such changes have brought with it an exponential increase in the worldwide piracy of media products and services. There are two interrelated factors that have caused the massive increase in international piracy. They include the relative ease of copying and distribution, and cultural attitudes towards theft of service.

The Relative Ease of Copying and Distribution

New media technologies, including VCRs and personal computers, not only expand the opportunities for the recording, storage, and dissemination of media software, but they likewise offer up multiple opportunities to abuse those systems. The illegal copying of media software is often done in the relative privacy of one's business or home. As a result, the international black market in software piracy has become pervasive. In some countries, an estimated 75 to 85% of all videotapes are pirated; that is, programs are recorded and distributed with no adherence to copyright laws.[26]

The sale and distribution of pirated (nonlicensed) software has cost international software producers billions of dollars in lost revenue. In 1994, software producers lost an estimated $15 billion from the illegal copying of audio, video, and computer software.[27] Several regions of the world including the Middle East, Asia, and Russia have become major markets for the sale and distribution of pirated software. Table 7.1 provides a comparison of software piracy among 10 nations in terms of lost revenue and their estimated rate of piracy.

The illegal pirating of program software has become the single most important problem facing international television and film producers. The problem is compounded by the fact that such countries as the United Arab Emirates (UAE) and Cyprus are major exporters of unauthorized videocassettes. The UAE is reportedly one of several countries that maintains highly sophisticated tape plant facilities. The UAE supplies countries like Saudi Arabia and other Arab and African states with low-cost media software.[28] Similarly, the country of China has a long history of engaging in state-sponsored piracy of music and computer software.

Cultural Attitudes Toward Theft of Service

What is termed the *private ownership* of media property is a concept that is not fully appreciated in many parts of the world. The piracy of both advertiser

TABLE 7.1
A Comparison of Software Piracy (10 Nations: 1994)

	Lost Revenue Due to Software Piracy—$ Millions	Estimated Rate of Piracy
United States	$2,877	35%
Japan	$2,076	67%
Germany	$1,875	50%
France	$771	57%
Brazil	$550	77%
Korea	$546	78%
Britain	$544	43%
Russia	$541	94%
China	$527	98%
Italy	$404	58%

Note. Source: *BusinessWeek*, Business Software Alliance.

and pay-supported television is oftentimes not looked upon as a criminal offense. Moreover, legislation to prohibit media and computer software piracy is difficult to enforce due to the nature of its use. The country of Saudi Arabia provides a good illustration of this problem. In Saudi Arabia, there are few public cinemas. The country's two national channels provide the vast majority of public television service. The VCR has become readily available and there is burgeoning demand for foreign television entertainment. The availability of copying machines prompted an enormous increase in pirated U.S. and British programming. The cost for such programming is considerably less than that which is officially licensed and sanctioned by the Saudi government. As Boyd (1993) pointed out:

> Several businesses operate in Saudi Arabia selling selected television programming taped in various American and British cities: so little attention is paid to the editing of their tapes that in many instances identifications from stations in New Orleans, Louisiana and San Francisco, California may be seen or heard.[29]

The country's middle and upper middle classes are among the biggest users of pirated programming. Many have traveled abroad and are quite familiar with Western media technology and entertainment. Ironically, they are the same people who endorse or tolerate the government's official position of censorship. Other beneficiaries of illegal pirated material are the many foreign business firms that operate inside the country. They have become willing customers who want access to such programming for the private use of their employees. In the end, the illegal import of VCR television and film programming has become a big business in Saudi Arabia and has effectively circumvented official government attempts to restrict the kinds of visual material that is shown within the kingdom.

DISCUSSION

The TNMC is the most powerful economic force for global media activity that the 1980s has produced. The TNMC is more likely to view transnational expansion and its effects in the context of whether it makes good business sense. Such concerns for obscenity, violence, and cultural trespass are often secondary considerations to the business of profitability. The host nation, for its part, is trying to balance free-market economics with the political and civic responsibilities of preserving national sovereignty. Clearly, the goals of the TNMC and the goals of the host nation are at times incompatible. It is, therefore, appropriate that we ask three questions:

1. Should the host nation treat the import of media and telecommunications products differently from other types of goods and services?
2. Should the host nation position itself as the guardian of culture?
3. When are the appropriate times that a host nation should impose restrictions on the import of media and telecommunication products?

We offer two perspectives.

International Media Trade: A Business Perspective

In a transnational economy, media entertainment and telecommunications services are viewed as commercial products that should be allowed to openly compete. The business of transnational media ownership is an industry characterized by high start-up costs and high risk. The decisions to invest in cable television or to launch a new magazine are high-risk ventures with few guarantees. Such efforts usually require a long-term investment in the host nation in terms of capital, technology, and resources.

The TNMC views the international export of media products and telecommunication services as a business. It is not done with the intention of trying to systematically exploit or culturally dominate other countries.[30] Attempts by host nations to impose trade restrictions or program quotas are considered a form of economic protectionism. Governments that impose program quotas are incorrectly assuming that each nation can function as a self contained island. As Poole (1977) suggested: "that kind of autarchy can be had only at a high price, (for even more than the flow of goods) each location has a comparative advantage only in a few activities. If a country tries to do everything for itself, it squanders resources, assuring only that it does nothing well."[31]

The Obligations of a Host Nation

As host nations seek to become part of an interdependent global economy, they have certain obligations and rights. One of those obligations is to protect the intellectual property of TNMCs and software distributors whose business is dependent on the fair and legitimate use of their software product. Illegal piracy and/or copyright infringement is contrary to all forms of legitimate business practices. Another obligation is that a host nation should not engage in power politics by targeting specific companies or countries with specially imposed rules. A host nation should avoid arbitrary and capricious behavior that involves the establishment of unilateral restrictions and/or rigid quotas.

Equally important, it is not the responsibility of host nations and their government ministries to position themselves as the guardians of culture. Specifically, a host nation should not attempt to micromanage the television-viewing and music-listening habits of it citizens. It is virtually impossible for a 21st-century country to function in isolation without some degree of external influence. In an age of instantaneous communication, the combination of transnational media and highly sophisticated network technology precludes this possibility. As Ang (1990) concluded, "the dissemination of the transnational media system is an irreversible process that cannot be structurally transcended, only in concrete cultural contexts." The movement is forward and cannot be reversed.[32]

International Media Trade: A Host Nation's Perspective

The TNMC has become an integral part of the global economic landscape. The TNMC raises the specter of policy issues considerably, given its unique ability to influence national politics, economic priorities, and social opinion. The confluence of transnational media products is eroding the cultural soil of host nations. The erosion is not deliberate, nor is it being caused by one nation or company. The changes are slow and barely perceptible. But the net effect is that transnational media in the form of music, television, film, and news is yielding a homogenized world culture. The resulting globalization of culture requires both government and policymakers alike to consider the long-term implications.

The Rights of a Host Nation

When are the times that countries should exercise this right? The appropriate times to impose such restrictions are when the said media products represent a direct threat to the privacy and cultural integrity of a nation and its citizens. Specifically, a sovereign nation should safeguard the privacy of its citizens by restricting the easy access and transfer of personal records to those companies that would use such information for direct marketing purposes.

Media entertainment and telecommunication services are a form of commercial trade. If that is true, than a sovereign nation should exercise the right to impose quality control standards as they would for any other product import. To that end, sovereign nations should develop systems of evaluation or general guidelines that establish reasonable standards for media imports. If a TNMC fails to exercise critical judgment when it comes to the export of program software, then it becomes the responsibility of the host nation to do it for them.

Media restrictions may also be appropriate when environmental and cultural resources are at risk. In traditional land use management, the use of appropriate zoning laws are designed to ensure that public and cultural resources are maintained. Sovereign nations and local communities routinely impose zoning laws in order to preserve national parks, historic downtowns, and important landmarks from unacceptable forms of environmental and cultural trespass. These specially designated areas are protected from such things as incompatible building design, intrusive billboard, or improperly designed signage. Let us suggest a form of cultural zoning, including the use of public funds, in order to preserve public broadcasting and national arts programs. In a world that is becoming increasingly privatized, advertiser-supported media provides no assurance that narrowly focused media and arts programs are sustainable. It becomes the responsibility of sovereign nations to ensure their continuation and development.

There are few international laws to govern the conduct of TNCs. International deregulation and privatization is admittedly a delicate balancing act that requires a government and its representative agencies to properly function as a nation's defenders of the public interest while participating in an interdependent global economy. The goals of profitability and economic sovereignty are not mutually exclusive. The basic underpinnings for successful international trade require mutual cooperation and respect between the TNC and the host nation. In the end, it remains the responsibility and right of all sovereign nations to monitor and regulate the business practices of those companies engaged in FDI.

ACKNOWLEDGMENTS

An earlier version of this chapter first appeared in James Jaksa, Michael Pritchard (Eds.) *Ethical Communication in Risk Technologies*, (Cresskill, NJ: Hampton Press, 1995). The author wishes to thank Hampton Press.

NOTES

[1] Peter Drucker, *The New Realities*, (New York: Harper & Row, 1989), Leonard Glynn, "Multinationals in the World of Nations," *The Multinational Enterprise in Transition*, (Eds.) Phillip D. Grub, Fariborz Ghadar, and Dara Khambata (Princeton, NJ: Darwin Press, 1984), pp. 70–71.

[2] Hamid Mowlana, "The Multinational Corporation and the Diffusion of Technology," *The New Sovereigns: Multinational Corporations as World Powers*, (Eds.) A. A. Said & L. R. Simons (Englewood Cliffs, NJ: Prentice-Hall, 1975), pp. 77–90.

[3] Ben Bagdikian, "The Lords of the Global Village," *The Nation*, 12 June, 1989, p. 807.

[4] L. R. Beltran and E. Fox. De Cardona, "Latin America and the United States: Flaws in the Free Flow of Information," *National Sovereignty and International Communication*, (Eds.) K. Nordenstreng and H. Schiller, (Norwood, NJ: Ablex, 1979), pp. 33–64; D. Boyd & O. Barrett, "Media Imperialism: Toward an International Framework for the Analysis of Media Systems," *Mass Communication and Society*, (Eds.) J. Curran, M. Gurevitch, and J. Woollacott, (Beverly Hills, CA: Sage, 1977); C. Lee, *Media Imperialism Reconsidered* (Beverly Hills, CA: Sage, 1980); J. Tunstall, *The Media are American: Anglo American Media in the World* (New York: Columbia University Press, 1977); K. Nordentreng and T. Varis, Television Traffic—A One Way Street. *Reports and Papers on Mass Communication # 70*, (Paris, UNESCO, 1974); T. Varis, "The International Flow of Television," *Journal of Communication*, 34(1), 1984, pp. 143–152.

[5] During the post-World War II period, several different researchers began to link media production and exports with the term *imperialism* made popular by Lenin in the early 1920s. In 1971 and 1975, research by Mattelart and Dorfman resulted in highly popular work entitled *How to Read Donald Duck*. The book was a stinging criticism of the Hollywood film industry and its ability to culturally manipulate the people of Latin America.

[6] Herbert I. Schiller, "Transnational Media and National Development," *National Sovereignty and International Communication*, (Eds.), K. Nordenstreng and H. Schiller, (Norwood, NJ: Ablex, 1979), p. 30.

[7] E. McAnany and K. Wilkinson, "From Cultural Imperialists to Takeover Victims," *Communication Research*, 19(6), 1992, pp. 724–748.

[8] Herbert I. Schiller, "The Global Commercialization of Culture," *Directions PCDS*, 4, 1990, pp. 1–4.

[9] Bernard Miege, *The Capitalization of Cultural Production*, (New York: International General, 1989).

[10] "The New Publishers' Row," *Newsweek*, 21 February, 1994, pp. 64–65.

[11] Noreene Z. Janus, "Advertising and the Mass Media in the Era of the Global Corporation," *Communication and Social Structure*, (Eds.) E. McAnany, J. Schnitman, and N. Janus, (New York: Praeger, 1981), p. 306.

[12] Michael H. Anderson, *Madison Avenue in Asia: Politics and Transnational Advertising*, (Rutherford, NJ: Fairleigh Dickinson University Press, 1984).

[13] According to Lerner, the spread of frustration can be seen in the imbalance between achievement and aspiration. The modernization process occurs with new forms of public communication (i.e., radio, television, and magazines) that stimulate people's desires. The problem of rising frustrations occurs when people in a society want far more than they can hope to achieve. See Daniel Lerner, "Toward a Communication Theory of Modernization: A Set of Considerations," *Communications and Political Development*, (Ed.) L. W. Pye, (Princeton, NJ: Princeton University Press, 1967), pp. 327–350.

[14] F. H. Cardoso and E. Faletto, *Dependency and Development in Latin America*. (Berkeley: University of California Press, 1979); E. De Cardona, "Multinational Television: Forms of Cultural Dependency," *Journal of Communication*, Spring, 1975, pp. 122–127; R. Salinas and L. Paldan, "Culture in the Process of Dependent Development: Theoretical Perspectives," *National Sovereignty and International Communication*, (Eds.) K. Nordenstreng and H. Schiller, (Norwood, NJ: Ablex, 1979), pp. 82–97.

[15] Omar Oliveira, "Mass Media, Culture and Communication in Brazil: The Heritage of Dependency," *Transnational Communications: Wiring the Third World*, (Eds.) G. Sussman and J. Lent, (Newbury Park, CA: Sage, 1991), pp. 200–201.

[16] Manley R. Irwin & Michael J. Merenda, "Corporate Networks, Privatization and State Sovereignty," *Telecommunications Policy*, (13) December 1989, pp. 333–334.

[17] Warren Freedman, *The Right of Privacy in the Computer Age*, (New York: Quorum Books, 1987), pp. 10–12.

[18] "Rethinking the Nature of Privacy," *Technology Review*, May/June 1985, pp. 47–48.

[19] G. R. Bassiry, "Business Ethics and the United Nations: A Code of Conduct," *SAM Advanced Management Journal*, Autumn 1990, pp. 38–41.

[20] Reed Moyer, *International Business: Issues and Concepts*, (New York: Wiley, 1984).

[21] J. Tsalikas and O. Nwachukwu, "A Comparison of Nigerian to American Views of Bribery and Extortion in International Commerce," *Journal of Business Ethics*, (10) 1991, pp. 85–98.

[22] "A World of Greasy Palms," *Business Week*, 6 November, 1995, pp. 36–37.

[23] "A World of Greasy Palms," pp. 36–37.

[24] Ben Bagdikian, *The Media Monopoly*, (Boston: Beacon Press, 1990). pp. 244–245.

[25] Anthony Smith, *The Age of the Behemoths: The Globalization of Mass Media Firms*, (New York: Priority Press Publications, 1991). p. 31.

[26] Christine Ogan, "Media Imperialism and Videocassette Recorder: The Case of Turkey," *Journal of Communication*, 38(2), 1988, pp. 99–100.

[27] "The World's Top Pirates," *Business Week*, 5 June, 1995, p. 4.

[28] National Telecommunications and Information Administration, *Globalization of the Mass Media*, (U.S. Department of Commerce, NTIA Special Publication: 93–290, 1993), pp. 98–101.

[29] Starting in the late 1970s, VCR television and film products were licensed through international agreements with major TNMC producers. Initially, the country's customs inspectors were accommodating. They did not fully understand VCR technology or the programming that went with it. Nor did they have any means for previewing such material at the point of entry. As the Ministry of Information became more familiar with the potential consequences of VCR technology, they became very strict in the censoring of such programs. In response, local importers of television and film programming went underground and simply used high-speed duplicating equipment to meet the demand. See Douglas A. Boyd, *Broadcasting in the Arab World*, (Ames: Iowa State University Press, 1993), pp. 164–166.

[30] William H. Read, *America's Mass Media Merchants*, (Baltimore: Johns Hopkins University Press, 1976).

[31] Ithiel de Sola Poole, "The Changing Flow of Television," *Journal of Communication*, 27(2), 1977, pp. 139–149.

[32] Ian Ang, "Culture and Communication: Towards an Ethnographic Critique of Media Consumption in the Transnational Media System," *European Journal of Communication*, (5), 1990, p. 257.

II

Transnational Media: The Players

8

Time Warner Inc.

HISTORICAL OVERVIEW

In July 1989, Time Inc. and Warner Communications completed a corporate merger that would make it the largest media company in the world. The merging of Time Inc. and Warner Communications has to be understood in the context that it was part of a larger worldwide movement toward transnational economic consolidation. The purpose of the Time Warner merger was perhaps best summarized in the company's first annual report to its stockholders:

> In the Eighties we witnessed the most profound political and economic changes since the end of the Second World War. As these changes unfolded, Time Inc. and Warner Communications Inc. came independently to the same fundamental conclusion: globalization was rapidly evolving from a prophecy to a fact of life. No serious competitor could hope for any long-term success unless, building on a secure home base, it achieved a major presence in all of the world's important markets.[1]

Also important to recognize about the Time Warner merger were the personal motivations and unique contributions of a few select men who were intimately involved in the planning process. Those individual personalities would have a profound influence on the final outcome of the agreement and the long-term future of the newly combined company.

The Creating of a Journalistic Tradition

Time Inc. was founded in 1922 by Henry Robinson Luce in order to publish a newly created magazine called *Time*. It was the first weekly news magazine of its kind. Henry Luce was passionate about politics. His cause celebre was the emerging U.S. role in the 20th-century political landscape. Luce used his magazines to promote the cause of the American century. As David Halberstam wrote:

> His American century was a noble concept, convinced as he was of the rectitude of our culture and our values and our energy; the world would want these same things, on our terms and by our definitions, and it was our clear duty to spread

them. He would stand watch to ensure that our politicians matched and fulfilled their responsibilities.[2]

Luce was a restless man who was fascinated by ideas and the people who made things happen. He would become a major force in U.S. journalism with the founding of such later publications as *Life Magazine, Fortune,* and *Sports Illustrated.* Luce and his eventual seven magazines would become an important voice for conservative U.S. politics and social center.

One direct consequence of the Luce legacy was the fostering of a magazine priesthood. The journalists of both *Time* and *Life* were writers with a mission. *Life* magazine, for one, elevated photojournalism to new heights during the 1940s and 1950s. Journalists were required to work hard, but not to concern themselves with the company's finances. There was a clear separation between the company's writing mission and its business operations.[3] For the first 50 years of its history, the business of Time-Life was print journalism.

Home Box Office (HBO)

It is not surprising that the Time-Life journalistic priesthood was initially resistant to the company's entry into video communications in 1972. Television was viewed as something that was contrary to the purpose and mission of a print media organization. On November 8, a fledgling operation named Home Box Office (HBO) began supplying movies to 365 subscribers on the Service Electric Cable TV system in Wilkes Barre, Pennsylvania. That night, Jerry Levin, then vice president for programming and future CEO, introduced viewers to the debut of HBO. Within a year, Time Inc. demonstrated its confidence in the young company by acquiring HBO as a wholly owned subsidiary. By May 1974, HBO had emerged as the largest pay cable program supplier in the United States.[4]

From the beginning, HBO developed a number of strategies that helped promote its rapid growth, including premium movies and sports entertainment. The service was marketed with a monthly per-channel fee, rather than the technically complex pay per view approach that had been unsuccessfully tried before by several early pay television ventures. In addition, HBO was the first U.S. company to use satellite communications for the transmission of television programming. That decision not only reshaped its own method for distributing programming, but it transformed broadcast and cable television forever. HBO's use of satellite communications laid the groundwork for future satellite cable networks, including Ted Turner's Superstation WTBS and Cable News Network. In the words of cable analyst, Paul Kagan, "Rarely does a simple business decision by one company affect so many. In deciding to gamble on the leasing of satellite TV channels, Time Inc. took one catalytic step needed for the creation of a new national television network designed to provide pay TV programs."[5]

The future of video communications within the Time corporate structure was firmly established.[6] By 1978, HBO and American Telecommunications Corporation (ATC), the company's cable system operations, were responsible for generating more than half of all company revenues. Time Inc. was later reorganized into two main divisions including print and video communications.

The success of HBO and the entire video division subsequently launched the careers of J. Richard Munro, Nicholas J. Nicholas and Jerry Levin into the top executive posts at Time Inc. Munro became the president and CEO of Time Inc. in 1982. He later appointed Nicholas as president and CEO in 1986. As president, Nicholas would recast Time Inc. into a financially driven TNMC with the emphasis on profitability. The house that Luce built had become, in the words of Nicholas himself, "a superb collection of franchises in key market positions."[7]

Warner Communications

Prior to its merger with Time Inc., Warner Communications was often referred to as Steve Ross' company. What began as a patchwork quilt of different companies—including his father-in-law's funeral parlor combined with a car rental business—later evolved into a highly profitable set of service industries. Ross took the company public as Kinney National Services in 1962. The company's entry into entertainment began with the purchase of Warner Brothers Seven-Arts in 1969. That occasion marked an important change in the future direction of Ross' many diverse business holdings. A year later, Kinney National Services was renamed Warner Communications to reflect the company's primary focus in communications and entertainment. Throughout the decades of the 1970s and 1980s, Warner Communications evolved into a highly diverse entertainment company that included television and film studios, cable television, music, and publishing.

Ross has often been described as an entrepreneur and a consummate dealmaker. He was well respected for his financial acumen as well as his generosity to Warner senior staff executives. Warner's corporate officials were among the highest paid in the industry. In describing Ross, Bruck (1990) wrote:

> Many who have watched Steve Ross over the years believe that it is his ability to win people over that may account, as much as all the rest, for his success.... He is a master of the thoughtful gesture, large or small: calling those involved when a movie has failed dismally, sending flowers for a birthday to the spouse of someone whom he is keeping late at the office, awarding a bonus (instead of a loan) to cover an employee's financial need, supplying the Warner plane or sending a hard-to-find gift to a star—ceaselessly spreading largesse.[8]

Ross' entrepreneurial spirit was particularly evident in the area of cable television. Warner Communications achieved a number of firsts, including Qube; the first U.S. interactive cable television system. Warner Communications, in conjunction with American Express, founded Qube in Columbus, Ohio in 1978. Warner's promotion of interactive television enabled the company to later win important cable franchises in several key U.S. cities. The Qube system demonstrated the possibilities for future PPV technology.

Warner also achieved an important first in cable television programming as well. The company was responsible for the debut of the Music Television Network (MTV), America's first 24-hour rock music television service. The MTV network demonstrated cable television's ability to narrowcast an entire service to a particular audience segment. MTV proved to be a highly successful business operation because the primary source of programming was rock videos supplied to the MTV network for free.[9]

Time Inc. and the Need for a Future Growth Strategy

The early 1980s was a critical period for Time Inc. Revenues from the magazine division had leveled off to a steady 5.7% with no major growth in sight. Worse still, Time's reputation for launching successful magazines was severely tarnished with the debut of TV-Cable Week, which became an instant failure that cost the company $47 million. Pay television revenues were also flat. HBO faced a major downturn in pay cable revenues, resulting from the growing success of videocassette rentals. The newly emerging tape rental industry would prove to be an important source of revenue to Hollywood's film industry.[10] The combination of events prompted many Wall Street analysts to undervalue Time Inc. and to speculate that the company was ripe for a takeover.

Time Inc.'s principal strengths were in publishing and cable television. As a company, Time Inc. had assumed a more cautious growth strategy when compared to such TNMCs as Bertelsmann, News Corp, and Maxwell Communication. The latter companies were more global and diverse. In 1983, only 10% of Time's revenues came from overseas investments. Time Inc. needed a global strategy that would enable it to compete head-to-head with the world's leading media companies. Any plan for future growth would have to include greater involvement in original television and film production.

Time's senior management reasoned that a merger or acquisition would be the most efficient way for the company to expand its entry into the entertainment side of the business. Between 1985 and 1988, Time Inc. held discussions with CBS, the Gannett Company, and Capital Cities/ABC. Differences in corporate philosophy and future management control made negotiations difficult. By 1987, it became clear that there were only a handful of companies that provided the right strategic match. They included Warner Communications and Paramount (then called Gulf & Western). A chance meeting between Time Inc's Nick Nicholas and Warner's Steve Ross occurred in May 1987.[11]

During the subsequent meetings that followed, talks centered around areas of common interest to both companies, most notably, cable television. Time Inc. and Warner Communications, respectively, had the second- and fifth-largest cable MSOs in the United States. A cable partnership between both companies would make them a formidable player within the industry. Also on the table for discussion was a possible joint venture between HBO and Warner Brothers Studios.

The talks continued over the next year. The talks primarily focused on a joint cable venture. During that time, a number of issues began to surface that threatened to undermine the progress being made. Privately, both Levin and Nicholas had begun to consider the possibilities of a more comprehensive merger agreement. In a confidential memo to J. Richard Munro, Levin wrote, "I am now convinced our primary objective should be a merger. Like IBM or GE, its size and range of solid franchises would make it an institutional 'must carry' stock..."[12]

An internal strategy group was formed and given the task of assessing the company's long-term future. The report seemed to confirm what Levin had been thinking. Munro and Nicholas, in a subsequent report to Time's Board of Directors, noted:

> Our recent internal review concluded that if we want to remain the preeminent source of information and entertainment we must acknowledge the increasing dominance of video as the medium of choice worldwide. We do not believe, however, that Time Inc. has the experience and depth of management to evolve into a fully integrated major motion picture and television company. Thus we have concluded that the only practical means to achieve this goal is to acquire or merge with a major studio. To that end we have been examining some form of combination between Time Inc. and Warner Communication, but to date have reached no conclusions. Warner is characterized by excellent, stable management.[13]

In June 1988, Nicholas raised the stakes considerably by proposing a full-scale merger agreement between Time Inc. and Warner Communications. Ross took about a week to consider the proposal and agreed to it in principle.

Warner Communications: Planning for the Future

Ross was in his late 50s at the time serious negotiations between Time Inc. and Warner Communications got underway. The motivation to consider such a deal was prompted by a desire to secure the future of his company. Ross had no heir apparent and his own health was failing. Here was an opportunity to forge a strategic partnership between two highly successful companies. A less clear motivation may have been the deal itself. For Ross, the proposed merger would be the consummate deal, the crowning achievement to a long and highly successful business career.

Surmounting the Differences in Corporate Philosophies

Munro spent the summer of 1988 meeting individually with Time's board of directors. The members of the board were divided in their support of the proposed merger. There were three major sticking points. The first had to do with the preservation of Time Inc. as a journalistic enterprise. Several members expressed concern that the separation of business and editorial activities be preserved under any proposed arrangement. The second area of concern had to with Ross' character. Ross was the embodiment of Hollywood glamour and showmanship that ran counter to the staid Ivy League tradition of Time Inc. There was also the question of compensation. In addition to a base salary of $1.2 million, Ross would be guaranteed $193 million under an amended 10-year contract that would include $70 million in cash and $123 million in deferred payments.

The issue of governance was the third and perhaps the most divisive issue that separated the two companies. The issue became so highly charged that on August 11, 1988, Ross pulled out of the talks after an emotional meeting at his Park Avenue apartment. A major sticking point was that Time's board of directors insisted that Ross accept a finite term as co-CEO with the understanding that Nicholas would eventually succeed as the sole CEO. During discussions, Time's attorneys displayed an obvious lack of sensitivity by referring to Ross' tenure as transitional. Ross, for his part, felt unwanted and not trusted by the Time board. His principal fear was that he would be relegated to a lame duck status with no authority.[14]

After the talks broke down, Mike Dingman, an influential member of Time's board of directors, met with Ross for dinner to see if he could get the discussion back on track. The conversation prompted Ross to make a clear decision about his future. By his own admission, Ross was not interested in managing the company's day-to-day affairs. Instead, he wanted some flexible role that would allow him the ability to explore new business opportunities and meet with key people.

In a statement of principles, Ross agreed to retire as co-CEO in 1994 and remain as sole chairman of the board of the combined company for another 5 years, through 1999. Both the Time and Warner boards approved the merger agreement on March 3, 1989. Although technically Time was acquiring Warner, it was understood between both parties that the term *acquisition* was not to be used. As Clurman (1994) reported:

> The merger is a true combination of two great companies. For either company to be looked upon as anything but an equal partner in this transaction would sap that company of its vitality and destroy the very benefits and synergy that the combination is intended to achieve.[15]

Under the terms of the agreement, there would be no cash purchase, but rather an exchange of stock with an agreed-on exchange ratio.[16] The newly proposed Time Warner board of directors would consist of 24 members with equal representation from both sides. Both Steve Ross and Richard Munro would serve as co-CEOs of the newly formed company. N.J. Nicholas would replace Munro in 2 years as co-CEO and become sole chairman of the company 5 years after that.

Paramount's Hostile Bid to Purchase Time Inc.

At the time of the announced merger, there was a clear recognition by Time's investment advisors that the proposed all-stock merger was vulnerable to a high cash bid by an an outsider. The company's fears were soon realized when Paramount Studios hired Morgan Stanley to prepare for a financial raid on Time Inc. in May. Time officials were genuinely surprised and angered because Martin Davis, president and CEO of Paramount, was a friend and business associate of Munro. Only weeks before, Davis had made clear his intention not to make a run on the company. In a letter to Paramount's Davis, Munro charged: "On a professional level, you've changed the name of your corporation [from Gulf & Western to Paramount Communication] but not its character. It's still 'engulf and devour.' Hostile takeovers are a little like wars. Once they start, it's impossible to tell where they'll end."[17]

Davis, for his part, felt that the announced merger was a betrayal because Munro had said on past occasions that Time Inc. was not interested in owning a movie studio. Davis was also concerned with what a Time Warner combination would mean to the future of the movie industry. Specifically, he was concerned that such a company would be formidable, especially with Steve Ross at the helm.

Paramount's tender offer to buy Time Inc. at $175 per share would severely undermine the original all-stock (no cash/no debt) exchange that was at the center of the financing arrangement between Time Inc. and Warner Communications. The Paramount offer was 40% above market price for Time stock and was clearly a better deal for those stockholders who were interested in realizing an immediate profit. It should be pointed out that a high percentage of Time stock was held by financial institutions and trusts whose first consideration is to make the most money that it can for its investors. On June 23rd, Davis raised his offer to $200 a share, a move that was fully anticipated by Time's directors. The Time board rejected the offer immediately. The $200-a-share offer, nevertheless, had the desired effect.

The challenge for Time's senior management would be to convince its stockholders to view the proposed Time Warner merger as a better long-term solution to the company's future. The reality was that had a vote been put forth to its stockholders, the Paramount offer would have been overwhelmingly approved. The only way to circumvent a stockholder vote would have been for Time Inc. to purchase Warner Communications outright. The total cost for acquiring Warner Communications would be $14.9 billion.

One of the more telling features of a buyout arrangement was that both Ross and Warner Communications (including employees and stockholders) stood to gain over $1 billion in payments as well as millions in potential stock options. Time Inc.'s senior executives including Munro, Nicholas, and Levin would likewise be highly compensated. Time's employees and stockholders, however, were not so fortunate. They received no cash and stockholders saw the value of their stock drop from a premerger high of $182 to $70 per share. Time's senior management became the target of severe criticism for its rejection of the $200-a-share cash offer. Paramount, shortly thereafter, filed suit against Time Inc. in the state of Delaware.

Paramount Communications v. Time Inc.

The state of Delaware is the official registration site for many of America's top corporations due to its liberal laws governing liability complaints as well as its favorable taxing structure. In *Paramount Communications v. Time Inc.*, Paramount argued that Time had put itself up for sale the moment they decided to merge with Warner Communication. The plaintiffs further argued that Time's unwillingness to consider the Paramount offer was clearly an act that was contrary to the best interests of the company's stockholders. By refusing to consider Paramount's bid, Time's senior executives were enriching themselves at the stockholder's expense.

As part of its defense, Time argued that the proposed merger was a carefully thought-out business plan that was 2 years in the making. Paramount's decision to bid on Time Inc. did not include the right to stop the proposed deal. If Paramount had not proceeded with its last-minute offer, the Time Warner merger would have gone through as scheduled.[18] Time's legal counsel also argued that there was nothing to prevent Paramount from bidding on the future Time Warner corporation. In the end, the court agreed with Time's defense. Chancellor William T. Allen, in his court opinion, wrote that the situation would be chaotic if shareholders were able to take legal action each time they disagreed with corporate policy. He said, "corporate law does not operate on the theory that directors, in exercising their powers to manage the firm, are obligated to follow the wishes of a majority of shareholders."[19]

In July 1989, Time Inc. and Warner Communications completed the final details that would make the combined organization the largest TNMC in the world.

Postmerger Integration and Beyond

The challenge of comanaging an organization as large and complex as Time Warner was going to be difficult under the best of circumstances. Differences in business priorities and professional operating styles were likely to make the transition long and difficult. The differences finally surfaced in March 1992 when co-CEO Nicholas was removed by an official vote of Time Warner's board of directors. With Nicholas away on vacation, the board convened in Manhattan and voted to request Nicholas' resignation. Vice Chairman Gerald Levin was named his successor. The main reason for the change in leadership had to do with differences in management style and corporate strategy.

Nicholas' "bottom line" mentality soured both Ross as well as the company's executive staff. Both Ross and Levin were in favor of selling minority stakes in Time Warner whereas Nicholas favored selling off assets like cable as a way to pay down debt. The Time Warner board of directors felt confident that an executive partnership between Ross and Levin would prove more amicable.

In December 1992, Ross died of prostate cancer at the age of 65. The change in leadership signaled an important shift in the company's future. Levin represents a new generation in Time Warner leadership, having built his early career at HBO and the video group. Levin is regarded as someone who values Time's print media tradition as well as the importance of new technology. Levin has played a decisive role in promoting Time Warner's future entry into broadband video services, most notably, its Full Service Network.

Marketplace Realities and the Preservation of Editorial/Creative Freedom

Prior to the merger agreement, there were already indications that the magazine division was not achieving significant increases in readership or profitability. *Time Magazine*, the company's flagship publication, still retained enormous respectability but was losing readership. The causes were not necessarily the result of some perceived fault in the magazine. The decline in subscribership could be attributed to a variety of factors, including changes in the marketplace and consumer lifestyle. The combination of more highly specialized magazines, combined with narrowcasted cable services had made the field of publishing a far more competitive environment than was true in past years.

When the Time Warner merger was first announced, the magazine division at Time Inc. was especially concerned with the potential effect that a merger agreement would have in preserving editorial independence and creative freedom. Would the company's various magazines receive the financial backing necessary to ensure their continued successful operation? Or would a new bottom line results-oriented approach be the new stock phrase at Time Warner?

U.S. news operations such as CBS, NBC, CNN, and Time Inc. have historically been allowed to operate with a greater degree of latitude than their entertainment counterparts. Author Ken Auletta suggests that the years 1984 to 1987 marked a significant change in the management of large media organizations. This period was characterized by an increased effort to make news operations more financially accountable. This was particularly true at the three U.S. television networks (CBS, NBC, and ABC) where news operations sustained significant losses in personnel.[20] The same concerns for cost consciousness were being felt in the newspaper and magazine industries as well. Two years after the merger agreement, the first signs of a problem for the company's magazines began to surface. In the fall of 1991, Time Warner announced a 10% budget cut across the board that included the elimination of more than 600 jobs from the company's magazine division.

A related concern had to do with the future of editorial policy. Would a vertically integrated Time Warner promote a policy that encourages the use of the company's magazine division to promote the cause of Time Warner artists, performers, and media products? Similarly, would there be administrative or business pressure to discourage those news stories or creative efforts that might offend Time Warner's many advertisers and/or pose a conflict for the company's overall operation?

Events surrounding the July 1992 release of the song "Cop Killer" on the album *Bodycount* by rap singer/artist Ice-T may serve to illustrate the problems cited. The controversial song was released shortly after the acquittal of four Los Angeles policemen accused of beating up Black citizen Rodney King. The song encourages violence and retaliation against police. Citizen and police reaction to this song was swift. They held demonstrations and supported a public ban against Time Warner products. They argued that it was the responsibility of senior management to raise the moral level of media products and advertising, regardless of its potential for profits.[21]

Time Warner was initially very resistant to such protests, claiming the importance of First Amendment rights. In the meantime, Time Warner stock dropped, partially due to the controversy. As protests increased, including critical comments from former U.S. President George Bush as well as the company's own board of directors, there followed an abrupt change in policy. Time Warner announced its intentions to reissue the album *Bodycount* without the song "Cop Killer." In a released statement, Time Warner officials indicated that it was musician Ice-T, himself, who had requested that the song be pulled from the album. The decision, in fact, came from the top and was motivated largely out of a concern for how the adverse publicity would affect Time Warner's reputation and long-term profitability.[22] A similar situation occurred in 1995 when the company came under fire by the U.S. Senate and the National Political Congress of Black Women for failing to exercise critical judgment when it came to promoting hate music, including the use of violent and vulgar lyrics.

Despite such events and (early predictions about the harmful effects of corporate mergers), there is no discernible pattern to suggest that the company's publications, video, and film entertainment divisions have either been helped or hurt by the merger agreement. Time Inc.'s long-standing tradition of separating its editorial/creative efforts from its business operations seems to continue unabated. The history and tradition of Time Inc. would suggest that senior management is not likely to involve itself in routine editorial and creative decision making.

ORGANIZATIONAL STRUCTURE

Since 1989, Time Warner has undergone several organizational changes as the two companies have become more fully integrated. Today, there are two major divisions that comprise Time Warner Inc. They include Time Warner, which is responsible for all activities related to publishing and music. The second division is Time Warner Entertainment (TWE) Group, which includes filmed entertainment, HBO programming and cable. Table 8.1 provides an overview of Time Warner media products and services, including partial investments.

BUSINESS STRATEGY AND PHILOSOPHY

Vertical Integration and Complementary Assets

The Time Warner merger was originally intended to take the philosophy of vertical integration to whole new level in terms of strategic planning and operations.[23] In principle, Time Inc. could control an idea from its appearance in a book to its debut on HBO as well as gaining additional press coverage through the company's own magazines. In practice, the combining of Time Inc. and Warner Communication did not achieve the once hoped for synergies. The Time Warner organization endured several difficult years of postmerger integration. As a result, there was a tremendous amount of in-fighting between various Time and Warner divisions. Although individual divisions performed well, there was not the level of cooperation between divisions that was originally expected. As an example, Warner Brothers studios and HBO did not build the kind of cooperative arrangement that would have benefited both companies. In fact, just the opposite was true.

Despite such postmerger difficulties, both companies were highly complementary in their assets. Time Inc. brought to the merger agreement such notable magazines as *Time, Life, People, Fortune, Money, Sports Illustrated*, and *Southern Living*. In 1988, the magazine group was the largest magazine publisher in the United States. In addition, Time Inc. was the leading U.S. pay-television programmer with Home Box Office and Cinemax. The company also owned the nation's second largest cable MSO, American Television & Communications, which served an estimated 4.5 million subscribers in 33 states.

Warner Communications brought to the merger agreement a major presence in television/film studio production, including Warner Brothers Studios (one of Hollywood's top three studios) and Lorimar Television Entertainment (the leading producer of television programs in the world). In addition, Warner Brothers studios was a key supplier of programming to the cable industry, including Time's HBO and Cinemax cable services.[24] In the area of music entertainment, Warner Communications had a strong presence as well, including Warner Brothers Records, Atlantic Records, and Elektra Entertainment. Warner Communications was also a major player in cable television. Prior to the merger agreement, Warner Cable was America's fifth largest cable MSO. Table 8.2 provides a comparison of what Time Inc. and Warner Communication brought to the merger agreement in terms of companies and product groupings.

TABLE 8.1
Time Warner Media Holdings (1994–1995)

TIME WARNER

Magazines

Time	Parenting
Life	Baby Talk
Fortune	Southern Living
Sports Illustrated	Martha Stewart Living
Money	Hippocrates
People	Asiaweek
Sports Illustrated for Kids	President
Entertainment Weekly	Dancyu
Progressive Farmer	Who
Southern Accents	Vibe
Cooking Light	Sunset
In Style	Health

Book Publishing / Warner Music

Book Publishing	Warner Music
Little Brown	Warner Brothers Records
Warner Books	The Atlantic Group
Time Life	Elektra Entertainment Group
Book of the Month Club	Warner Music International
Oxmoor House	
Sunset Books	

THE ENTERTAINMENT GROUP

Filmed Entertainment	Time Warner Cable
Warner Brothers Television	
Warner Brothers Studios	**Time Warner U.S. Investments**
Witt-Thomas Productions	19% investment in Turner Broadcasting Systems
The WB Television Network	55% investment in Court TV
Warner Brothers Domestic Pay-TV	50% investment in Comedy Central
Cable and Network Features	33% investment in the Sega Channel
Warner Home Video	15% investment in Black Entertainment Television
HBO Cable Programming	14% investment in Hasbro Corporation
Home Box Office	25% investment in Atari Corporation
Cinemax	50% investment in Catalog 1

Note. Source: Time Warner, Inc.

TABLE 8.2
The Time Warner Merger Agreement A Comparison of Companies and Product Groupings (1988)

Time Revenue: $4,507,000,000		Warner Revenue: $4,206,100,000	
Magazines	39%	Filmed entertainment	37%
Cable	18%	Recorded music and publishing	49%
Programming	23%	Cable and broadcasting	11%
Books	20%	Publishing and related dist.	3%

Note. Source: Time Inc. and Warner Communication 1988 Annual Reports.

The merging of Time Warner was originally expected to generate synergies that would ultimately boost the value of the combined stock. The merger agreement called for a plan to forge massive alliances in Europe and Asia as a way to enter these markets. The plan would require that these partners invest in a limited partnership as a way to gain an equity stake in Time Warner's assets. The money would then be used to pay down the company's debt.[25]

The sale of limited partnerships has been reasonably successful to date. In November 1991, Time Warner entered into an agreement with Japan's Toshiba Corporation and C. Itoh, a well respected trading company. The latter companies agreed to purchase a 12.5% stake in Time Warner Entertainment (TWE) for $1 billion. TWE consists of HBO and Time Warner Cable. Through this arrangement, Time Warner obtained an important source of capital as well as gaining greater access to Japanese markets. In May 1993, RBOC US West invested $2.5 billion in TWE. The resulting strategic alliance has enabled Time Warner to move ahead with plans to develop and market the first in a series of integrated community networks called Full Service Network (FSN).

The first prototype began operation in Orlando, Florida in 1995. For its part, US West has aggressively moved into cable television, announcing plans in March 1996 to purchase Continental Cablevision for $10.8 billion. This, in turn, will bring the number of combined cable customers now managed by US West and its partner Time Warner to 16.2 million.

In addition to selling limited partnerships, Time Warner has moved aggressively into international markets. The company's magazine group, Warner Music Group, and HBO have become major players in the overseas market. In 10 years, Time Warner's FDIs have grown from less than $740 million in 1984 to more than $4 billion in 1994. The result has been a compounded annual growth rate of 20%.

Time Warner and Turner Broadcasting Systems

In September 1995, Time Warner announced that it would merge with Turner Broadcasting Systems, involving an $8 billion stock swap. In exchange, Ted

Turner would receive $2.5 billion and a 11.3% stake in Time Warner, thus making him the company's largest stockholder.[26] In addition, Turner would serve as vice chairman of Time Warner and would remain CEO of Turner Broadcasting System. Through its affiliate, Liberty Media, John's Malone's TCI would emerge as Time Warner's second largest share holder.[27] The proposed merger was subsequently approved by the U.S. Federal Trade Commission.

The rationale behind the proposed merger is to combine the news and programming assets of Turner Broadcasting with the highly complimentary assets of Time Warner. According to Levin, "The complimentary nature of the two organizations will allow us to maximize the value of our assets and distribution systems and position us as the leading media company in an increasingly competitive global marketplace."[28]

The merging of the two companies will require a major reorganization of both companies. The combining of Time Warner and Turner Broadcasting would be divided into three major divisions, including entertainment, news, and telecommunications. Table 8.3 provides a comparison of assets between companies.

Time Warner's proposed merger with Turner Broadcasting will require an altogether different operating philosophy than was true in the past. According to Levin:

TABLE 8.3
Time Warner and Turner Broadcasting (Comparison of Assets)

Turner Broadcasting	Time Warner
Entertainment	
TBS	Warner Brothers:
Turner Network Television (TNT)	(Movies, TV, cartoons, video, DC Comics)
Castle Rock Entertainment	Warner Music Group
Cartoon Network	Home Box Office
New Line Cinema	
Hanna-Barbera Cartoons	
Atlanta Braves Baseball	
Atlanta Hawks Basketball	
News	
Cable News Network	Time Inc. (40+ magazines)
Telecommunications/Cable	
	Time Warner Cable plus the future addition of US West/Continental Cablevision's 16.2 million subscribers

This transaction compels a kind of teamwork. In the past, I've never used the word 'synergy' because there was more financial mileage in growing individual businesses. But now, anybody who isn't on the team is out. . . . I've made it very clear that I'm not going to make the same mistake that we made with Time Warner; that is, we negotiated an organizational structure as part of the merger. There was no sensitive appraisal of the needs of the situation. [This time] no one has a fixed assignment. It's going to get worked out in an understanding fashion so that there is an organization that is less hierarchical and more team oriented.[29]

It is expected that the merger agreement will enable CEO Levin to exert more authority by having a stronger board of directors (including Turner and Malone) who are more supportive of his actions.

FINANCIAL PERFORMANCE AND ANALYSIS

International Recession and Financial Risk

If given the choice, Time Inc. would have much preferred to consummate its merger with Warner Communication under the terms of the original agreement; that is, an all-stock exchange, no cash deal. Instead, the Paramount bid on Time forced the company to come up with an alternative, albeit more costly, approach to financing its merger/acquisition of Warner Communications. Time Inc.'s willingness to purchase Warner Communications for $14.9 billion and assume an $11.2 billion debt load came at a time when market conditions were aggressive and being highly leveraged was considered an acceptable business practice for long-term financing.

What could not be anticipated was the worldwide recession that began to unfold during the early 1990s. The recession was especially difficult for Time Warner, given its high debt load.[30] The company was affected at two levels, including slower than anticipated growth and a decrease in advertising revenue. Cash infusion in the form of limited partnerships by Toshiba, C. Itoh, and US West has helped to reduce the debt load for the Time Warner Entertainment.

The combined revenues of Time Warner have steadily increased each year. The individual performance of such divisions as Warner Brothers Music, Time Warner Cable, and Filmed Entertainment have demonstrated a strong performance in the international marketplace. However, the company's steady increase in revenues has to be viewed against a backdrop of staggering debt obligations. To further complicate matters, Time Warner purchased a minority interest in American Telecommunications Corporation in 1992 at a cost of $1.3 billion. A year later, the company retired some $57 million of its corporate debt. Table 8.4 examines Time Warner's financial financial performance for the years spanning 1989 to 1994.

TABLE 8.4
Time Warner Inc. Financial Performance (1989–1994, in Millions)

	1994	1993	1992	1991	1990	1989
			Time Warner			
Publishing	$430	$372	$328	$246	$366	$295
Music	$720	$643	$585	$560	$558	$500
			Entertainment Group			
Filmed ent.	$565	$549	$410	$390	$377	$312
Programming (HBO)	$257	$230	$215	$195	$182	$166
Cable	$989	$1,035	$977	$872	$769	$644
EBITDA[a]	$2,961	$2,829	$2,515	$2,263	$2,252	$1,917
Total revenue[b]	$15,905	$14,544	$13,070	$12,021	$11,517	$10,779
Net income[c]	$(91)	$(221)[d]	$86	$(99)	$(227)	$(432)

Note. Source: Time Warner, Inc.
[a]EBITDA = Earnings Before Interest, Taxes, Depreciation, and Amortization. EBITDA is designed to show the operating income of Time Warner's business segments before depreciation and amortization expense. The major portion of Time Warner's amortization charges relate to the $14 billion acquisition of Warner Communications in 1989 and the $1.3 billion purchase of the minority interest in American Television and Communications Corporation in 1992.
[b]Total Revenues includes the combined revenues of all business segments of the Time Warner Corporation—in millions.
[c]Parentheses indicate net loss for the year.
[d]The net loss for 1993 includes an extraordinary loss on the retirement of debt of $57 million and corresponding tax liabilities.

Although combined revenues have steadily increased each year, the earnings before interest, taxes, depreciation, and amortization (EBITDA) have left the company with a net loss in 5 out of the 6 years under review. The result has been corresponding decline in the value of Time Warner stock. The company's financial statements for fiscal years 1993 and 1994 are laced with qualifiers that attempt to explain the reasons for the net income loss. According to company documents, there are a combination of factors that include after-tax charges, retirement of debt, corporate restructuring charges, and capital investment in plant and equipment.

The challenge for Time Warner will be whether it can meet its long-term debt obligations by generating sufficient revenues each year or be forced to sell off assets. In 1995, Time Warner sold its Six Flags amusement park operations in an effort to pare down its debt and raise cash. All this comes at a time when Time Warner is simultaneously trying to purchase Turner Broadcasting. Shortly after the agreement was announced, US West unsuccessfully filed a lawsuit in an attempt to block the proposed merger. US West cited numerous conflicts of interest and a concern that the value of its 25% interest in TWE would be substantially devalued. For company stockholders, (and industry analysts) a bigger question remains; namely, Time Warner's ability to absorb added debt at a time when its finances are just beginning to stabilize. The purchase of Turner Broadcasting will add an additional $2 billion to the company's debt structure for a combined total of $10.8 billion.

DISCUSSION

The Time Warner merger was conceived as a global strategy in order to position the company to compete head-to-head with the world's leading media companies.[31] During the mid-1980s, senior management at Time Inc. came to the realization that the company needed to be revitalized. At the time, Time Inc.'s principal strengths were in publishing and cable television. Specifically, the magazine division and HBO were viewed as mature industries with limited growth potential. It was clear that Time Inc. had been overly cautious in its development plans when compared to such transnational media rivals as Bertelsmann and NewsCorp. Ltd. The latter companies were more global and diverse whereas only 10% of Time's revenues came from international sales.

What was needed was a long-term growth strategy that would enable the company to compete head-to-head with the world's leading TNMCs.[32] Warner Communications provided the right strategic match by offering Time Inc. greater involvement in original television and film production. The combined Time Warner Communications has indeed become the most highly diverse TNMC in the world. Since the merger agreement, international sales now account for 40% of the company's total revenues.

One important goal for the future is the company's commitment to its Full Service Network concept.[33] Time Warner is positioning itself in the years ahead to be an industry leader in terms of owning both program software and the method for distribution to the home. The FSN will allow for a kind of one-stop-shopping approach whereby, customers will be offered both Time Warner and competitive products via an electronic supermarket. The future FSN design will allow for the full integration of voice data and video services and (for the second time in its corporate history) redefine the nature of television programming.

Still to be determined will be the success and final outcome of its merger with Turner Broadcasting. In principle, Turner Broadcasting offers Time Warner an excellent fit in terms of complimentary assets. A future merging with Turner Broadcasting provides multiple opportunities for combining strengths, especially in the area of news, sports entertainment, and children's programming. In addition, there are significant opportunities for cross-marketing as well as increasing the combined company's international profile. At the same time, a proposed merger with Turner Broadcasting brings with it a significant increase in debt that has caused stockholders and industry analysts alike to question the financial soundness of the merger agreement.

What is clear, however, is that the combining of Time Warner and Turner Broadcasting will require an altogether different approach than was the case with the original Time Warner merger. CEO Jerry Levin readily acknowledges that the proposed merger will fundamentally change the future of the organization: I finally want to make a clear break with the past because so far it has been nothing but people getting upset. It will never be the old Warner or the old Time again. It's going to be something totally different, as it must be."[34]

NOTES

[1] Time Warner Annual Report to Stockholders, (New York: Time Warner Corporation, 1989), p. 1.

[2] David Halberstam, *The Powers That Be*, (New York: Alfred A. Knopf, 1979), p. 48.

[3] One indication of this was that the executive editor from the magazine group was an equal to the company's president and held a seat on the company's board of directors.

[4] Richard A. Gershon and Michael O. Wirth, "Home Box Office," *The Cable Networks Handbook*, (Ed.) R. Picard, (Riverside, CA: Carpelan Press, 1993), pp. 114–115.

[5] Paul Kagan, remarks contained in *The Pay TV Guide: Editor's Pay TV Handbook*—a Publication of Home Box Office, Inc. (1984).

[6] In retrospect, the 5-year $7.5 million contract with RCA was a tremendous gamble for HBO and its parent company, Time Inc. For Levin, the commitment to use satellite communications represented a kind of corporate rite of passage. Time Inc. was responsible for the satellite time regardless of whether there was going to be one earth station used or a thousand.

[7] "Time's Nick and Dick Show," *Business Week*, 3 August, 1987, p. 55.

[8] Connie Bruck, "The World of Business: Deal of the Year," *The New Yorker*, 8 January, 1990, p. 67.

[9] The only blemish on what is otherwise an impressive business history was Warner's purchase of Atari video games in 1980. At the time, Warner recognized a potentially lucrative market for home video games. The initial sale of the Atari home video games series was highly profitable. By 1983, rather than holding back on product inventory, Warner saturated the market with an oversupply of Atari software cartridges. This came at a time when there was a marked slowdown in demand. The Atari debacle cost the company close to $1 billion in a 9-month period. The experience was particularly sobering for Ross, who was criticized for taking a rather hands-off approach to the Atari affair.

[10] The early success of HBO proved to be a constant source of irritation to many of Hollywood's more successful studios. Hollywood was criticized for failing to recognize the future importance of pay cable television. HBO was the premiere pay television service. The company was also recognized for being tough in negotiations. In short, Hollywood's major studios had missed out on the opportunity to launch an equivalent pay television service. The later success of video rentals provided Hollywood with a second opportunity to enter the business of pay television. This time, they would be ready.

[11] Bill Saporito, "The Inside Story of Time Warner," *Fortune*, 20 November, 1989, p. 170.

[12] Richard M. Clurman, *To the End of Time*, (New York: Simon & Schuster, 1992), p. 151.

[13] Ibid., p. 156.

[14] Saporito, "The Inside Story of Time Warner," p. 183.

[15] The Statement of Principles was informally referred to as the Liman letter—after Ross' attorney, Arthur Liman. See Clurman, *To The End of Time*, p. 189.

[16] Warner stockholders would exchange each of their shares, in a tax free transaction, for 0.465 shares of Time stock. Time Inc. had approximately 56.6 million common shares outstanding,

and Warner had 177.2 million common shares outstanding. Although the transaction was technically Time's acquisition of Warner, current Warner shareholders would end up with approximately 60% of the shares of the new company.

[17] Clurman, *To the End of Time*, p. 221.

[18] The raid on Time Inc. cost Paramount an estimated $80 million in pretax earnings.

[19] Judith H. Dobrzynski, "From One Decision Flow a Lot of Hard Lessons," *Business Week*, 31 July, 1989, p. 28.

[20] Ken Auletta, *Three Blind Mice*, (New York: Random House, 1991), pp. 9–72.

[21] "Just What are Our Values?" *Industry Week*, 17 August 1992, p. 7; "Momma Dearest," *The New Republic*, 10 August, 1992, p. 50.

[22] "All Claiming Victory in Cop Killer Battle," *Variety*, 3 August, 1992, p. 48; "Ice-T, Mr. Nice Guy Cuts the Controversy," *New York Times*, 2 August, 1992, p. E2.

[23] Consider that in 1990, Time Warner realized revenues in excess of $10 billion. In the area of television film entertainment alone, the newly formed Time Warner Communications brings together Warner Brothers studios, one of the top three Hollywood studios; Lorimar Telepictures, the world's largest producer of television product; the Time Magazine group, the largest magazine publisher in the United States; Warner Brothers Records, the largest record company in the United States; ATC, the second-largest cable MSO in the United States; Warner Cable, the fifth-largest cable MSO in the United States; and HBO, the largest pay cable television programmer in the United States.

[24] "Time Inc. and Warner Communication: Media Giants Strike Merger Deal," *Broadcasting*, 13 March, 1989, p. 30.

[25] "Time Warner," *Business Week*, 22 July, 1991, pp. 70–72.

[26] "It's TBS Time," *Broadcasting & Cable*, 25 September, 1995, pp. 8–10.

[27] Tele-Communications Inc. CEO John Malone owns 22% of TBS.

[28] Time Warner Inc, "Time Warner Inc. and Turner Broadcasting System, Inc. Agree to Merge, Creating the World's Foremost Media Company," press release, September 22, 1995.

[29] "Chairman Levin Defends the Time Warner-TBS Merger," *Business Week*, 9 October, 1995, p. 38.

[30] In a free market economy, advertising is at the heart of mass media products and service. In times of recession, advertising is often one of the first places that business looks to save money. This, in turn, affects all areas of advertiser supported media. In the United States alone, television network advertising fell 7.1% in the first half of 1991 from the same period in 1990. Similarly, magazine ad revenue was down 5% for the first half of 1991 and newspaper ad revenue was down 7%. "What Happened to Advertising?" *Business Week*, 23 September, 1991, p. 23.

[31] Tim Boggs, Vice President of Public Affairs, Time Warner Corporation, Presentation to the Annenberg Washington Conference on Cable Communication, Washington, DC: January 11, 1991.

[32] Tim Boggs, January 11, 1991.

[33] In addition, Time Warner has begun to explore telephone communication by establishing the first cable based telephone system in Rochester, New York.

[34] "The Unlikely Mogul," *Business Week*, 11 December, 1995, p. 87.

9

The Sony Corporation

HISTORICAL OVERVIEW

The Sony Corporation is a leading TNMC and ranks as a world leader in new product development and sales. The introduction of its Walkman product and related broadcast equipment have defined an entire generation in the field of consumer electronics. The company has carved out a distinct niche by providing consumers with products they did not know they wanted, including everything from the now famous Walkman to related audio and video equipment. In less than 40 years, the company has evolved from a small transistor radio maker to a world-class manufacturer of broadcast equipment, compact discs, digital audiotape, and HDTV.

The Early Years

The Sony Corporation was founded by Masaru Ibuka in the aftermath of Japan's defeat during World War II. In September 1945, Ibuka left the countryside where he had sought refuge from the bombings, and returned to the war-torn capital of Tokyo to begin a new business. Shortly thereafter, in October, Ibuka established the Tokyo Tsushin Kenkyujo or Tokyo Telecommunications Research Institute. At the time, his fledgling company was nothing more than a:

> ... narrow switchboard area on the third floor of Shirokiya Department Store (now Tokyu Department Store) in Nihonbashi. It became the workshop for Ibuka and his newly founded group. Having barely survived the fires during the war, the building had cracks all over its concrete exterior. Without windows, the new office was small and bleak.[1]

In the days and months that followed World War II, Japan's citizens had an urgent need for news information. During its initial start-up, Ibuka's shop was primarily in the business of radio repair. Ibuka and his small group of engineers also made short-wave adapters that could convert medium-wave radio receivers into superheterodyne (or all-wave) receivers. The short-wave adapters caught the attention of the public, and a feature article appeared in the *Asahi*

Shimbun newspaper. One such reader was Akio Morita, who had returned home to Kosugaya in Aichi Prefecture. Morita knew Ibuka from their past association with Japan's Wartime Research Committee. During the war, Ibuka worked as a radio engineer for the Nissoku munitions factory, specializing in submarine detection systems. Morita served as a Navy technical lieutenant in thermo-optical weapons. The article prompted Morita to write to Ibuka. Ibuka replied at once and urged Morita to come to Tokyo and join him in the start-up of his new business venture.[2]

On May 7, 1946, Ibuka and future chairman Morita officially incorporated the new company as the Tokyo Tsushin Kokyo *Totsuken*, or the Tokyo Telecommunications Engineering Corporation, starting with a capital investment of 190,000 Yen, or $500. The founding of Totsuken spoke directly to the challenges of postwar Japan and the need to rebuild. At the time, Ibuka was 38 and Morita 25. Both were knowledgeable and enthusiastic engineers, and both recognized the importance of what high technology meant to the future of Japan and to their company in particular. In his dedication address, Ibuka noted, "We must avoid the problems which befall large corporations, while we create and introduce technologies which large corporations cannot match. The reconstruction of Japan depends on the development of dynamic technologies."[3]

As a start-up company, Totsuken's most immediate problem was financing. The company was able to secure loans, but it routinely suffered from rising costs and inflationary spirals. The problem of cash flow was compounded by the government's new currency policy that placed restrictions on the withdrawal and use of old currency. In order to meet payroll, Totsuken manufactured both communication and noncommunication devices, including electric rice cookers and heat cushions. The electric rice cooker was a commercial failure. In its first year, Totsuken made a profit of $300 on sales of less than $7,000.

One of Totsuken's first important communication contracts was issued by Japan's NHK, who had an urgent need to restore its national broadcasting network. This included the repair of its many studios and transmitters. It would mark the beginning of a long-standing business relationship between the future Sony corporation and NHK. Throughout the late 1940s, the engineers at Totsuken concentrated on the development of consumer electronic goods, including Japan's first-ever tape recorder.[4]

The initial demand for the tape recorder remained quite low until Ibuka accidentally came across a U.S. military booklet entitled *Nine Hundred and Ninety-Nine Uses of the Tape Recorder*. The booklet was translated into Japanese and became an effective marketing tool for customers who did not understand the tape recorder and its many potential uses. The first significant order for the G-type tape recorder came from Japan's Supreme Court. Among Totsuken's many other customers was the Academy of Art in Tokyo. The academy was responsible for purchasing many of the new recorders. Norio Ohga, a music student at the academy, wrote several letters to Morita criticizing the sound quality of the recorders. Morita was impressed with the detailed comments and suggestions and invited Ohga to participate in the development of a new recorder as a consultant. The future Sony president was said to have the most demanding ears in the company.

Establishing the Sony Name

During the early 1950s, Japanese products suffered from a public perception of poor quality. The description *made in Japan* evoked an impression of inferior product quality in design and manufacturing. American-made products, on the other hand, had a reputation for high quality. U.S. products were available worldwide, and sales by U.S. companies skyrocketed as a result. At the time, Morita reasoned that if Sony was going to enter into the manufacturing and sales of electronic equipment, it was necessary to establish a market presence in the United States.[5] In 1952, Morita made the first of two trips to the United States to examine how American companies manufactured and marketed tape recorders. He also wanted to examine potential market opportunities for future Totsuken exports. During Morita's second trip in 1953, he acquired the licensing rights to the transistor patent that was invented at AT&T's Bell Laboratories. Due to Morita's effort, Totsuken was the first company in the Far East to be licensed by AT&T to manufacture and use the transistor in new product designs. In 1955, Totsuken developed the TR-55 transistor radio in Japan and introduced it to the U.S. market that same year.[6]

A year later, Totsuken was able to successfully improve on the transistor radio and produced the TR-63, the world's smallest pocket radio. The newly developed radio had the Sony logo affixed to it. The name Sony soon became more familiar in the world of international electronics than the parent company. At the time, Morita believed that Tokyo Tsushin Kogyo (or Totsuken) was not a name that was easily understood overseas. Thus, despite much internal disagreement, the company's name was officially changed to Sony in January 1958.

Sony's Entry Into World Markets

Early on in his tenure, Morita developed the kind of business skills that allowed him to successfully enter into foreign markets. He did not initially have a global strategy in mind. Instead, he operated in those markets that he believed were important and where Sony's products would be most readily accepted. The United States clearly fulfilled both sets of objectives. The first phase of Sony's globalization plan was the formation of the Sony Corporation of America in 1960. The company established its first showroom in New York City. During the next few years, Sony established Sony Switzerland, U.K. Limited, Sony Deutchland, and Sony France.

All during the 1960s, the Sony Corporation achieved a number of firsts in product design and innovation, including the transistor TV, the portable videotape recorder, the transistor condenser microphone, and the integrated radio circuit. One of the more notable discoveries came in 1968 when Sony engineers had developed a new approach to color television technology. The newly conceived Sony Trinitron set used one electric gun, for more accurate beam alignment, and one lens, for better focus. The result was a clearer television image than had been produced to date using the conventional three gun and three lens set approach.

As so often happens, a company's successful entry into a foreign market can largely be the result of one important contract and/or its involvement in the design and manufacture of one piece of equipment. During the 1970s, a large percentage of U.S. broadcasters used video tape recorders as part of their electronic newsgathering effort. The CBS network, in particular, experimented with Sony's U-matic video tape recorder (VTR). They found the equipment potentially useful, but it was heavy and inconvenient to use. Sony was approached with the idea of designing similar equipment that could provide picture quality equal to film and that was lighter and more portable to use. Thus began Sony's serious entry into the field of broadcast equipment.

In 1976, Sony introduced its U-matic BV series of electronic newsgathering equipment, consisting of the BVP 100 color camera, the BVU 100 and 200 video cassette tape recorder, and the BVE-500 auto electronic editing unit. The equipment was an immediate success. Soon thereafter, recognition came in the form of an Emmy award that was presented to the Sony Corporation for Outstanding Technological Development. The real sign of acceptance was the industry's wholesale adoption of Sony's term *ENG* to describe an altogether new category of electronic newsgathering equipment. In 1981, Sony made another important breakthrough by introducing its Betacam ½-inch broadcast camcorder, which combined both the camera and recorder into one unit. As a result of these technical contributions, the Sony name became closely aligned with broadcast equipment.

Failure and Setback

Being first does not always ensure success. By the late 1970s, the VCR for home use was beginning to take off. In the United States, there was no industry standard for home VCR use. As early as 1975, Sony had already begun promoting its own standard with the introduction of its ½-inch Betamax VCR. In the meantime, several of Japan's other major consumer electronics companies, most notably Panasonic and Japan Victor, rallied around a different standard called VHS. After several years of competition, VHS became the de facto standard, largely due to cost and widespread availability.

In retrospect, Sony made two critical errors in planning. The first was the lack of television and/or film programming that was exclusively available on the Betamax format. The second mistake was to propose Betamax as an industry standard while insisting that every Betamax VCR carry the Sony name. JVC, by contrast, promoted the VHS standard and let others manufacture its system under license. As the VHS format became more commonly accepted, several of Hollywood's premiere film studios would no longer release films using the Betamax format.[7] By 1984, VHS had acquired 90% of the world market.

The resulting failure cost the Sony corporation millions of dollars in lost revenue and time. It also caused a major management shake-up at the top. Masaru Ibuka stepped down as chair and was replaced by Akio Morita as the new chairman of the board. Norio Ohga was named as the new president of the company.[8] The lessons of the Betamax experience, however, proved very instructive. In the future, Sony would make a firm commitment to software development as a critical leverage for selling its technical equipment. It has been under Ohga's leadership that Sony has begun the process of looking at balancing technical competency with software development.

ORGANIZATIONAL STRUCTURE

The Sony Corporation was led, until 1989, by cofounder and chairman of the board Morita. Morita was responsible for much of Sony's early success by introducing the transistor radio to the U.S. market. It was during his tenure as CEO that Sony achieved international recognition for many of its consumer electronic products, including the Walkman portable stereo and the Trinitron television set. His handpicked successor as CEO was longtime friend Norio Ohga. Ohga came up through the ranks of the tape recording division and participated in the 1968 CBS/Sony joint ENG equipment venture, and later became President of Sony in 1982.

The Sony Corporation divides its worldwide operations into four geographic zones, including Japan, the United States, Europe, and International. There are two primary business areas that comprise the Sony Corporation. They include electronics and entertainment. The electronics product group is divided into four divisions: video equipment, audio equipment, television, and others. The entertainment product group is divided into two divisions: the music group and the pictures group. Sony's organizational structure and primary business areas are highlighted in Table 9.1.

BUSINESS STRATEGY AND ECONOMIC PHILOSOPHY

The Sony Corporation is a traditional Japanese company. There is a sense of family and/or missionary zeal that is uniquely Japanese in approach. All of Sony's top officials are Japanese and together they share in the company's collective mission. Sony carefully grooms its future leaders over many years of service. Loyalty to the company is a value that is cultivated at all levels of the organization. In his book, *Made in Japan*, Morita wrote:

> There is no secret ingredient or hidden formula responsible for the success of the best Japanese companies. No theory or plan or government policy will make a business a success; that can only be done by people. The most important

TABLE 9.1
The Sony Corporation: Organizational Structure and Primary Business Areas

Electronics	Product Categories
Audio equipment	CD players, the MD system, DAT recorders, hi-fi components, minicomponent stereos, radio cassette tape recorders, tape recorders, radio car stereos, car navigation systems, transmission receivers, professional use audio equipment, and audiotapes.
Video equipment	Home-use VTRs, laserdisc players, video equipment for broadcast and professional use, HDTV and related equipment, still image video cameras.
Televisions	Color televisions and monitors, HDTV-related equipment, satellite broadcast reception systems, projector systems, professional use displays, and large-screen display systems.
Others	Optical pickups, electronic components, floppy disk drives, information-related equipment, and telephones.
Entertainment	**Product Categories**
Music group	is represented by Sony Music Entertainment Inc. (SMEI) which consists of the following recording labels: Columbia, Epic, Epic Associated, Epic Soundtrax, CHAOS Recordings, Sony Classical, Soho Square, Tristar Music Group, and Sony Wonder. Artists range in music types and genres. Some of their best known performers include Michael Bolton, Mariah Carey, Michael Jackson, and Sade. In Japan: Kome, Kome Club, and Dreams Come True.
Pictures group	includes all television and film products; represented by Sony Pictures Entertainment Inc. which consists of the following studios: Columbia Pictures, TriStar Pictures, Sony Pictures Classics, Triumph Releasing, Columbia TriStar Film Distributors, Loews Theatre Management Corp., and Sony Pictures Studios.

mission for a Japanese manager is to develop a healthy relationship with his employees, to create a family-like feeling with the corporation, a feeling that employees and managers share the same fate.[9]

As Sony becomes more transnational in its planning and operation, the ability to maintain a familylike orientation may prove difficult, if not impossible, to achieve. The vast majority of its worldwide employees are not Japanese. They have not been part of the company's cultural fabric or history. There is a clear recognition among international managers and workers alike that opportunities for professional advancement are somewhat limited by the fact that they are not Japanese.

To that end, Sony officials recognize that in order to be more globally competitive, the company will need to promote greater responsibility and autonomy in the field. The promotion of Michael P. Schulof as senior vice president of Sony America and Jacob K. Schmukli of Sony Europe represent important steps in this direction. Both Schulof and Schmukli were the highest ranking non-Japanese executives in the Sony corporation.[10] Since then, Schulof has left the company. Sony is perhaps more transnational in its approach to management than are some Japanese companies. However, in the end, final decision making clearly rests in the hands of senior management in Tokyo.

Research and Development

The field of consumer electronics and engineering exacts a demand on a company to invent or innovate products at a faster pace than is true with other products and services. It is not surprising, therefore, that Sony has a disproportionately higher commitment to research and development (R & D) when compared to other TNCs.[11] Between the years 1989 and 1994, Sony maintained a steady commitment to R & D, with approximately 6% of sales being used to support ongoing research. This is important when one considers that Matsushita (Sony's nearest competitive rival) devotes only 4%. In 1994 alone, despite a 2-year downturn in consumer electronics in Japan, Sony allocated a 6.2% R & D budget based on ¥230 billion in sales.[12]

Sony's R & D group is among the most prolific in the world. Each year the R & D group is responsible for some 1,000 new products. Approximately 800 of those are improvements and innovations on existing products and 200 are intended to create altogether new markets. Sony has a long history of being the first among product designers, which in past years has earned them the dubious title of "corporate guinea pig." There was a time when founder and honorary chairman Ibuka would have bristled at the comparison. In more recent years, he has come to appreciate the metaphor, for it speaks to Sony's core mission. According to Ibuka.

> One of our most important jobs is determining how to apply the latest developments in electronics to new consumer products. One has to be innovative. There are countless industries which can be built up from scratch if someone takes the right approach. In other words, by taking this guinea pig approach to products, there is always something new to challenge.[13]

The key to Sony's R & D group is flexibility. For a Japanese company that is otherwise traditional, the R & D group is surprisingly flexible. As part of its recruiting efforts, Sony's R & D mostly employs engineers who are generalists and that have the distinctive quality of *neyaka*, which suggests a person who is optimistic, open-minded, and wide-ranging in their interests. Throughout the years, Sony's R & D Group has adopted a policy called self-promotion, which encourages engineers to seek out projects elsewhere in the company. The intention is to encourage the kind of creative and intellectual fermentation that is fundamental to the company's success. Sometimes the idea for a new product concept comes from management and sometimes the ideas germinate from within the project teams. The ability to create ad-hoc, fast-paced project design teams is at the heart of Sony's R & D efforts.[14] Nowhere was this more evident than in the development of a portable, high-fidelity cassette player.

In 1979, Morita personally oversaw the development of a small, personal tape player called the Walkman. Morita took his inspiration from Ohga's desire to listen to music while walking. Morita put together a small project team and challenged them to design a compact, high-fidelity tape player that could be paired with the lightweight headphones already under development. The entire project took less than 5 months to complete and the result was the now-famous Sony Walkman. The name *walkman* has become the generic term used to describe all products of a similar design, including those produced by Sony's competitors.[15]

The Integration of Software and Hardware Design

The Sony Corporation firmly believes that ownership of music and entertainment provides greater leverage in promoting its technical business. The company's 1975 introduction of its Betamax videocassette recorders underscored the point that hardware design was not enough to ensure consumer acceptance. It was under Schulof's direction that Sony has ventured into the world of program entertainment with the $2 billion purchase of CBS Records Inc. in 1988 and the subsequent $3.4 billion acquisition of Columbia Pictures Entertainment in 1989. The Columbia purchase includes two film studios, a television unit, and the Loews theater chain. Sony's purchase of CBS Records and Columbia Pictures gives the company access to a variety of media properties in the form of proprietary licenses and agreements.[16]

Despite such efforts, Sony's foray into the world of television and film production has thus far proven highly unsuccessful. The idea is correct in principle, but achieving success has been an entirely different matter. Throughout the early 1990s, Sony Pictures Entertainment sustained repeated losses, culminating with its worst performance ever in 1994. Although the results have been disappointing, the Sony Corporation has no plans to exit the field of television and film production.[17]

A very promising avenue for the future lies in multimedia production. Newly appointed CEO Nobuyuki Idei is charting the company for an all-digital future. Sony is currently designing smart television sets that will enable users to access the Internet as well as Sony's proprietary video game software. One such prototype is PlayStation, which fully integrates the company's manufacturing capability with its entertainment software.[18]

FINANCIAL PERFORMANCE AND ANALYSIS

During the years 1989 to 1991, the Sony Corporation saw a steady increase in net income from ¥72 billion in 1989 to ¥120 billion in 1992. In the years that followed, the company has experienced a precipitous decline. Sony's consolidated sales and operating revenue for fiscal year 1994 decreased 6.5% from 1993 to ¥3,734 billion ($36,250 million). The decline in terms of net

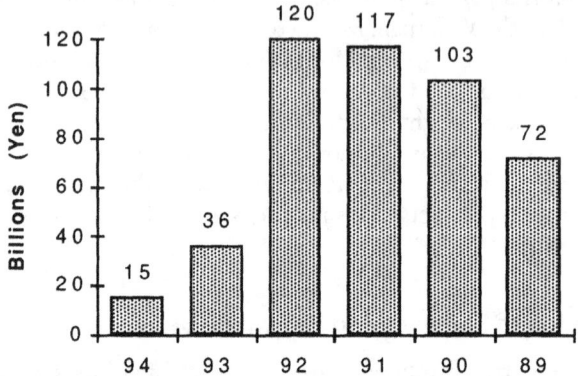

FIG. 9.1. Sony Inc. financial review: Net income (1989–1994).

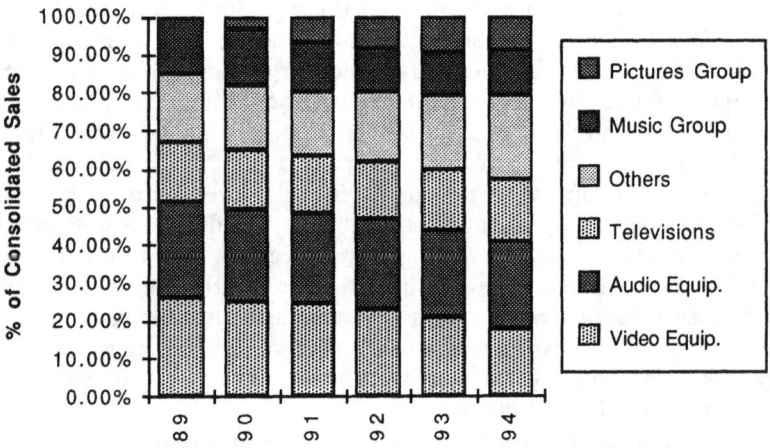

FIG. 9.2. Percentage of consolidated sales by product group: (1989–1994).

income was even more dramatic. During fiscal year 1994, net income fell 57.8% to ¥15 billion ($149 million). A review of Sony's financial performance between 1989 and 1994 can be seen in Fig. 9.1.

The decline in sales and net income can be partially attributed to worldwide recessionary conditions that were especially pronounced in both Japan and Europe. The Japanese audio market, in particular, recorded 4 consecutive years of negative growth. The problem was compounded by the disastrous performance of Sony Pictures Entertainment. In 1994, Sony Pictures Entertainment took a $2.5 billion write-off to cover bad projects and lawsuits. At the close of fiscal year 1994 (ending March 31, 1995), Sony experienced a $2.8 billion loss—the first in its corporate history.

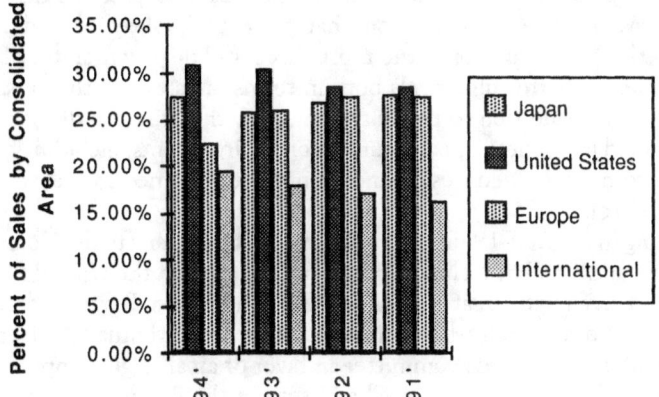

FIG. 9.3. Percentage of consolidated sales by regional location (1991–1994).

In 1994, the video and audio equipment divisions were responsible for 20.8% and 23.2% of company sales, respectively. Figure 9.2 provides a financial review of consolidated sales worldwide by product group. The review period covers the years 1989 to 1994.

In 1994, sales and operating revenue by geographic location remains fairly well divided, with Japan accounting for 27.4%; the United States, 30.9%; Europe, 22.3%; and international at 19.4%, respectively. Since 1992, sales and operating revenue have steadily increased in the United States, and there has been a corresponding decrease in Japan. The combined overseas markets account for approximately 72% of Sony's sales and operating revenues. Figure 9.3 provides a breakdown of sales and operating revenue by regional location.

DISCUSSION

The Sony Corporation is neither the largest hardware nor software producer of media products, but it is undoubtedly the most sophisticated in blending the two areas together. Sony's business imperative for the future will be media integration. The company not only wants a highly successful music and motion picture capability, but it also wants to manufacture the hardware delivery systems for such software products. The Sony Corporation, like many Japanese companies, adheres to the principle of long-term planning, which in the field of consumer electronics can mean a 10-year interval between product design and production.

The Sony Trinitron display monitor serves as the classic example of a device that took 10 years to develop and implement. The Trinitron was the culmination of what began as an earnest attempt to find a better way to produce a color television set.[19] For chairman and founder Ibuka, the Trinitron display monitor represents Sony's most successful business product design. Says Ibuka, "We bet the company on that basic technology."[20] And for good reason—the Sony Trinitron is the most successful display monitor of its kind worldwide, outperforming rivals both in terms of sales and the versatility of applications. In addition to personal home use, the Trinitron display monitor can be found in a variety of communication environments, including broadcast studios, computer-aided design and manufacturing, medical display, and air traffic control.

Starting in the mid-1980s, Sony was the first company to develop a HDTV prototype and standard. The product's introduction in the United States was initially received with great enthusiasm and anticipation. But despite its 5-year head start, Sony's analog-based Muse system was eventually rejected by a U.S.-appointed standards committee in favor of an all-digital approach. Sony has been in this position before. The lessons of the Betamax experience may ultimately prove beneficial. One of Sony's unique strengths is its ability to adapt to the vagaries of the marketplace. In 1993, despite its failed attempt to establish the Betamax VCR standard some 15 years earlier, the Sony Corporation led the U.S. market in high-fidelity VHS format VCRs.[21] Similarly, Sony can be expected to be a market leader in the production of HDTV sets. The real future for Sony lies in multimedia production. HDTV is at the heart of any proposed multimedia future.

During the next decade, Sony will continue to focus on a number of critical technologies, including its Video Hi-8 8mm camcorder, MiniDisc (MD) personal audio system, and digital audiotape (DAT) recorders and players. Sony will also continue its work with Japan's NHK in the ongoing design and implementation of the country's DBS system. Sony is also strong in several key technologies that will power next generation products. They include magnetic storage (i.e., CD-ROM formats), semiconductors, and wireless communication.

Sony's entry into the field of music entertainment has proven very successful during the past 5 years. The company has under contract several notable artists, including Mariah Carey, Michael Bolton, Michael Jackson, Pearl Jam, Billy Joel, Soul Asylum, Sade, and the Spin Doctors. In Japan, major artists include Dreams Come True and Yutaka Ozaki. In fiscal year 1994, music group sales increased 3.4% to ¥462 billion ($4,483 million), representing 12.3% of consolidated sales worldwide. The pictures group and the business of filmmaking, however, is an altogether different story. In fiscal year 1994, the pictures group achieved sales of ¥328 billion (or $3,182 million), accounting for 8.8% of consolidated sales. Yet, this represents a 14.8% decrease from the year before. After 5 years, Sony's entry into filmmaking can only be characterized as disastrous.[22] The Sony Corporation is not likely to abandon its investment in motion pictures. However, there is considerable speculation that Sony will consider a future partnership in the area of filmmaking and studio production.

Sony's business environment, for the short term, is expected to remain challenging due to prolonged recessionary conditions in Japan and Europe. The problem has been exacerbated by a volatile foreign exchange rate. The result has been a serious downturn in the Japanese audiovisual market. It is worth noting that many of these problems are not unique to Sony. All of Japan's leading consumer electronics companies, including Matsushita, Hitachi, Fujitsu, NEC, and Toshiba, have experienced a serious decline in sales in both 1992 and 1993.[23] All this comes at a time when Sony and Japan's leading consumer electronics companies are faced with increased competition from other Pacific Rim nations, most notably China and Korea, who are producing consumer electronics equipment at less cost. The ability to maintain product quality will prove challenging in light of such changes as more and more consumer electronic products are produced worldwide.

NOTES

[1] Sony Corporation, Inc., *Genryu: Sony Challenges 1946–1968*, (Tokyo: Sony Inc., 1988), p. 22.
[2] Sony Corporation, *International Directory of Company Histories*, (Vol. 2.) Chicago: St. James Press, 1990), pp. 101–103.
[3] Sony Corporation, Inc., *Genryu Sony*, p. 30.
[4] Sony Inc., "The Spirit Toward a New Excellence," *Sony's Innovation in Management Series*, (Vol. 5.) (Tokyo: Sony Inc., 1986), p. 3.
[5] Akio Morita, Mitsuko Shimomura, and Edwin M. Reingold, *Made in Japan*, (New York: Dutton, 1986), p. 74.
[6] Sony Corporation, Inc., *Genryu Sony*, p. 96.
[7] Anthony Smith, *The Age of the Behemoths*, (New York: Priority, 1991), pp. 34–35.
[8] Hiroyuki Muneshige, *Sony Morita Akio no Keiei Tetsugaku*, (Tokyo: Kodansha, 1991), pp. 16–121.
[9] Morita, Shimomura, and Reingold, p. 130.
[10] "Tamotsu Iba / Sony: Putting Foreigners in the Executive Suite," 21st Century Capitalism: Special Edition, *Business Week*, November, 1994, p. 90.
[11] "Japan as Global Superpower: An Interview with Sony Corporation Chairman Akio Morita," in *Der Spiegel*, reprinted in *World Press Review*, February, 1990, pp. 62–63.
[12] Sony Corporation, *1994 Annual Report to Stockholders* (Tokyo: Sony, Inc., 1994), p. 30.
[13] Sony Corporation, Inc., *Genryu Sony*, pp. 142–143.
[14] Brenton R. Schlender, "How Sony Keeps the Magic Going," *Fortune*, 22 February, 1992, pp. 77–78.
[15] Sony Corporation, *International Directory of Company Histories*, p. 102.
[16] "Media Colossus," *Business Week*, 15 March, 1991, pp. 64–65.
[17] The future integration of software and hardware can be seen in other forms as well. In December 1994, Sony America unveiled the first in a series of IMAX motion picture theaters that will enable people to view 3-D films on an 80-foot screen. The plan is to create an altogether new theater experience by outfitting attendees with wraparound gray plastic goggles that combine infrared sensors, liquid crystal lenses, and stereo speakers. What distinguishes IMAX from earlier attempts to introduce 3-D films is the level of commitment for software support.
[18] "Sony's New World," *Business Week*, 27 May, 1996, pp. 100–101.
[19] *Genryu*, pp. 202–221.
[20] Schlender, "How Sony Keeps the Magic Going," p. 82.
[21] S. Lubove and N. Weinberg, "Creating a Seamless Company," *Forbes*, 20 December, 1993, p. 154.
[22] "The Sony Scenarios," *Newsweek*, 28 November, 1994, p. 47.
[23] Brenton R. Schlender, "Japan: Hard Times for High Tech," *Fortune*, 22 March, 1993, pp. 92–94.

10

Bertelsmann A.G.

HISTORICAL OVERVIEW

Bertelsmann A.G. was founded by Carl Bertelsmann in 1835 and began as a small printing company in Gutersloh, Germany. For its first 80 years, the company concentrated on the publishing and printing of Protestant hymnals and religious pamphlets. With only 150 employees, the company managed to progress and develop until the start of World War II. Bertelsmann's support of a church resistance group during the ascent of Adolph Hitler led to the closure of the company in 1943. By war's end, most of Bertelsmann's assets had been destroyed. It was nothing more than a bombed-out printing factory.[1]

In 1946, Reinhard Mohn, a 22-year-old German lieutenant and great-grandson of Bertelsmann, returned to his hometown of Gutersloh in northern Germany. As Studemann (1992) wrote:

The scene he encountered there was repeated a thousandfold across post-war Germany: bombed out towns, hungry and helpless people. Mohn's father was ill, his brother still missing in Russia; little was left of the family printing business.[2]

Reinhard Mohn

Mohn's plan for rebuilding the family business can partially be attributed to his experience as an American prisoner of war in Concordia, Kansas. Mohn spent more than 2 years as a POW, having served as an officer in Field Marshal Erwin Rommel's Afrika Corps. On May 12, 1943, 250,000 German and Italian soldiers surrendered to the Allied Forces at the battle of El Alamein. One of those surrendering was the young German lieutenant, Reinhard Mohn.[3]

During his POW internment, Mohn got his first real taste of American life. He was drawn to the dynamism and openness of American society. He worked the Kansas wheatfields by day and studied engineering in his spare time. Mohn read about the life of Alfred P. Sloan, the former president of General Motors. He was deeply impressed with Sloan's philosophy of decentralization and entrepreneurship. It was during this same period that Mohn observed the start-up of a hot new trend in U.S. publishing called book-of-the-month clubs (or book clubs).

After the war, Mohn returned to Gutersloh with the intention of becoming an engineer. Mohn's father, who was deeply ill, convinced his son to rebuild the family printing business. Soon thereafter, Mohn assumed control of the family business and began the task of rebuilding. Mohn proved to be highly resourceful in tracking down the few available printing presses and sources of paper. In the beginning, this meant having to sort through the postwar ruins, retrieving old books from the rubble of bookstores and libraries and bartering anything he could for waste paper that could be used for print. He printed labels for a local distiller in exchange for whiskey. He then traded the whiskey for bricks.[4]

Mohn's plan was to pioneer the start-up of a similar type of book club in Germany. By 1950, Bertelsmann established its first German book club called Lesering. Within 4 years, the number of club members surpassed 1 million and the company's future was solidly launched. Book-of-the month clubs proved to be only the beginning. The company soon realized the possibility of applying the same concept toward records, and later, tapes. In 1962, Bertelsmann initiated the first in a series of foreign book clubs, starting with Spain and later expanding to 22 other countries. Under Mohn's direction, the ruins of a family business were steadily transformed into Europe's largest media company, and years later, the second largest TNMC in the world. Bertelsmann's remarkable transformation would serve as a classic example of Germany's postwar economic miracle.

The Purchase of Gruner & Jahr

The second business milestone for Bertelsmann occurred in 1969 when the company purchased a 25% interest in Gruner & Jahr, one of Germany's big four magazine publishers. Gruner & Jahr was home to Stern, then considered one of Germany's most influential magazines. During the next few years, Bertelsmann purchased the controlling interest.[5] Today, Gruner & Jahr publishes more than 70 magazines and newspapers in seven countries. Some of its more notable titles include Femme Actuelle in France, Prima in the United Kingdom, and Geo in Spain. Since German unification, Gruner & Jahr has also expanded into newspapers in the east and publishes Berlin's largest regional daily.

Failure and Setback

Bertelsmann, when compared to other TNMCs, is one of the best managed media companies in the world. But for all its success, there have been a few notable failures. The first occurred in 1979 with Bertelsmann's unsuccessful attempt to launch a U.S. version of a high-quality German geographic magazine called *GEO*. The magazine failed to catch on and after 2 years was discontinued with losses estimated at $50 million. In 1984, the company tried to buy *U.S. News and World Report* but was outbid by real estate entrepreneur Mortimer Zuckerman. Both monetary setbacks, however, pale in comparison with the company's biggest embarrassment. In 1984, Bertelsmann's very own

Stern magazine published with great fanfare the Hitler diaries, only to discover soon thereafter that they were a hoax.[6]

The Next Generation of Leadership

In 1981, Mohn stepped down as CEO of Bertelsmann A.G., following his own rule that established 60 as the required age for retirement. Mohn was succeeded 2 years later with the appointment of Dr. Mark Wossner, who served as the former head of the company's printing operations. Wossner was given the full support of the former chair and a strict mandate to "preserve and expand" Bertelsmann's core business. In a rapidly expanding international market, this could only mean one thing—foreign direct investment into the United States.

Bertelsmann Entry Into the United States

A third important milestone was reached with Bertelsmann entry into the U.S. market. In 1977, Bertelsmann began the first in a series of FDIs with the purchase of 51% of Bantam Books (later increased to 100%). The next year, the company purchased Arista Records from Columbia Pictures. Under Wossner's direction, the most aggressive move into the U.S. market occurred in 1986 with two major acquisitions, including Doubleday publishing ($475 million) and RCA Records ($330 million). These two deals vaulted the low-profile German media company into the lofty postion of becoming the world's second-largest TNMC. Equally important, Bertelsmann A.G. became a major force in U.S. publishing virtually overnight. The company gained immediate access to Doubleday's book club business, which then boasted a membership of 2.5 million subscribers.

The RCA Records label was founded in 1901 as the Victor Talking Machine Company. Over the years, RCA Records was home to several of America's legendary music performers, including Duke Ellington, Benny Goodman, Elvis Presley, and the Jefferson Airplane. Bertelsmann's 1986 acquisition of RCA Records firmly established the company in the field of U.S. music recording and distribution. The next year, Bertelsmann consolidated RCA Records and its other record labels into a new division called Bertelsmann Music Group (BMG). The newly formed music subsidiary would consist of Arista Records, Ariola, and RCA.[7] Since 1987, BMG has has added several newer labels to its music portfolio including investments in Zoo Entertainment, Windham Hill, and Imago Recording.

The importance of the U.S. market was perhaps symbolized in 1992 with the purchase of a $200 million office building on prestigious Broadway in New York City. This building now serves as the world headquarters for BMG and is home to the Bantam-Doubleday-Dell Publishing Group as well. At the building's dedication, Honorary Chairman Mohn had a chance to peer out from the 22nd floor of the Bertelsmann building to the New York City landscape and to an America that had taught him well.

ORGANIZATIONAL STRUCTURE

Bertelsmann A.G. is the second-largest TNMC in the world. The company's central headquarters is based in Gutersloh, Germany. Bertelsmann is the most transnational of the world's leading media companies. Two-thirds of its business is done outside Germany. The company's management style is highly decentralized. The company adheres to a strict philosophy of autonomy that allows each subsidiary to determine its own performance objectives. Each subsidiary retains its own name, which helps to partly explain why the Bertelsmann name is not well known in the United States and certain parts of the world.

Starting in 1992 through 1993, Bertelsmann underwent a major organizational change by consolidating its seven corporate divisions into four product line groups. The four major product groups include Book, BMG Entertainment, Gruner & Jahr, and Industry.

In all, these four product line groups oversee more than 200 companies around the world. Figure 10.1 provides an overview of Bertelsmann's four product line groups and their respective areas of business.

The Book Product Line

Bertelsmann Book A.G. combines the two former book divisions and the Publishing Group International. The book division publishes and distributes books on a wide variety of topics, including fiction and nonfiction (encyclopedias, dictionaries, scholarly literature, maps, travel guides and medical information services). Bertelsmann Book A.G. is the world's largest book publishing

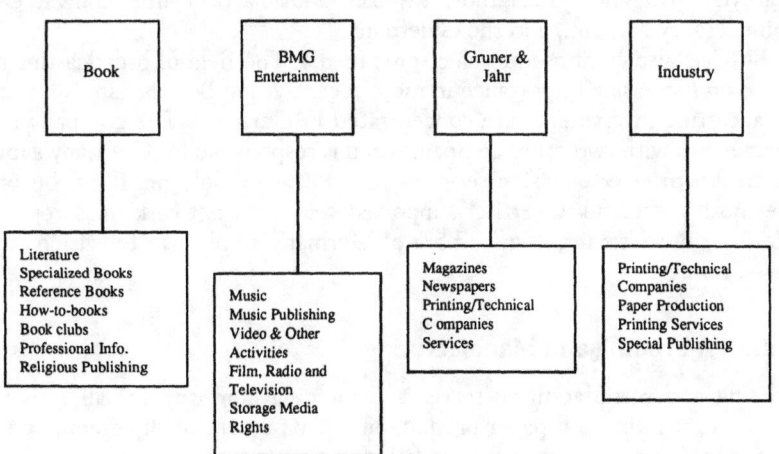

FIG. 10.1. Bertelsmann A.G. four major product line groups.

and distribution organization. In the United States, alone, Bertelsmann owns Bantam Books, Doubleday Corporation, Dell Publishing, and the Literary Guild. John Grisham and Danielle Steel are two of the more prominent authors who write for Bertelsmann. In 1993, Grisham's legal thrillers, including *The Firm*, *A Time to Kill*, and *The Pelican Brief* sold an estimated 22 million copies.[8] Grisham's bestsellers were responsible for boosting the sales of book clubs in the United States by 33%.

BMG Entertainment

The Bertelsmann Music Group (BMG) consists of music and electronic media. BMG is headquartered in New York City and is comprised of several major recording labels including Arista Records Inc., RCA Records U.S., BMG Classics, and Zoo Entertainment. BMG also has major investments in smaller recording labels such as Windham Hill (50%), BMG Victor (90%), Private Music (50%), and Imago Recording (20%). The music and distribution for BMG can be found in 37 countries and is handled through BMG International. BMG's recording labels are home to variety of international artists that include Annie Lennox, Lisa Stansfield, David Bowie, Udo Jergens, SNAP, Vaya Con Dios, Eros Ramazzotti, Rainhard Fendrich, Peter Maffay, and ZZ Top. The Arista recording label is the most successful of the company's multiple music labels, accounting for some 7.4% of sales in the United States. Some of the more notable U.S. artists who perform on the Arista recording label include Whitney Houston, Kenny G., the Grateful Dead, Carly Simon, Aretha Franklin, Barry Manilow, and Alan Jackson. In the area of classical music, BMG Classics is home to several of the world's best known classical musicians including Van Cliburn, Pinchas Zukermann, Evegny Kissin, Alicia de Larrocha, Marilyn Horne, and Ofra Harnoy, as well cross-over artists James Galway, Cleo Laine, Henry Mancini, and the Chieftains.

BMG is also composed of electronic media. The field of broadcasting has taken on increasing importance in more recent years. Bertelsmann's primary broadcasting investments are concentrated in Germany. The company is in partnership with two other companies and is responsible for Germany's most successful private television service—RTL Plus—in Cologne. It has become the most successful advertiser-supported television network in Europe. In addition, Bertelsmann owns 37.5% of Germany's only pay television service—Premiere.

Industry: Printing and Manufacturing

Printing and manufacturing serves as a holding company for all activities related to printing and paper production. Fifty percent of all revenues come from printing magazines and advertising materials such as catalogs or direct mail flyers. Thirty-two percent of revenues in this group result from the printing of books and calendars. Germany represents the biggest market for printing and manufacturing, contributing 63% to overall revenues followed by Italy at 12%.

Gruner & Jahr

Gruner & Jahr comprises all magazine and newspaper holdings. The product line group produces over 34 magazines in Germany and seven other countries, including *Stern* and *Brigette* in Germany, *McCalls* and *Family Circle* in the United States, *Best* and *Prima* in Great Britain, and *Femme Actuelle* in France. A complete listing of Gruner & Jahr's magazine holdings can be seen in Table 10.1.

BUSINESS STRATEGY AND PHILOSOPHY

Gutersloh, Germany is a quiet town in the northern plains of Germany with a population of 80,000. There is no airport within 100 miles and the express trains do not stop there; it is an unlikely place for a TNMC. As Studemann (1992) wrote, "But it was from there that the Bertelsmann family printing business, in ruins after the Second World War, was built into a global media empire with interests ranging from books and magazines to music and television."[9]

From the very beginning, Mohn set out to create a highly decentralized organization in which managers were ultimately responsible for their unit of operation. The approach seemed to combine two important experiential threads from his past. The first was based on his POW experience in Concordia, Kansas, where Mohn was deeply impressed with the innovative thinking of General Motor's Alfred P. Sloan, who stressed the importance of entrepreneurship and decentralization. To that end, Mohn would later create a company of semiautonomous profit centers that would operate within a broad framework established by the parent corporation. The second important thread was the direct result of his experience as an Army lieutenant, where Mohn was exposed to the military principle of *Auftragstaktik*; that is, assigning a mission to a commander and giving him the freedom to decide how to make it succeed.

During the early start-up of his company, Mohn encouraged his managers to be entrepreneurs. He created dozens of semiautonomous profit centers to encourage competition among the groups. As Mohn slowly discovered, such competition can wreak havoc on an organization. By making each division semiautonomous, organizational growth was erratic and there was significant overlap between divisions. In the early days, it was not uncommon to find company salespeople competing among themselves for the same customer. The same autonomy led to some far-flung purchases in the 1960s that included poultry farming. By the 1970s, Mohn refocused the company's attention on the business of mass media.

TABLE 10.1
Bertelsmann: Gruner & Jahr Magazine Holdings (1993–1994)

International Magazines		Magazines in Germany
France	**Great Britain**	Art
Ca m'interesse	Best	Brigitte
Capital	Prima	Brigitte YOUNG MISS
Cuisine Gourmande	Focus	Capital
Femme Actuelle		Eltern
Gala	**Italy**	Essen & Trinken
GEO	Focus	Flora
Guide Cuisine	Vera	Frau im Spiegel
Tele Loisirs		Frau im Spiegel Raten & Prima
Voici	**United States**	Gala
Prima	Parents	Geo
	YM	Geo Saison
Spain	Family Circle	Geo Special
Cosmopolitan	McCalls	Hauser
Dunia	American Homestyle	Impulse
Geo	Fitness	Impulse ost
La Casa Marie Claire	Child	Marie Claire
Marie Claire		Max
Mia	**Poland**	Mein Kind und ich
Muy Interasante	Claudia	Neues Wohnen
Natura	Moje Mieszkanie	P.M. Magazin
Ser Padres Hoy		P.M. Logik-Trainer
		P.M. Perspektive
		P.M. Das historische Ereignis
		Prima
		Sandra
		Schoner Essen
		Schoner Wohnen
		Schoner Wohnen Decoration
		Sports Life
		Stern
		Wochenpost
		Yps

Bertelsmann Today

Bertelsmann A.G. is a low-profile company that ranks as one of the best managed TNMCs in the world. CEO Wossner believes that Bertelsmann's success can be attributed to long-range strategic planning and decentralization, a legacy that Mohn instilled in the company before his retirement in 1981. That philosophy is captured in the company charter, which stresses entrepreneurial leadership and decentralization of operations, creativity and innovation at every level of the corporation, continuity and dynamic growth on a sound financial basis, and commitment to being a valued corporate citizen of the communities in which Bertelsmann companies operate.[10]

In practice, Bertelsmann's strategic decision making and corporate policies are developed by the company's executive board, which consists of the company's seven division heads. In turn, each business unit is responsible for developing its own business plan, including control over assets, human resources, and contribution to overall profitability. In keeping with this structure, the company business units retain their distinct identities by creating their own products and implementing their own separate marketing plans. Each business unit is accountable for fulfilling its business objectives at the end of the fiscal year. According to Bertelsmann spokesman Helmuth Runde, "We want people to feel as though they are working for themselves so they are given as much responsibility as possible."[11]

Bertelsmann A.G. is the second-largest TNMC in the world. Yet, according to Wossner, the real goal for Bertelsmann is quality and not size: "I'm not interested in size. We should be the best. If we were the most excellent media company in the world, and we could measure it, that I would find interesting."[12]

Wossner describes Bertelsmann's business philosophy as elegantly simple:

> Our concept for expansion is always the same. We never go into a business in which we don't have self-reliant knowhow and experience. If we do go into a business which is a little bit strange for us, we do it mostly in markets where we have an outstanding infrastructure and leading positions for financing and recruiting top management.[13]

This approach has usually meant launching the new business venture in Germany and replicating the experience in other markets. As an example, Bertelsmann's entry into book clubs began in Germany and was later transferred into 22 markets worldwide. Similarly, Gruner & Jahr's production of a top women's magazine, *Femme Actuelle*, has been replicated several times over throughout the many countries where the company engages in magazine production.

Another important reason why the company is able to promote the level of entrepreneurship can be directly linked to the company's ownership pattern. The Mohn family holds about 89.3% of the company stock, with the remaining portion held by Mr. Gerd Bucerias, a well-known Hamburg publisher. As a result, there is not the same institutional pressure to achieve short-term profits at the expense of long-term strategic plans. Here again, is another Mohn legacy.

During the early 1950s, Mohn's expansion plans were so ambitious that many of Germany's leading banks were reluctant to lend him the needed capital. So Mohn turned to his employees and outside investors, who were encouraged to buy nonvoting, profit-sharing certificates in the company. Bertelsmann, thereby, obtained the needed financing and employees have been getting a 15% yearly return ever since. Mohn subsequently initiated a nonvoting, profit-sharing plan with company employees. It is also one of the principal reasons why unions have not been very successful at Bertelsmann.[14]

FINANCIAL PERFORMANCE AND ANALYSIS

Bertelsmann A.G. is financially a very strong company. During fiscal year 1994, the company's total revenue increased by 7.2% to DM 18.4 billion. Bertelsmann has demonstrated a consistent pattern of growth during the previous 5 years, with an annual growth rate of 7%. A review of Bertelsmann's financial performance between 1989 and 1994 can be seen in Fig. 10.2.

In 1993 and 1994, sales and operating revenue by geographic location was fairly evenly divided with Germany accounting for 36.3%; Europe excluding Germany, 31.3%; the United States, 24.4%; and international, 8.0%. Evidence during these past 5 years would suggest that Bertelsmann is becoming increasing transnationalized with a greater percentage of its revenues coming from the United States and other international markets. Figure 10.3 provides a breakdown of sales and operating revenue by geographical location for fiscal years 1993 to 1994 and 1992 to 1993.[15]

In 1993 to 1994, BMG Entertainment was responsible for the largest

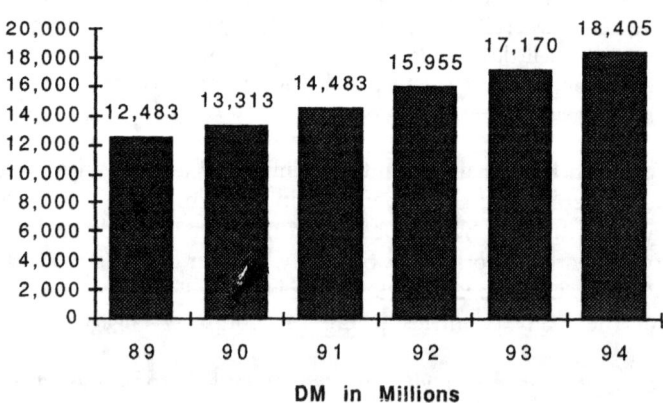

FIG. 10.2. Bertelsmann A.G. Financial performance (1989–1993).

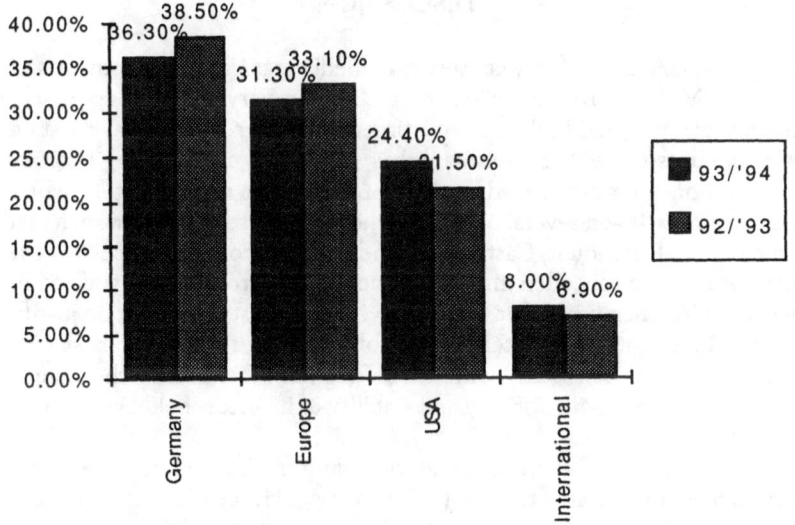

FIG. 10.3. Bertelsmann A.G. total sales by region.

TABLE 10.2
Bertelsmann A.G. Worldwide Revenues by Product Line (DM in Millions)

	1992/1993	1993/1994	Change in Total Percentage
Book	6,049	6,294	4.1%
BMG Entertainment	5,127	5,944	15.9%
Gruner & Jahr	3,755	3,848	2.5%
Bertelsmann Industry	2,987	3,103	3.9%
Total Revenue	17,918	19,189	7.1%
Intercompany Sales	–748	–478	4.8%
Consolidated Revenues	17,170	18,405	7.2%

Note. Source: Company reports.

growth increase, where revenues increased by 15.9% to DM 5.9 billion. BMG's impressive performance was largely due to increased sales in the United States. The book product line that includes, book publishing, clubs, and professional information increased 4.1% to DM 6.3 billion. Revenues for Bertelsmann Industry increased by 3.9% to DM 3.1 billion. Lastly, revenues for Gruner & Jahr were up 2.5% to DM 3.8 billion.[16] Table 10.2 provides a financial review of Bertelsmann's four major product line groups for fiscal years 1992 to 1993 and 1993 to 1994 based on worldwide sales and operating revenue.

DISCUSSION

Bertelsmann A.G. is a fairly conservative media organization in comparison to other TNMCs. In recent years, it has taken a very cautious approach to strategic planning and FDI goals. At a time when other TNMCs have sustained large amounts of debt, Bertelsmann has shied away from paying exorbitant sums of money for overpriced media properties. As a result, Bertelsmann has been unsuccessful on several occasions when it came to bidding on such media companies as Paramount, Castle Rock, and Virgin Records, to name only a few. Bertelsmann also cancelled impending cooperative projects with such companies as MCA when it was felt that the investment costs could not be justified. At the same time, the Bertelsmann debt-to-equity ratio is the best among TNMCs. This is consistent with CEO Wossner's belief that the company should be defined by the quality and stability of its media holdings and not by the size.

In his book, *In Search of Excellence*, author Tom Peters spoke of the importance of being able to stick to the knitting. His central thesis is that the best managed companies are those that can strengthen and deepen what they know how to do best.[17] Bertelsmann is the embodiment of this philosophy. The company's conservative and patient approach has enabled it to be a consistent earnings performer throughout the past 7 years. Bertelsmann's decision to enter the U.S. market in 1988 with the purchase of RCA and Doubleday has paid off handsomely. The formation of BMG Entertainment is fast becoming a primary engine that will drive the company in the years to come.

The real question for Bertelsmann is whether the company's conservative approach will allow it to adapt to a rapidly changing media marketplace. If experience is any indication, Bertelsmann is likely to continue doing what it does best—publications and music. At the same time, Bertelsmann's plans for the future will also include electronic media and, specifically, pay television. To that end, Bertelsmann has already undertaken a number of electronic media projects in Germany. The company has teamed up with Deutsche Telekom and the Kirch Group to begin developing a series of cable television systems in select markets. This effort is consistent with Wosnner's belief that Germany should provide the proper testing ground before expanding internationally. The long-term strategy is to develop cable television throughout Germany, Eastern Europe, and the Far East.[18] To that end, Bertelsmann has teamed up with France's Canal Plus to begin marketing a European-wide pay television service.

NOTES

[1] Reinhard Mohn, *Erfolg durch Partnerschaft*, 2nd ed. (Berlin: Siedler, 1993), p. 402.

[2] Frederick Studemann, "Europe's Great Communicator," *International Management*, September 1992, p. 34.
[3] Milton Moskowitz, "Bertelsmann A.G." *The Global Marketplace*, (New York: MacMillan, 1987), p. 69. See also "Reinhard Mohn," *The Nation*, 12 June, 1989, p. 810.
[4] "Reinhard Mohn: The Alfred P. Sloan of Publishing," *Forbes*, 5 October, 1987, p. 124.
[5] "Bertelsmann: The Media Company that Makes Murdoch's Empire Seem Small," *The Economist*, 19 April, 1988, p. 63.
[6] "Reinhard Mohn," *The Nation*, p. 810.
[7] "Bertelsmann's US Invasion May be Just Beginning," *Business Week*, 10 August, 1987, p. 72.
[8] "An Overnight Success After Six Years," *Business Week*, 19 April, 1993, p. 52.
[9] Studemann, "Europe's Great Communicator," p. 34.
[10] Bertelsmann A.G., "Bertelsmann: A World of Experience," (New York: Bertelsmann Marketing and Public Relations, 1993), p. 7.
[11] Studemann, "Europe's Great Communicator," p. 36.
[12] "Bertelsmann's Stairway to Stardom," *International Management*, November, 1987, p. 36.
[13] Ibid., p. 37.
[14] "Bertelsmann: The Media Company That Makes Murdoch's Empire Look Small," *The Economist*, 19 April, 1988, pp. 63–64.
[15] Bertlesmann A.G., *1994 Annual Report to Stockholders*, (New York: Bertelsmann, Inc.).
[16] Ibid.
[17] Thomas J. Peters, *In Search of Excellence: Lessons From America's Best-Run Companies*, (New York: Warner, 1984).
[18] "Bertelsmann Records Worldwide Revenues of $8.3 Billion," *Publishers Weekly*, 12 October, 1990, p. 9.

11

The Walt Disney Company

HISTORICAL OVERVIEW

At the end of World War I, Walter Elias Disney returned to the United States after serving as an ambulance driver for the American troops overseas. Prior to his enlistment, Disney trained as a commercial artist, having studied at the Kansas City Art Institute. Disney's plan, on his return, was to pursue a career as a commercial artist. In 1919, Disney formed his own animated cartoon company in partnership with artist Ub Iwerks. Despite several attempts, the 4-year partnership proved unsuccessful. The company went bankrupt and Disney left to join his brother, Roy, in Hollywood. Together, they formed the Disney Brothers Cartoon Studio in 1923.[1] Walt Disney would be responsible for the creative side and brother Roy would devote himself to the business end.

Soon thereafter, word came from New York that M. J. Winkler, a film distributor, was interested in buying the rights to a series of Disney's live action cartoon reels, later to be called *Alice Comedies*. Winkler offered $1,500 per reel. Disney agreed and soon became Winkler's production partner. In 1927, Disney began developing a series of animated films called *Oswald the Lucky Rabbit*. The series was an instant hit with the general public. However, *Oswald the Lucky Rabbit* was copyrighted in Winkler's name. As a result, Disney did not receive the full recognition or commercial benefits of his success. It was the last time that Disney would relinquish creative control and the copyright to one of his character inventions.

It was during this same period of time that Disney conceived of an altogether different type of animated character. This time it was a mercurial mouse named Mortimer—later shortened to Mickey. Disney drew up several sketches and together with his brother Roy invested their own money in the production of two Mickey Mouse films. The third Mickey Mouse film represented a major step forward with the introduction of sound. The film *Steamboat Willie* was a technological achievement and went on to become an all-time classic.

The Mickey Mouse sequence of films quickly became a stellar success in the field of cartoon animation. They allowed Disney to pursue other projects, including several full-length motion picture films and advances in Technicolor film. Throughout the late 1930s and early 1940s, Disney produced a number of award-winning animated films, including *Snow White & the Seven Dwarfs* (1937), *Pinocchio* (1940), *Fantasia* (1940), *Dumbo* (1941), and *Bambi* (1942). The mid-1940s also saw the release of several live action films, including *The Reluctant Dragon* and *Song of the South*.[2] It was during this same period that Disney lent assistance to the war effort by using several Disney characters for purposes of information and public relations.

Starting in the early 1950s, Disney formed a new distribution company called Buena Vista. Among the first films to be released under the Buena Vista name was *20,000 Leagues Under the Sea* and *The Living Desert*. The decade of the 1950s also saw the advent of television. Disney recognized the potential of the new medium and served as host to a new series called *Disneyland* that premiered in 1954. Each week, some 4 million Americans tuned in to watch live action drama combined with film clips from various Disney cartoons and specials. The effect on America's youth was enormous. As an example, Disney made a national hero out of frontiersman Davy Crockett when he made the folk hero the subject of a three-part series. In a matter of weeks, the Disney company was making a fortune on the sale of coonskin caps and other Crockett merchandise. That experience taught Disney an important lesson in the value of program software and tie-in merchandising. The success of Davy Crockett set the stage for a new era in Disney live action adventures that included such 1950s hits as *The Great Locomotive Chase*, *Westward Ho*, *Old Yeller*, and *The Light in the Forest*.[3]

In October 1955, *The Mickey Mouse Club* debuted on the ABC television network. Throughout the late 1950s, Disney virtually owned late afternoon television viewing among American school-aged children. *The Mickey Mouse Club* improved the popularity of ABC and likewise provided a popular forum through which Disney could promote its new amusement park in Anaheim, California.[4] In 1961, Disney switched to the NBC television network and premiered a new hour-long show entitled *Walt Disney's Wonderful World of Color*. The program aired for 20 years. An entire generation of American school children grew up watching both the *The Mickey Mouse Club* and *Walt Disney's Wonderful World of Color*. The combination of Disney television and film entertainment left an indelible impression in the minds of the public that Disney meant family entertainment. As Newsweek wrote:

> What is the Walt Disney Co. but a dream machine, a teller and seller of fairy tales? And at the heart of every Disney saga are some of life's most basic themes: friendship, family and the struggle for independence. The Little Mermaid defies her father for love. Simba the lion cub flees home, finds friendly refuge amid the wilderness and overcomes an evil uncle to assume his rightful place as king. Always, the young hero breaks away, triumphs over great dangers and returns to the fold. All is forgiven, there's always a happy ending . . .[5]

Theme Parks and Leisure Entertainment

For some time, Walt Disney had been conceiving of an amusement park where traditional rides and entertainment could be combined with the character inventions of his television and film programs. To that end, the Walt Disney company purchased 250 acres in Anaheim, California. Thus was born Disneyland, which opened its gates to the public on July 17, 1955. What gave Disneyland its distinctive flavor was the project's special ability to interweave Disney's classic characters with the actual rides and attractions available at the park. Disneyland became the first theme park of its kind, a concept that would eventually be imitated many times over throughout the world.

Walt Disney died on December 15, 1966. Shortly before his death, the company purchased 28,000 acres in Orlando, Florida for what was then referred to as the Disney World project. The entire 28,000 acres was purchased for a mere $5.5 million. The real costs associated with Disney World would be closer to $400 million by the time the company opened its doors to the public. Roy Disney supervised the first phase of the project, culminating with the opening of the Magic Kingdom in October 1971.

Nine thousand workers took part in the construction effort that eventually included a 200-acre man-made lake, two 18-hole golf courses, two hotels, the Magic Kingdom, and a highly efficient transportation network that connected the various elements. Given the complexity of the project, Disney planners understood the importance of three vital elements: comfort, safety, and accessibility. Disney would set the standards for a then-unknown field called leisure management.

A Change in Leadership

The Walt Disney Company fared well in the immediate years following the opening of Disney World. However, during the late 1970s, and early 1980s, the company encountered a period of decline evidenced by falling attendance at its theme parks, the production of several unsuccessful films, and questionable leadership at the top. In March 1984, Roy E. Disney, Walt's nephew, resigned his position on the board of directors, citing his dissatisfaction with the company's financial performance. His action invited a swarm of potential raiders, including the Bass brothers from Texas, who wound up with 25% of the company. Together, with Roy E. Disney, they put in a new management team consisting of CEO Michael D. Eisner (former president of Paramount) and Frank Wells (former president of Warner Brothers).[6] Eisner and Wells reorganized the company by putting together a new management team. One of their first charges was to change the name of the company from Walt Disney Motion Pictures and Television to the Walt Disney Company.

What Eisner and his team of managers had inherited was a large, undermanaged company. The real challenge from the start was to find ways to more fully realize the potential of the Disney name and the company's unique mix of tangible and intangible assets. One of Eisner's first moves was to raise the admission price to the two theme parks, which had been kept artificially low. The result was immediate. By 1986, the increase in ticket revenues was responsible for 59% of the company's revenues and 94% of its earnings growth.[7]

Disney, under its former management, had been woefully lax in producing new animated films and expanding on its existing franchise of cartoon characters.[8] Eisner immediately increased the budget for new animated film productions. The 1988 animated cartoon *Who Framed Roger Rabbit?* became an animated classic. It was followed by a whole new series of animated films, including *The Little Mermaid, Beauty and the Beast, Aladdin,* and *The Lion King.*

Another Eisner move included the start-up of a new film production company called Touchstone Pictures, which was created for the production of mainstream and adult film entertainment. Touchstone Pictures was largely built on good scripts and lesser known actors. The result was a string of successful films at lower cost, including *Down and Out in Beverly Hills, Ruthless People, Three Men and a Baby, Good Morning Vietnam, The Color of Money, Outrageous Fortune,* and *Pretty Woman.* In a matter of 4 years, Disney's combined film studios went from last place to first among the eight major U.S. film studios.[9]

Leisure Management Comes of Age

By the time Eisner set out to reorganize the company, Walt Disney World was fast becoming one of America's most popular vacation sites. As was mentioned, Disney had seriously undermanaged the theme parks prior to Eisner's arrival. In addition to undercharging admission fees, the company had overlooked the burgeoning hotel business. Disney's three existing hotels had occupancy rates well above the national average. Thus, the newly transformed Walt Disney Company embarked on an ambitious building plan that included the construction of six new hotels.

What Eisner and his team of managers brought to Disney was the unique ability to combine creativity with strong financial discipline. The Team Disney approach established a creative climate that allowed good projects to be conceived and executed without a lot of encumbrance. Since 1984, The Walt Disney Company has seen a sevenfold increase in profitability. The value of Disney's stock has been equally impressive, having climbed 750% during the same time period.[10] The Walt Disney Company has now positioned itself as one of the most successful and creative forces in the entertainment industry. The combination of Disney television and film entertainment and the theme parks have left an indelible impression in the minds of the public that Disney means family entertainment.

Organizational Changes

Starting in 1994, a combination of natural events, organizational changes, and financial decisions had cast a shadow over what had otherwise been a stunning financial performance. The starting point for these changes can be found in the organizational leadership itself. The Disney management team that had so smoothly navigated the company through the decade of the 1980s and early 1990s, was about to end. In April 1994, Frank Wells, chief operating officer, died in a heli-skiing accident in Nevada. Wells was a seasoned veteran and the man credited with giving the company strong financial leadership. He was the consummate negotiator and handled much of the company's behind-the-scenes administrative work. His death left Eisner with a personal loss and a difficult void to fill. One possible choice to fill that vacancy was Jeffrey Katzenberg, then head of Disney Studios.

In September 1994, after a long and difficult power struggle, Katzenberg resigned his position when it became clear that he would not be named to fill the CEO position. Katzenberg's departure was all the more difficult when one considers that he and Eisner worked together for 19 years. This was understandably a difficult period for Eisner. Only 6 weeks before, Eisner had been hospitalized and underwent quadruple bypass surgery. The combination of natural and human events shook the very foundation of what many considered to be the best management team in the field of media and entertainment. Finding replacement positions was not going to be easy. As an example, the company had been in the process of consolidating its television and telecommunications divisions into one unit headed up by Richard Frank, a long-time Disney executive. In less than 6 months, Frank had resigned his position as well.

Disney Purchases Capital Cities/ABC

On July 31, 1995, the Walt Disney Company announced plans to purchase Capital Cities/ABC for $19 billion. The proposed merger combined the Walt Disney Company with the most profitable U.S. television network, including its ESPN sports cable service.[11] The deal was said to have originated at a business conference in Sun Valley Idaho. According to Eisner, "I literally passed Tom Murphy on the street and said, 'Tom I think the time is right now. Every part of your company is working. Every part of our company is working.'"[12]

Shortly thereafter, Cap Cities Chairman Tom Murphy met with his long-time friend and founding partner, Daniel B. Burke, to develop a proposal that would allow Disney to buy Cap Cities/ABC through a combination of stock and cash. After that, serious meetings got underway between both companies with all details kept secret until the announced merger.

The merging of Disney and Cap Cities/ABC represented the second largest merger in U.S. corporate history, second only to the $25 billion deal between RJR Nabisco and Kohlberg Kravis and Roberts. The merging of both companies transformed the Walt Disney Company into a TNMC giant. The combined company has a major stake in both program software and distribution technology, and thus is a formidable player in the transnational media landscape.

It is interesting to note that the Disney and Cap Cities/ABC combination exhibits many of the same features characteristic of the Time Warner merger, where again the deal was engineered by a small group of ambitious chief executives and influential advisors. For Cap Cities/ABC's Murphy, the merger agreement was the final chapter to a long and successful business partnership between himself and Burke that began in 1954. For Disney CEO Eisner, the Disney–Cap Cities/ABC merger represented a personal triumph after a year of business setbacks and personal loss.

The purchase of Cap Cities/ABC brought to the merger agreement a well-respected, highly profitable television network. ABC has some of the most highly rated television shows in the industry and has the most well-respected news operation. In addition, ABC will ensure a steady audience for Disney programs and offer numerous cross licensing and marketing opportunities. The Walt Disney Company brought to the merger agreement a highly creative culture committed to developing and distributing original television and film programs. The company also has unparalleled skill in the field of marketing. Disney's creative and marketing contributions should make ABC a more formidable rival to its broadcast and cable network counterparts. And for both companies, the Disney–Cap Cities/ABC merger brings Disney full circle from the 1950s when Walt Disney Studios got its start on the fledgling ABC television network.

ORGANIZATIONAL STRUCTURE

The Walt Disney Company is divided into three major divisions, including Walt Disney Studios, Walt Disney Attractions, and Walt Disney Consumer Products. Figure 11.1 provides an overview of the Walt Disney Company in terms of its three major divisions.

Walt Disney Studios

Walt Disney Studios produces live action and animated motion pictures for distribution to theatrical, television, and home video markets. Motion pictures are produced under three separate film production companies including Walt Disney Animation, Touchstone Pictures, and Hollywood Pictures. Walt Disney Studios also produces original television products for network television and first-run syndication markets. Walt Disney Studios also operates The Disney Channel, a 24-hour pay cable television service. The Disney Channel began in 1985 with approximately 50% of its programming based on Disney's vast library holdings. The library now accounts for only 23% of the program schedule, with the remaining portion filled with original and acquired pro-

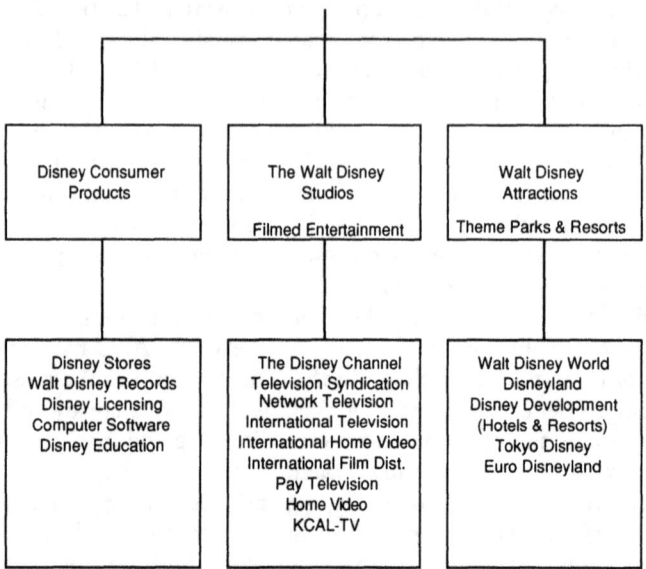

FIG. 11.1. The Walt Disney Company.

gramming. Walt Disney studios also owns and operates television station KCAL-TV in Los Angeles, California.

Walt Disney Attractions

Walt Disney Attractions is responsible for the operation of the company's theme parks and corresponding venues. The two primary theme parks are Disneyland and Walt Disney World. The Disneyland theme park is located on 250 acres in Anaheim, California. It features the original Magic Kingdom as well as numerous rides and attractions. In 1995, Disneyland unveiled its Indiana Jones Adventure after 11 years of planning and development. The 4-minute ride takes visitors in a military transport vehicle on a trip through highlights from the various Indiana Jones films.

The Walt Disney Company also owns and operates Walt Disney World, located in Lake Buena Vista, Florida. The Walt Disney World resort features three major theme parks: the Magic Kingdom, Epcot Center, and MGM Studios. In addition to its theme parks, Walt Disney World also includes its Pleasure Island Water Park, nine hotels, a complex of villas, the Disney shopping village, conference centers, campgrounds, golf courses, and other recreational facilities.

Walt Disney Attractions is also an equity investor in Euro Disney, located in the suburbs of Paris, France. Euro Disney opened its doors to the public in the spring of 1992. The company also has a licensing agreement with Tokyo Disneyland, located in Japan. The latter is the only company theme park that

Disney does not own and operate. Disney licenses the operation to a Japanese company and collects royalties.

Walt Disney Consumer Products

The Consumer Products division is responsible for licensing the Walt Disney name and its literary properties, animated characters, and music to various manufacturers, retailers, and publishers. Each year, the consumer products division licenses more than 16,000 separate items of merchandise worldwide. Disney also produces audio and computer software for the children's market as well as film and video products for the educational market. Many of these product items are available in catalogs and are distributed internationally. Another important distribution vehicle for the Consumer Products division is the Disney Stores that serve as retail outlets for the company's merchandise. The Disney stores are located throughout the United States, Great Britain, Japan, Canada, Puerto Rico, and France.

What Capital Cities/ABC Brings to the Merger Agreement

The rationale behind the merger agreement between Disney and Cap Cities/ABC is to own both the program content and distribution outlets alike. For Disney, the purchase of ABC also represents an opportunity to nearly double the company's size by purchasing assets that are entirely complementary. In 1995, Cap Cities/ABC was the premiere television network leader in terms of programming and the top national newscast, *World News Tonight with Peter Jennings*. The ABC television network consists of 228 television affiliates and 21 radio stations. Cap Cities/ABC is among the top five of American broadcast groups with eight owned and operated television stations with 23.5% U.S. coverage.[13] Table 11.1 provides a look at Capital Cities/ABC's owned and operated stations.

TABLE 11.1
Capital Cities/ABC: Owned and Operated Stations 8 Stations/23.463% of the U.S. Market

Station	City	Channel	Market Rank
WABC-TV	New York	Ch. 7	1
KABC-TV	Los Angeles	Ch. 7	2
WLS-TV	Chicago	Ch. 7	3
WPVI-TV	Philadelphia	Ch. 6	4
KGO-TV	San Francisco	Ch. 7	5
KTRK-TV	Houston	Ch. 13	11
WDTV	Durham-Raleigh, NC	Ch. 11	32
KFSN-TV	Fresno, CA	Ch. 30	57

Note. Source: *Braodcasting and Cable*.

In addition, Cap Cities/ABC holds a number of publishing interests, including the *Kansas City Star* and the *Fort Worth Star Telegram* newspapers. The company also owns Fairchild and Chilton trade publications.

BUSINESS STRATEGY AND PHILOSOPHY

The Walt Disney Company is first and foremost in the business of family entertainment. CEO Eisner has a natural feel for the product he is trying to sell. What distinguishes Eisner from other TNMC CEOs is the fact that he is first and foremost a creative executive. Eisner has on occasion been described as being more Walt than Walt. According to one executive who knows him well:

> Genius is an overworked word in our business, and its something you often hear about Michael. But he's no genius. He's a very smart man who happens to believe very strongly in the kind of products Disney produces. Probably from the time he started working in this industry, he wanted to run Disney. So what you have is a man perfectly in tune with the values of the company he's running.[14]

Team Disney

For his part, Eisner considers one of his chief duties at Disney to be that of a creative leader; that is, to be a thinker, inventor, and cheerleader for new ideas. Says Eisner: "Every CEO has to spend an enormous amount of time shuffling papers. The question is, how much of your time can you leave free to think about new ideas? To me, the pursuit of ideas is the only thing that matters. You can always find capable people to do almost everything else."[15]

To that end, Eisner tries to promote a familylike camaraderie; hence the name *Team Disney* to describe the collegial approach he wants to engender among his top managers. Team Disney tries to promote an environment that allows its creative team to come up with ideas that can be easily set into motion with unusual speed and agility. All this is tempered with a strong financial discipline. As an example, Disney's average cost for producing a film before prints and advertising is well below the industry average. When the company goes after big name stars, it does so when their careers have stalled, attracting them with long-term contracts that include offers to produce or direct.

Every creative effort, from filmmaking to hotel construction is carefully reviewed by a six-person strategic planning group that reviews all project proposals. The group's responsibility is to consider the financial soundness of the project, which includes putting together financial projections and a schedule. The project proposal is then sent on to the chief financial officer and Eisner, who sign off on the project.

Does the Team Disney approach apply to the rank-and-file employees who work for the company, especially those who directly support the company's massive Disney World operation? Creating the Disney experience is largely dependent on the 35,000 Walt Disney staff members. They are responsible for translating the Team Disney approach into action. The Walt Disney Company employs one of the most sophisticated employee training programs in the world.

Training begins with an appreciation for the fact that appearance is everything. It is not surprising, therefore, that Disney employees are referred to as cast members. The presentation includes everything from the way in which Disney employees interact with the public to the clothes they wear. In creating the right appearance, cast members are taught to be polite. They are taught to understand that park attendees are to be treated as guests, and that helping a guest often means going the extra mile. In addition, Disney employees are expected to follow a dress code and are not permitted to eat, drink, smoke, or chew gum in front of guests.[16] At all levels, Walt Disney World is about creating an impression that the park is safe, accessible, and fun.[17]

Less visible to the public is the massive infrastructure that goes to support the Walt Disney World operation. It is not Jahad the sorcerer who keeps Disney World's multibillion-dollar consumer business operating. Rather, it is a highly sophisticated, labor-intensive warehouse operation that relies heavily on just-in-time manufacturing and delivery techniques.

This year, as in previous years, millions of people will visit Disney World, considered to be one of the most popular family vacation spots in the world. Not a single visitor, it is safe to assume, will wonder how every retail shop and fast food stand manages to keep the shelves fully stocked. On a single night, during the height of tourist season, the warehouse staff must deliver thousands of line-item products to several hundred locations within the park, and it must be accomplished during the off hours when the park is closed.

The retail outlets within the park order through a centralized computer system that handles all order entry and purchasing. The exacting requirements are further complicated by the fact that all merchandise must be priced and marked uniformly before it is distributed to the park's multiple venues and shops. In other words, an item that is purchased in the Magic Kingdom must cost the same at all other attraction sites located throughout Walt Disney World. It is important that visitors never get the feeling that they need to shop around in order to get the best price. Rather, the intention is to make every venue and shop appear as though it is part of the Disney World experience.[18]

Cross-Licensing and Marketing

The Walt Disney Company has a history and a product name that is one of the mostly easily identifiable in the world. Disney takes full advantage of its name and is able to leverage it throughout the entertainment field. Disney's three divisions synergize each other in a variety of ways. It begins when the animation studio creates a character such as Simba the Lion for use in the film *The Lion King*. The same character is later cross-licensed to merchandisers, who turn

Simba the Lion into stuffed animals and/or print the character on t-shirts and other products that can be sold in the Disney theme parks and the company's multiple retail store outlets. Several of Disney's more notable animated film characters, including Beauty and the Beast, Aladdin and Jasmine, Pocahontas and John Smith, reinforce character recognition and are regularly featured in the theme parks. And in the case of Simba the Lion, they can become the basis for an altogether new form of media technology such as electronic video games.

The Technology of Animation

Disney's animation artists are among the best in the world. The company has developed a variety of computer-aided animation techniques that digitize animators' drawings so that cartoon illustrations can be dramatically reduced both in terms of time and the cost of production. Computer-aided animation makes it possible to create an animated television series, such as *Aladdin* and *The Little Mermaid*. The series can be produced at a fraction of the cost due to technology and a staff of artists.

FINANCIAL PERFORMANCE AND ANALYSIS

CEO Michael Eisner's financial growth strategy for the 1980s was to maximize the value of existing assets and to begin laying the groundwork for long-term projects and investments. Between 1984 and 1989, The Walt Disney Company experienced a sevenfold increase in profits, including a $703 million net income in 1989, based on revenues of $4.6 billion. Between 1989 and 1990, the company experienced a 27% increase in revenues for the year, hitting an all-time high of $5.8 billion. The value of Disney's stock was equally impressive, having climbed 750% between 1984 and 1990.[19]

The Walt Disney Company has steadily increased the value of its asset base. Most of the company's growth during this time period was the result of internal investment rather than acquisition. According to Gary Wilson, former chief financial officer for Disney:

> The reason [Disney] is worth so much more is because a talented group of people, through their creativity, have taken the Disney franchise and made it hum. We have opened retail stores, marketed the parks better, built hotels and made hit movies. It's amazing how much value can be created by giving people responsibility for a great but undermanaged franchise like Disney.[20]

Since 1990, the Walt Disney company has experienced impressive growth in its annual revenues, although not as dramatic as the years between 1987 and 1990. The one exception is 1993. That year, the company sustained a $514 million loss on its Euro Disney investment. A 9-year review of the Walt

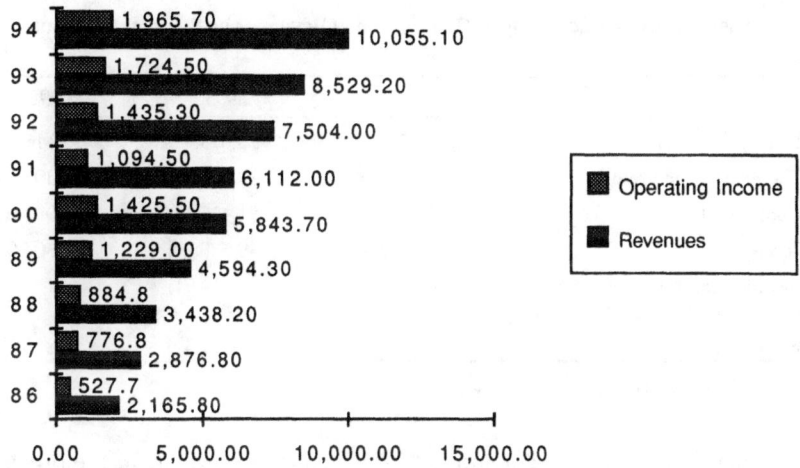

FIG. 11.2. The Walt Disney Company financial performance, 1986–1994 (in millions).

Disney Company's financial performance between 1986 and 1994 can be seen in Fig 11.2.

One of the company's strategic objectives has been to lessen its dependency on any one area of the company's three primary business segments and to create a more balanced revenue flow. In 1989, for example, Disney's theme parks and resorts contributed 64% to the company's total operating income. Filmed entertainment was responsible for 21% and consumer products 15%. In 1994, the relative contributions of each business segment had achieved more balanced proportions, with theme parks and resorts contributing 35%; filmed entertainment, 43%; and consumer products, 22%. Table 11.2 provides a comparison of revenues by business segments for fiscal years 1992, 1993, and 1994.

DISCUSSION

Starting in 1984, the Eisner management team brought financial acumen and vision to a company that was essentially undermanaged. Disney's senior management initiated major changes by increasing the number of animated film productions. Under Jeffrey Katzenberg's direction, Walt Disney Studios turned out a series of box office animated hits, including *The Little Mermaid, Beauty and the Beast, Aladdin,* and *The Lion King.* In addition, the Walt Disney World theme park was reinvigorated with new attractions and the construction of several new hotels. And lastly, the company became more aggressive in the cross-licensing and merchandising of Disney products. The results were startling. In a few short years, the Walt Disney Company was transformed from

TABLE 11.2
The Walt Disney Company: A Comparison of Revenues by Business Segments
(in Millions)

	1994	1993	1992
Filmed entertainment	$4,793.3	$3,673.4	$3,115.2
Theme parks and resorts	$3,463.6	$3,440.7	$3,306.9
Consumer products	$1,798.2	$1,415.1	$1,081.9
Total	$10,055.1	$8,529.2	$7,504.0
Income (Loss) from investment in Euro Disney	(110.4)	(514.7)	
Net income	$1,110.4	$671.3	$816.7

Note. Source: The Walt Disney Company

an ailing $2 billion company into a $22 billion colossal giant. In the process, Disney's management team added value to the company and enriched its stockholders. In less than a decade, The Walt Disney Company reclaimed its title as one of America's premiere entertainment companies.

Creating New Market Opportunities

Riding a winning streak for any company is difficult. As early as 1990, it became apparent that Disney would be unable to sustain the 20% growth rate that had been a constant throughout the 1980s. In years to come, the formula for success would prove more challenging, especially in the international arena. Nowhere was this more evident than in the company's debut of its Euro Disney theme park in 1993. In a small suburb 20 miles east of Paris, Disney unveiled its much-heralded Euro Disney project at a cost of $2.6 billion. Disney's investment in the project was fairly modest by comparison. The company began with an investment of $350 million in planning the park and an additional $145 million for 49% of the project's equity. In 1993, the company's investment in Euro Disney resulted in a loss of $514.7 million. The Euro Disney project (now Disneyland Paris) was subsequently refinanced in 1994 through the efforts of the French government and 63 international banks.

There are several reasons that help explain the early failure of the Euro Disney project, including a major economic recession that devastated the European economy. A second contributing factor was a strong French franc that was forced to compete against a devalued pound, lira, and paseta, making the price of admission, food, and lodging comparatively high for European visitors. This translated into lower spending per guest for food and merchandise.

In retrospect, the Euro Disney project was a misstep from the beginning. Critics point to a number of factors that led to the park's modest reception, including the Paris weather, which during the winter months can be very cold.

Nor has the cold been confined simply to the weather. There has also been a cultural backlash. Euro Disney was been described by one French writer as a "cultural Chernobyl." Since World War II, France has never been a warm host to American culture. Euro Disney is viewed by many as an arrogant attempt to export American culture into the very epicenter of French life and culture. Other writers point to the fact that if Europeans want to experience Disney, they would prefer to travel to the United States rather than have it in their own backyard.

The preservation of culture is by no means a uniquely French phenomenon. In 1992, The Walt Disney Company announced plans to create Disney America, a recreation of the American Revolutionary and Civil War past. The proposed site was near several Civil War battlefields in Virginia. Reaction to the proposed plans was angry and swift. Historians and long-time Virginia residents opposed the plans on the grounds that Disney's attempt to inject play and fantasy would trivialize the United States' historical past. In the end, Disney withdrew its plans to build the controversial theme park. All this points to the difficulty of ensuring success even with the name of Disney. For the short term, Disney has announced plans to build an additional fourth theme park to its existing Walt Disney World in Orlando, Florida. The new Disney Zoo theme park is scheduled to open in 1997. What is less clear is whether the new theme park will attract a sufficient number of new and return visitors to more than offset the high cost of construction and development.

Strategic Planning Issues

The challenge for Disney and Eisner in particular is how to build the organization and keep the success going. The first part of Eisner's task is to build the next generation of Disney leadership. The death of Wells and the defection of several key Disney executives undescored the importance of securing a future management team. On August 14, 1995, Michael Ovitz, chairman of Creative Artists Agency Inc., accepted an offer to become the president of the Walt Disney Company. Ovitz is known throughout Hollywood to be one of the industry's most influential talent agents. He is well liked and brings to the position a clear understanding of the entertainment business.[21] Earlier that year, Eisner appointed Joseph Roth to head Walt Disney Motion Pictures. The purchase of Cap Cities/ABC is also expected to provide the newly combined company with additional sources of management talent, including Robert Iger, ABC's president and chief operating officer.

The Disney–Cap Cities/ABC merger provides some important answers to the all-important question—where will Disney's future growth come from? Although earnings were up by 30% in fiscal year 1994 to 1995, the main contributing reason was the enormous success of the *The Lion King*, which has achieved revenues in excess of $1 billion. The Walt Disney Company will continue to do well in such traditional areas as filmed entertainment and its theme parks. Likewise, the purchase of Cap Cities/ABC is expected to generate increased revenues with assets that are fully complementary. Cap Cities/ABC brings to the merger agreement a highly successful television news operation and distribution network. It is further expected that Cap Cities/ABC will be instrumental in helping Disney to become more transnational in its operations. According to Sanford M. Litvak, Disney COO, "We're not sure what the world will look like in five years, but having a broad array of assets certainly positions you better."[22]

Although movies, theme parks, and ABC television will become the primary engines driving the company, Disney also wants to promote its entry into travel and lodging. Disney has committed itself to a new concept called the "Disney Vacation Club," whereby Disney will build a number of vacation resorts throughout the world. The intention is to create a series of resort facilities with the same distinct feel and quality as their resort hotels located in Disney World. Building on the Disney name and reputation, the proposed set of guest facilities is expected to attract families who are looking for the same consistent value that they associate with other Disney products.

A variation of this theme is the planned construction of Celebration, Florida, a planned housing development 15 minutes from Orlando. Celebration is a 4,900-acre housing development that is modeled after pre-World War II Southeastern towns, featuring a number of architectural styles. The planned community will include housing, shopping facilities, schools, and recreation areas.

The Transnationalization of Walt Disney

The Walt Disney Company of the future will become more transnational in purpose and design. In 1984, Disney's international revenues totaled $142 million or 8.4% of consolidated revenues. The gradual expansion of Disney's worldwide operations including motion pictures, television, home video, product licensing, publishing, and retailing business has contributed to a significant increase in international revenues. In 1994, Disney's international revenues totaled $2.4 billion or 23% of consolidated revenues.[23] According to Richard Frank, former Disney programming executive, "I think the growth of [Disney's operations] will become more international. . . . Our business will move to be probably 50% international and 50% domestic over the next few years. The Disney shows are in some 30 different countries now. I think you'll see that expand."[24]

The Walt Disney Company has become a transnational media giant in the fullest sense of the term. Although the company has become more highly diverse, there remains a clear recognition that entertainment is at the heart of the Disney media empire. Entertainment remains the fundamental currency that will drive the company forward. At the same time, there is a strong appreciation for marketing and distribution evidenced by the purchase of Cap Cities/ABC. The Disney 2010 strategy requires a highly efficient marketing and distribution capability that will enable the company to sell its products and services throughout the world. This is the underlying rationale behind the creation of the Disney Store concept. Today, there are more than 350 Disney Stores worldwide. In closing, Eisner noted:

> As always, we see ourselves primarily as entertainers, providers of programs these new media will need. If we have any concern, it is only that no one business entity be allowed to control access to the new systems. Therefore, it not impossible that we will be strategically affiliated with hardware providers. . . . We must protect our access to the home, and in addition, where our creativity can come into play and we can benefit, we would like to be a partner in shaping the new environment.
>
> What we will not do is become an investor in technology as a sole means to an end. . . . We remind ourselves always that it is the software that is important, the software that we continue to produce in the form of Disney animated classics, live action movies, TV series and specials, animated cartoons and Disney Channel offerings.[25]

NOTES

[1] Ron Grover, *The Disney Touch*, (Homewood, IL: Irwin, 1991), pp. 1–7.
[2] "The Walt Disney Company," *The International Directory of Company Histories*, (Ed.) Lisa Mirable, (Chicago: St. James, 1990), p. 172.
[3] Ibid.
[4] Christopher H. Sterling and John M. Kittross, *Stay Tuned*, (Belmont, CA: Wadsworth, 1990), p. 329.
[5] "Of Mice and Men," *Newsweek*, 5 September, 1994, p. 41.
[6] "Putting Magic Back in the Magic Kingdom," *Fortune*, 5 January, 1987, p. 65.
[7] The cost of a 1-day adult ticket to a theme park in Disney World cost $23 in 1986. That same ticket in 1995 costs $38.
[8] "Reality Intrudes into the Magic Kingdom," *The Economist*, 21 April, 1990, p. 71.
[9] "Michael D. Eisner, The Walt Disney Company," *Financial World*, 21 April, 1987, p. 62.
[10] "Disney is Looking Just a Little Fragilistic," *Business Week*, 25 June, 1990, p. 52.
[11] "Disney Buys ABC for $19B," *USA Today*, 1 August, 1995, pp. 1A–2A.
[12] Bernard Weintraub, "For Disney Chairman, a Deal Quenches a Personal Thirst," *New York Times*, 1 August, 1995, p. A1.
[13] "Cap Cities/ABC Tops the TV Groups," *Broadcasting & Cable*, 10 July, 1995, p. 8.
[14] "Michael D. Eisner, The Walt Disney Company," p. 62.
[15] Christopher Knowlton, "How Disney Keeps the Magic Going: Corporate Performance," *Fortune*, 4 December, 1989, p. 115.
[16] Walt Disney issues prospective employees a set of guidelines that provides very specific information about appearance. Staff members are expected to read and follow the said guidelines as a condition of employment. As an example:
The Disney Look:
Costumes: In keeping with the Disney traditions, very careful attention has been given to every aspect of every part of the Show at Walt Disney attractions.
We are all aware of how human nature works and realize that it is normal to look at clothing in a very personal manner. But our costumes must satisfy the needs of all conditions, situations, and cast members, and it is important that all of our people reflect the "Disney look" to our

guests through their appearance.
See "The Disney Look: A Set of Guidelines Issued to New Employees," *Harpers Magazine*, June 1990, p. 40.

[17] Lorri L. McGough, "Definitive Disney," *Association Management*, March, 1992, pp. 87–88.

[18] E. J. Muller, "Behind the Magic Kingdom," *Distribution*, January, 1988, pp. 63–64.

[19] "Disney is Looking Just a Little Fragilistic," p. 52.

[20] Geraldine E. Willigan, "The Value Adding CFO: An Interview with Disney's Gary Wilson," *Harvard Business Review*, January/February, 1990, p. 88.

[21] "Disney: Room for Two Lion Kings?" *Business Week*, 28 August, 1995, pp. 28–29.

[22] "Disney's Kingdom," *Business Week*, 14 August, 1995, pp. 32–33.

[23] The Walt Disney Company, *1994 Annual Report to Stockholders*, (Burbank, CA: The Walt Disney Co., 1994), pp. 21–22.

[24] "Frank Talk About Disney and TV," *Broadcasting and Cable*, 12 September, 1994, p. 39.

[25] The Walt Disney Company, *1993 Annual Report to Stockholders*, (Burbank, CA: The Walt Disney Co., 1993), p. 4.

12

News Corporation Ltd.

HISTORICAL OVERVIEW

More than any single person of his generation, Keith Rupert Murdoch, president and founder of News Corporation Ltd., is an empire builder in the tradition of the great press barons of the 19th century. What began as a small newspaper in Adelaide, Australia would in the course of more than 40 years become a media empire that spans four continents. News Corp. Ltd. today is a highly diverse TNMC. The story of News Corporation Ltd. is the story of Murdoch and his ambitious climb to the top. It is also a story about shrewd business gamesmanship and the art of winning.[1] In a 1984 article for *Forbes* magazine, author Tom O'Hanlon wrote:

> To a degree that few people, least of all his fellow journalists, yet understand or even want to admit, Rupert Murdoch is an authentic heir of some great publishing figures of the past, of William Randolph Hearst, of Henry Luce, of Joseph Pulitzer, of Britain's Lord Beaverbrook. While most media corporations today are run by relatively colorless, numbers-oriented businessmen, Rupert Murdoch, Australian born, British educated, but now domiciled in New York, almost alone among them combines a zest and feel for the product with a shrewd sense of the bottom line.[2]

News Corporation Ltd. (News Corp.) can trace its origins to the year 1923, when News Limited was established for the purpose of publishing a daily newspaper in the city of Adelaide, Australia. In 1949, a minority interest in News Limited was purchased by Sir Keith Murdoch, father of Keith Rupert Murdoch. News Corp. Ltd. was formally incorporated in South Australia on October 5, 1979.

Taking Over the Family Business

Shortly after his graduation from Oxford University, Murdoch served less than a year's apprenticeship at two English newspapers, the *Birmingham Gazette*, and Fleet Street's *Daily Express*. At age 22, he returned to his native Australia to assume control of the family-owned *Adelaide News*. Sir Keith Murdoch had died earlier that year. At the time, trustees of his father's estate wanted young Murdoch to sell off the newspapers. It became soon apparent that Sir Keith Murdoch did not own much of what he had built. For most of his working career, Sir Keith had been publisher and managing editor to several of the Melbourne Herald Group newspapers. He was singularly the most influential and successful newspaper man in Australia, having spent much of his life building up the editorial and circulation efforts of the Herald Group newspapers. In later years, however, Sir Keith would deeply regret having not obtained greater ownership in the newspapers that he managed. So it was that the *Adelaide News* and *Brisbane Courier-Mail* were purchased in later years as a last-minute attempt to give young Murdoch an entre into the field of Australian journalism, and a place to begin his career as a publisher.[3]

And yet, it was hardly a sure thing. The *Adelaide News* found itself in direct competition with the more successful *Advertiser*, a Herald Group owned newspaper. In those days, newspapers engaged in a variety of bare knuckles tactics to eliminate the competition. Equally difficult was the fact that Murdoch found himself having to answer to a mostly outside board of trustees who who were neither supportive or impressed with the young man's abilities to manage the *Adelaide News*. As it was, the same board of trustees was responsible for having persuaded Elizabeth Murdoch (Rupert's mother) to sell the *Brisbane Courier-Mail* during his absence while at Oxford.

The combination of experiences provided Murdoch with an important future lesson on the importance of control. In spite of the competition and internal rancor among board members, Murdoch pushed ahead with his plans. In 3 years, Murdoch consolidated his operation and was competing head-to-head with some of Australia's most established newspaper owners, including the Fairfax family (owners of the Herald Group of newspapers) and Frank Packard, who published the *Women's Weekly* and the tabloid *Sydney Telegraph*. The Murdoch formula from early on was to borrow and buy. By the age of 30, Murdoch had managed to purchase a radio station, obtained a television license for a station in Adelaide, started a TV magazine, and bought the Sydney based newspaper, the *Mirror*. Newspapers like the *Mirror* were clear tabloid. In contrast, on July 14, 1964, Murdoch launched what would become Australia's first national newspaper, *The Australian*. It was a risky venture for Murdoch and it pushed him into national prominence.

Newspapers and Great Britain

Rupert Murdoch has, on several occasions, indicated that he does not operate with a master plan. The evolution of News Corp. Ltd. has to a large extent been shaped by where Murdoch could fully exploit a potential business opportunity. In 1969, Murdoch was notified about the possibility of buying into the London-based *News of the World*. The latter newspaper was considered Britain's most salacious Sunday paper, featuring a high gloss of sex, crime, politics, and excellent sports coverage. The paper had been run since the 1890s by the Carr family. In 1969, William Carr, Sr. was in bad health and the family was looking for an outside investor. At that time, Robert Maxwell had been vying for the newspaper as well. Maxwell had a notorious reputation in Great Britain for being dishonest, boisterous, and rude. The Carr family was so intent on not letting Maxwell acquire a controlling interest that the company's board of directors agreed to let Murdoch become the principle investor and partner even though he was offering less money. When all was said and done, Murdoch had no intention of being simply a silent partner. The Carr family was quickly relegated to the sidelines. As soon as the takeover battle was complete, Murdoch assumed immediate control of *News of the World* and began a total transformation of the paper. Despite written promises and Murdoch's assurances, the Carr family felt betrayed.

Later that same year, Murdoch had a chance to bid on a failing newspaper called the *Sun*. It had been launched in 1964 as a makeover of an earlier publication called the *Daily Herald*. The latter publication had been highly successful in the 1930s and was considered a serious left-wing newspaper. By 1969, the *Daily Herald* had seen a major decline in its circulation, from 1.5 million to 850,000 readers. At the time, Great Britain's trade unions were dead set against Maxwell, who had also expressed an interest in buying the newspaper. The unions felt that Murdoch had a better plan for keeping the newspaper viable and union jobs intact. Murdoch, for his part, wanted the same financial terms as Maxwell, and managed to acquire the *Sun* at a fraction of its true cost.

In very short order, Murdoch set out to transform the newspaper into a tabloid. Many in Great Britain's newspaper establishment were quick to criticize Murdoch for pandering to the public's worst side. Murdoch dismissed the comments and set about to assemble a team of journalists and promotion specialists including many from Australia to turn the *Sun* into a daily version of *News of the World*. By the end of the 1970s, the *Sun* had become Great Britain's most widely read newspaper, with an increase in circulation to well over 1.7 million. The *Sun*, today, boasts a circulation of over 4 million readers.

The Decade of the 1980s

Murdoch, throughout his career, has held to the single principle that he should maintain control of the companies that he purchased. In order to accomplish this, he would adopt a borrow-and-buy philosophy that would enable him to debt leverage his way to the top. Each successive purchase would yield greater rewards, but would likewise require greater patience. Nowhere was this more evident than in the launching of the Fox television network and British Sky Broadcasting (BSkyB). Both investments would experience enormous losses before seeing a return on investment.

Table 12.1 provides an overview of News Corp. Ltd. and several of the company's major global media purchases between the years 1977 and 1988.

TABLE 12.1
News Corporation Ltd. Global Media Purchases (1977–1988)

Media Property	Date	Purchase Price
New York Post (Newspaper)	1977	$30 million
New York Magazine and Village Voice (Newspaper)	1977	$17 million
Times of London and Sunday Times	1981	$28 million
20th Century Fox	1985	$600 million
7 Metromedia television stations	1985	$2 billion
Herald and Weekly Times Group (Australia)	1987	$1.6 billion
Harper & Row Publishers	1987	$300 million
Triangle Publications: TV Guide, Seventeen Magazine, and The Daily Racing Form (U.S.)	1988	$2.8 billion

TABLE 12.2
News Corporation Ltd. Purchase of Seven Metromedia Stations (1986)

Station	City	Mkt. % of U.S.	Market Rank	Stations in Market	Rank in Market
WNEW	New York	7.7	1	9	4
KTTV	Los Angeles	5.1	2	7	3
WFID	Chicago	3.5	3	9	5
WCVB	Boston	2.3	6	9	1
WTTG	Washington, D.C.	1.8	8	7	3
KNBN	Dallas	1.7	9	9	7
KRIV	Houston	1.6	11	7	4

Note. Source: A.C. Nielsen Co.

News Corporation and Its Entry Into U.S. Television

In 1985, Murdoch entered the U.S. market with the purchase of seven television stations from Metromedia Inc. for $2 billion. The purchase allowed News Corp. the ability to lay the foundation of what would become the future Fox Television Network. These television stations were all highly ranked stations in 7 of the top 11 U.S. markets. Table 12.2 identifies the seven stations that were purchased from Metromedia, including their market rank and competitive position.

A year later, News Corp. Ltd. bought 20th Century Fox for $1.55 billion. From the very beginning, Murdoch understood the importance of vertical integration as the basis for launching a new business. In 2 short years, Murdoch had ensured himself a steady source of programming with ready-made distribution outlets. In April 1987, Murdoch launched the Fox Television Network with 108 affiliates. Barry Diller was hired as the new chair and CEO of the Fox Network.

Under Diller's direction, the Fox Network was more highly differentiated than the other three U.S. networks. The programming was directed at a younger, more urban set of viewers. The approach was very similar to the ABC television network in the mid-1970s. Fox programming was decidedly counterculture and irreverent. There were three distinguishing program formats that characterized the Fox Network, including: reality based programming (e.g., *America's Most Wanted*), counterculture (e.g., *The Simpsons, Married With Children*), and tabloid television (e.g., *A Current Affair*).

The Fox Television Network experienced sizable financial losses during the first 5 years of development. In 1988 alone, the Fox network absorbed a $95 million loss. By 1990, however, the Fox Network was able to reach 91% of the United States through a combination of VHF and low-powered UHF stations. In addition, the network moved from three nights of programming to five. In June 1991, Fox earned an impressive $550 million from the sale of advertising.[4]

In 1988, News Corp. purchased Triangle Publications, publishers of *TV Guide, The Daily Racing Form* and *Seventeen Magazine* for $3 billion. The purchase of *TV Guide* was especially important given the fact that it was the largest-selling weekly magazine in the U.S., with a circulation of 17 million copies. Equally important was the fact that *TV Guide* would provide an important vehicle for promoting the Fox Television Network and its new lineup of programs.[5]

Ownership and the Challenges of Debt Financing

Throughout its history, News Corp. Ltd. has managed to navigate itself through a variety of financial crises and setbacks. However, the problems associated with debt financing reached a critical point in 1991, when the company was carrying an estimated debt of $8.3 billion. The problem was compounded by the significant cash drains from Fox Television and the BSkyB DBS service. All this came at a time when the media industries in general were falling deeper into a worldwide economic recession. Two of the TNMC players that were hardest hit were Maxwell Communication and News Corp.

Murdoch, for his part, came very close to bankruptcy. He was forced to restructure the company's debt by having to sell off several of his media properties including *New York, Premiere, Seventeen Magazine, The Daily Racing Form*, and a 49% interest in *The South China Morning Post*. In addition, he cut his international workforce by some 18%, to 31,186 people. The worldwide economic recession created a buyer's market; that is, potential buyers were less willing to pay top dollar for media properties. For News Corp., this meant having to sell assets at a time when their market value was in decline. This, in turn, meant having less capital to reinvest in ongoing projects as well as having the inability to service its existing debt. By one estimate, News Corp. took a $150 million pretax loss on the sale of three magazines alone. Murdoch was finally able to restructure his debt after several long and arduous meetings with 146 investors. In the end, Murdoch was able to obtain the necessary financing but it would require News Corp. to repay $2 billion during fiscal years 1992 and 1993 with an additional $6 billion due in February 1994.[6]

In summarizing Murdoch's business activities throughout the 1980s, the *Economist* wrote, "Nobody exploited the booming media industry in the late 1980's better than Mr. Rupert Murdoch's News Corporation—and few borrowed more money to do it.[7]

ORGANIZATIONAL STRUCTURE

News Corp. is a highly diversified TNMC. The company is principally engaged in the production and distribution of newspapers, motion pictures, television programming, books, and magazines. News Corp. acts as a holding company, whereby all of its businesses are conducted through subsidiaries and affiliates. The company's primary business activities are located in the United States, Great Britain, Australia, and the Asian Pacific region.[8]

Keith Rupert Murdoch, president and CEO, is responsible for all strategic decision making. Those who have worked closely with Murdoch indicate that he has a tremendous grasp for details, which is rather unusual in an age where TNMCs are typically managed by an assembled team of media managers. Each Friday, Murdoch is given a blue book that contains a weekly financial summary of his worldwide operations. The legendary blue book has become an essential information tool and is very critical to Murdoch and his ability to track News Corp.'s transnational media operations.

Transnational Media Operations

News Corp. can rightfully make claim to the fact that the company has the highest newspaper circulation in the world. In Australia alone, Murdoch controls two thirds of all newspaper circulation. News Corp. is parent company to the country's only national newspaper, *The Australian*, as well as the largest daily newspaper in terms of circulation, *The Herald Sun* in Melbourne. News Corp.'s presence can be found in every province located throughout the country. This includes such major publications as *The Daily Telegraph Mirror* in Sydney and *The Courier Mail* in Brisbane.

In England, News Corp. owns the nation's leading daily newspaper, *The Sun*, as well as the largest Sunday edition, *News of the World*. In addition, News Corp. owns several other British newspapers, including the *Sunday Times*. News Corp. is also the parent company to the world's largest set of DBS services, including British Sky Broadcasting (U.K.) and the Star Television Network (southeast Asia).

In the United States, News Corp. is parent company to the Fox Television Network, as well as eight owned-and-operated television stations. News Corp. also manages several publishing efforts as well, including HarperCollins publishers and such notable U.S. magazines as *TV Guide* and *Mirabella*.

In addition to its media holdings, News Corp. is also heavily involved in commercial printing, as well as a variety of other business enterprises that range from an Australian based East West Airlines to music recording company, Festival Records. Figure 12.1 provides an overview of News Corp.'s transnational media operations.

BUSINESS STRATEGY AND PHILOSOPHY

More than any person of his generation, Murdoch is an empire builder in the tradition of the great media press lords of the 19th and early 20th centuries. Murdoch's love of dealmaking and sense of gamesmanship may be every bit as important as are the highly diverse set of media properties that he steadfastly manages. News Corp. can rightfully make claim to the fact that the company has the highest newspaper circulation in the world and is the most aggressive player in the field of DBS communications. Through the years, Murdoch's continuing success and domination of the media has made him the target of

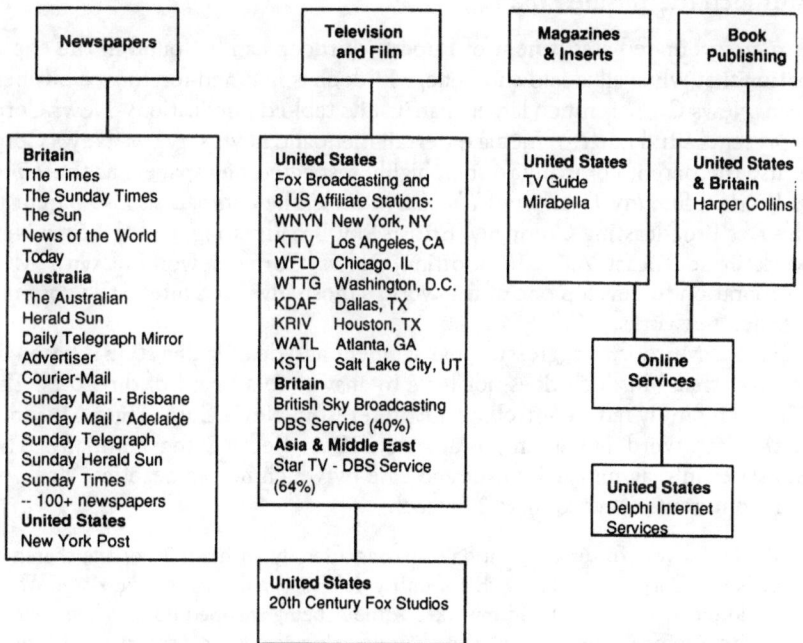

FIG. 12.1. News Corporation Ltd. Transnational Media Operations (Overview, 1995). *Note.* From News Corporation Ltd.[9]

much criticism among business rivals, government regulators, labor unions, and media analysts. Murdoch has been called everything from the "arrogant Aussie" to the "dirty digger."

The combination of Murdoch's aggressive dealmaking style, coupled with his reputation for promoting tabloid journalism, has made him a lightning rod for criticism among those who claim that he manipulates politics and is too preoccupied with the bottom line. Writing for the *Nation* magazine, author Ben Bagdikian observed:

> Rupert Murdoch may or may not be the most voracious media baron of them all, but he probably is the only one who ever prompted his critics to convene an entire conference devoted to dissecting him. This gathering of journalists and sundry others took place earlier this year [1989] in Sydney, Australia, where for three days various damning papers were presented, and the mood can best be summed up by the observation that Murdoch has become "the Magellan of the Information Age" splashing ashore on one continent after another.[10]

How does Murdoch respond to such charges? In a 1987 interview, Murdoch was asked whether he considered himself one who has debased and sensationalized the press. He answered, "No. But I can think of more important things than being loved by everyone."[11]

Murdoch the Businessman

A more grounded assessment of Rupert Murdoch can be found in the explanation that when all is said and done, Murdoch is first and foremost a businessman. News Corp. is much larger than just its tabloid publications. News Corp. represents a full range of media entertainment and news services. News Corp. is also the parent company to such highly respected newspapers as the *Times of London, Sunday Times,* and *The Australian.* The company is also parent to the Fox Broadcasting Company, British Sky Broadcasting, and the Star Network in southeast Asia. In addition, News Corp. is working with MCI Corporation to develop one of the world's most advanced integrated communication networks.

Part of Murdoch's aggressive management and dealmaking style is based on the fact that Murdoch does not have to answer to a board of directors. The Murdoch family has a controlling 43% interest in News Corp. Thus, Murdoch is the last word on all important decisions affecting the company. This translates into an unusual power and ease by which he can negotiate deals on four continents. According to Murdoch:

> I'm in the very fortunate position of having a family with a third of the shares of News Corp., and I enjoy that security. It also enables us to take risks. We could make a couple of bad mistakes without being snapped up or taken over by some company that wants to break us up. It's given us great security to know that while we can't be careless, we can take risks—and we have taken big risks thus far...[12]

Murdoch is the consummate business opportunist. To that end, there are four skills that have enabled him to successfully navigate the multifaceted world of media and telecommunications. First, Murdoch is the quintessential risk taker.[13] Murdoch has made a career of defying the odds, both financial and political. As early as 1964, Murdoch launched *The Australian*, the country's first national newspaper. That effort, in combination with his other newspaper holdings, has given News Corp. some 60% of Australia's metropolitan newspaper sales. Similarly, the start-up of the Fox Television Network came at a time when the conventional wisdom said that starting a fourth U.S. network was impossible. Likewise, the start-up of his BSkyB DBS network was launched well before the technology had proven itself in the marketplace. News Corp. suffered an estimated $1.2 billion loss on BSkyB between the years 1989 and 1993.

Second, despite his Oxford education, Murdoch has a good feel for popular taste, whether it be British, Australian, or American. Everything from the British-based *Sun* newspaper to Fox television's *The Simpsons* speaks directly to an appreciation for popular, albeit low-brow, taste. From his earliest days as a working publisher and son of a prominent newspaper man, Murdoch was well trained in the belief that newspapers should give readers what they want. According to Shawcross (1992), the origins of such thinking can be traced to British newspaper publisher Alfred Harmsworth (Lord Northcliffe) who once instructed Sir Keith Murdoch, Murdoch's father, that a "newspaper should be made to pay. Let it give the public what it wants."[14]

As Northcliffe's protege and having worked several years in England, Keith Murdoch returned to Australia and adopted a similar approach in his work with the *Melbourne Herald* and several other Australian newspapers. He was sometimes vilified by his critics for bringing yellow journalism to Australia. But no one could argue with the success by which he improved circulation at the *Melbourne Herald*. The same line of thinking and practical attitudes about the role of journalism was passed on from father to son. Rupert Murdoch embraced the belief that journalism should be accessible and profitable. In years to come, he would expand that basic working assumption to include television as well.

In London, News Corp. bought out an inconsequential liberal daily, *The Sun*, and in short order improved its circulation from 700,000 to more than 4 million. *The Sun's* new tabloid makeover featured screaming headlines and pictures of seminude women. During the Falklands War, for example, *The Sun's* banner headline read: "THE SUN SAYS: STICK IT UP YOUR JUNTA." In short order, *The Sun* became the largest selling English-language daily in the world. In the United States, News Corp. launched the sensationalist *Star* newspaper to compete with *The National Enquirer* in the supermarket checkout lines. News Corp. also owns the *New York Post*. In defense of tabloid journalism, Murdoch observes:

> Much of what passes for quality under these [European systems] is no more than a reflection of the values of the narrow elite which controls them—a view natural to all governing classes. Why should television be exempt from the laws of supply and demand any more than newspapers, journals, magazines or books.[15]

Third, Murdoch is a shrewd businessman who knows how to maximize his operations. Murdoch's politics are very pragmatic, as are his expectations regarding the work of his editors. When it comes to management and editorial control, Murdoch is very hands-on and displays little or no sentimentality. The one exception was the 1984 decision to purchase the *Melbourne Herald*, the newspaper that Sir Keith Murdoch helped to build. The makeover and start-up of several of his newspapers and broadcast services, including *The Sun, The New York Post*, and Fox Television all seem to follow a similar pattern. The publications and broadcast services begin as tabloids and are often quite irreverent toward the establishment. They appear somewhat radical at first. But over time, most of the senior managers (editors and producers) who were first involved in the start-up phase are slowly replaced by a more conservative management team. The start-up of the Fox Television Network, for example, is highly illustrative of this pattern. Once the Fox Network became stable, Murdoch became more directly involved in the company's day-to-day operation. As a direct consequence, Barry Diller, Fox president and CEO, resigned his position rather than face the prospect of comanaging the Fox Network.

Murdoch can, likewise, be very hard-nosed when it comes to cutting costs. His dealings with the newspaper labor unions in Great Britain's Fleet Street district has over the years demonstrated an unusual toughness with it comes to cutting costs and creating internal efficiencies. In 1985, Murdoch stood his ground against the labor unions and moved his printing operations to the London Docks area of Wapping. That action, with the full support of the Thatcher government, was the most significant challenge to Britain's printing unions ever. The combination of an open shop and updated technology enabled the company to streamline their operation. News Corp. was able to reduce the number of print workers from over 2,000 to 570. Company profits were up by 85% in the United Kingdom. In the end, the Wapping printing plant put an end to 80 years of printing strikes, bullying tactics, and featherbedding practices.[16]

In the United States, Murdoch continues to be a flash point for political and regulatory scrutiny. In May 1995, Murdoch was able to successfully deflect regulatory challenges to News Corp.'s 99% ownership of eight U.S. television stations, based on FCC regulations concerning foreign ownership. The FCC found the Fox Television stations to be in violation of the Commission's foreign ownership limits. However, the FCC granted Murdoch a waiver based on the company's 10-year record of serving the public interest.[17]

The fourth and perhaps the most important feature to Murdoch's approach to business is his ability to structure debt and to obtain global financing. In his desire to maintain control over his operations, Murdoch has developed a unique ability to manage debt at a higher level than most companies and organizations. The Murdoch formula is to carefully build cash flow while borrowing aggressively. In past years, Murdoch's excellent credit rating has been the essential ingredient to this formula. Each major purchase is expected to generate positive cash flow and thereby pay off what has been borrowed. Each successive purchase should be bigger than the one before, thereby ensuring even greater cash flow. All this presupposes an extraordinary ability to manage long term debt.

Debt Financing

Throughout the 1980s, Murdoch's borrow-and-buy formula was bolstered by the fact that market value of his media properties was growing faster than than their underlying cash flows. In addition, Australian accounting rules allow companies to revalue intangible assets, like newspaper mastheads and satellite transponders, without saying specifically how much each asset is worth. Critics point to the fact that such accounting practices are vague and misleading and can often give investors a false sense of confidence.

The problem with News Corp.'s debt financing reached crisis proportions in 1991, when the company was carrying an estimated debt of $8.3 billion. The worldwide economic recession created a buyer's market. For News Corp., this meant having to sell assets at a time when their market value was in decline. News Corp. Ltd. took an estimated $150 million pretax loss on the sale of *New York, Premiere, Seventeen Magazine*, and *The Daily Racing Form*. With the assistance of Citibank Corporation and Ann Lane, VP of finance, Murdoch was finally able to restructure the company's debt after several long and difficult meetings with some 146 investors. Murdoch was able to obtain the necessary financing, but not before the divestment of some important assets and an agreement to significantly pare down the company's debt load.[18]

It has taken 5 years, but News Corp. is on solid financial ground once more. In 1995, the company is making money on most of its media properties, including Fox Broadcasting and BSkyB. News Corp. has reduced its debt by almost half and has refinanced the remaining portion of its loans. It is not likely that Murdoch will engage in the level of risk taking and debt financing that he did in the late 1980s. Said Murdoch, "We've taken some gambles others might not have. But I don't want to keep betting the company. I'm certainly not going to bet the company again."[19]

FINANCIAL PERFORMANCE AND ANALYSIS

In the 4 years since News Corp.'s near bankruptcy, the company's fortunes have greatly improved. During that time, Murdoch has consolidated his media holdings. Combined revenues have increased by 23.8% between 1993 and 1994. The major sources of News Corp.'s new-found wealth are the highly profitable newspapers and the eight Fox-owned broadcast television stations. News Corp.'s newspapers are performing very well, having earned $2.2 billion in sales in 1995. Similarly, the company's television services, including Fox Broadcasting and BSkyB (40% investment) are expected to generate an estimated $3.2 billion in sales.

The United States holds the key to News Corp.'s long term global future. Since 1989, the United States has accounted for a substantially higher percentage of revenues when compared to the company's other geographic locations. In 1995, the United States accounted for 70% of the company's revenues, compared to the United Kingdom and Europe (17%), and Australia and the Pacific Basin (13%).

Between the years 1988 and 1995, News Corp. demonstrated a consistent pattern of growth. The year 1991 proved to be the exception. It was during this period of time that the company was engaged in a major restructuring of its debt load. Despite a strong financial performance, the financial drain on the company due to Fox Broadcasting and BSkyB resulted in a net loss that year of $307.5 million (A$392.9). A review of News Corp.'s financial performance between 1988 and 1995, based on total revenues, can be seen in Fig. 12.2.

News Corp. and Time Warner Communications operate with the highest debt-to-equity ratio among the world's leading TNMCs. In 1990, News Corp.'s debt ratio reached $8.2 billion, including interest payments as well as the high costs associated with Fox Broadcasting and BSkyB. What Murdoch did not foresee was the impact that a combination of events including a banking crisis, collapse in advertising, and an economic recession would have on his company. The result was an unprecedented tightening in credit. Unbeknownst to Murdoch was the fact that his entire debt load had been parceled out and reparceled among 146 creditors worldwide. In retrospect, Murdoch had made

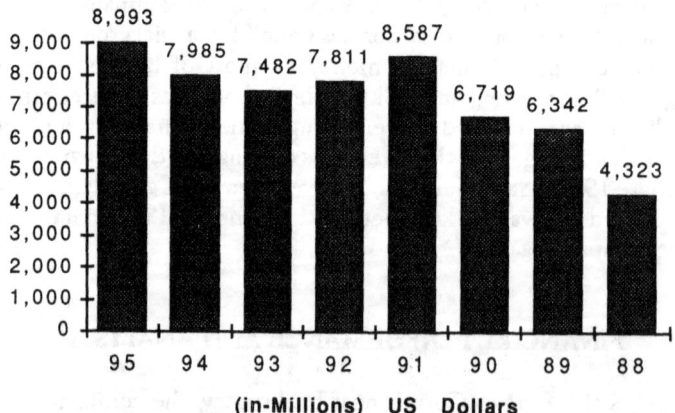

FIG. 12.2. News Corporation Ltd. financial performance (1988-1995): Total revenues.

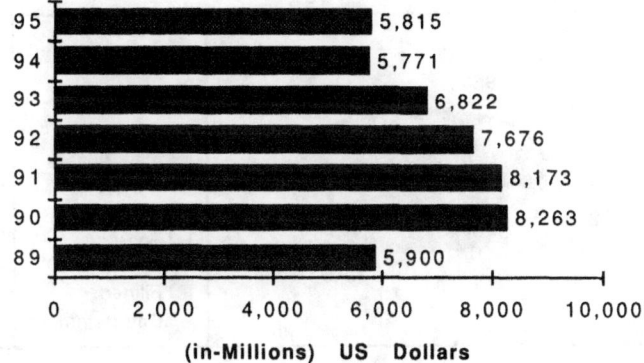

FIG. 12.3. News Corporation Ltd. financial position: Total debt, (1989–1995).

the mistake of assuming that short-term rates would go down and had, therefore, kept borrowing for the short term with the expectation of changing into a longer debt when the rates became cheaper. It never happened. Instead, international banking rates had started to rise sharply. News Corp. was now suddenly faced with repaying or rescheduling a $500 million short-term loan. The problem was compounded by an additional $2.9 billion loan that was due to mature between 1990 and 1991. News Corp. was eventually able to restructure its debt, but at a very high cost. The company was forced to sell off some critical assets in order to refinance its loan payment schedule. Since then, News Corp. has been able to reduce its debt considerably, due largely to the success of the company's newspapers and the Fox-owned broadcast television stations. Figure 12.3 provides a review of the company's financial position in terms of total debt for the years spanning 1989 to 1995.

News Corp. has an excellent mix of media properties. In 1995, operating income by product line groups was television, 30%; newspapers, 29%; magazines and inserts, 21%; books, 11%; and filmed entertainment, 9%. A review of operating income for fiscal years 1994 and 1995 by product line group can be seen in Fig. 12.4.

DISCUSSION

Television

News Corp.'s principal areas of operation are in the United States, the United Kingdom, and the Australia/Pacific region. The company currently derives 70% of its revenues from the United States, which will continue to be the major source of revenue for News Corp. The key to the U.S. market will be Fox Broadcasting. The plan is to move Fox beyond its image as a counterculture

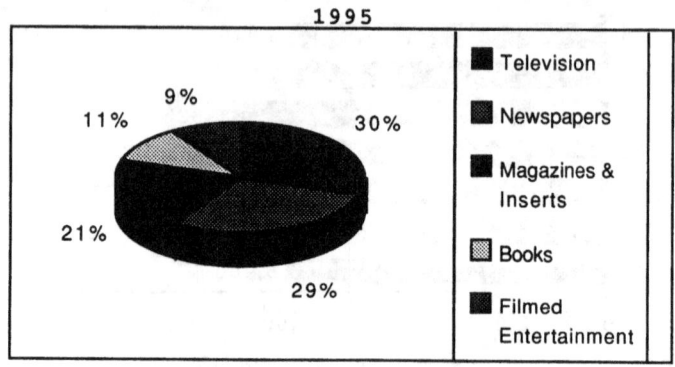

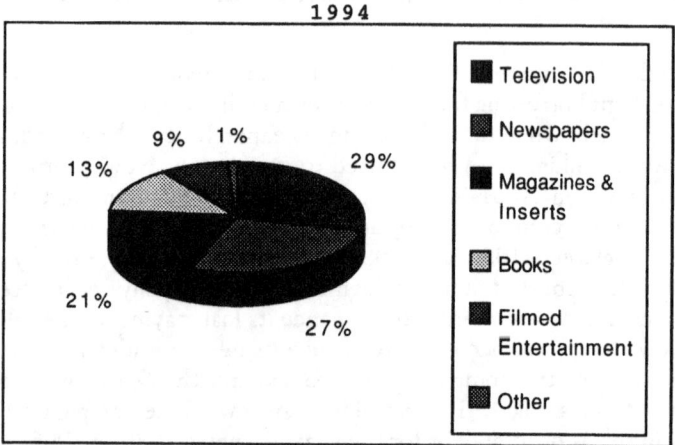

FIG. 12.4. News Corporation Ltd. operating income by business segments. From News Corp.[20]

network and to become a more conventional, albeit fully diverse, television service. According to Murdoch, "I think [Fox] has ambitions to grow into a conventional network in the sense that it would one day be able to provide programming for its affiliates pretty much around the clock."[21]

Fox did indeed become a more conventional network when in the fall of 1993, it acquired the television rights to the National Football League (NFL) by outbiding rival network CBS at a cost of $1.6 billion. The successful debut of NFL football on Fox has given the young network an added dose of credibility. In May 1994, Fox improved its affiliate position by paying New World Communications $500 million to break their 12-station affiliation agreement with the three major U.S. networks and to join with Fox Broadcasting instead. In exchange, Fox received 20% of New World's stock as well as improving its market position in 12 key cities. News Corp. subsequently purchased the remaining stock of New World Communications. Table 12.3 identifies the purchase of New World Communications and the 12 stations they represent.

The purchase of New World Communications caused a rippling effect that was felt throughout the entire broadcast industry. The three major networks, CBS in particular, were now forced to renegotiate their affiliation contracts with several important stations, given the possibility that they would break their existing affiliate contracts. In the meantime, the New World purchase has increased Fox's VHF penetration in the United States from 25% of the country to 40%. The number of Fox affiliate stations has increased from 138 to 184 television stations, thus providing market coverage to 98% of all U.S. households.

Between 1989 and 1993, News Corp. endured significant financial losses on its BSkyB DBS service. By agreeing to pay $456 million to telecast Premier League soccer games in 1992, BSkyB has increased its subscriber base to 4 million and is achieving profitability for the first time in its history. News Corp. plans to offer digitally compressed Sky signals sometime in 1996 and thereby increase channel capacity from 22 channels to 200. The sudden availability of new channels will enable the company to offer near video-on-demand PPV service.

In 1993, News Corp. paid $525 million for a 64% interest in Star Television in Asia. Star Television currently reaches an estimated 54 million homes.[22] The countries of China and India represent the largest set of Star television households, accounting for a combined 88% of program service subscribers.

TABLE 12.3
Fox Television Inc. and New World Communications Twelve-Station Affiliation Agreement (1994)

Station	City	Former Affiliation	Market Rank
KDFW	Dallas	CBS	8
WJBK	Detroit	CBS	9
WAGA	Atlanta	CBS	10
WJW	Cleveland	CBS	12
WTVT	Tampa, FL	CBS	16
KTVI	St. Louis	ABC	18
KSAZ	Phoenix	CBS	20
WDAF	Kansas City, MO	NBC	26
WTTI	Milwaukee	CBS	29
WGHP	High Point, NC	ABC	48
WBRC	Birmingham, AL	ABC	49
KTBC	Austin, TX	CBS	66

Note. Source: *New York Times*.

TABLE 12.4
STAR TV Households By Country (in Millions)

	1994	1993
China	35.0	30.4
India	12.0	7.3
Taiwan	2.8	2.4
Israel	0.7	0.6
South Korea	0.6	0.3
Hong Kong	0.3	0.3
Total	53.7	42.1

Note. From News Corp.[23]

Table 12.4 provides a breakdown of Star TV households by country for the years 1993 and 1994.

Star Television is not expected to achieve profitability for several more years. The problem, in part, is due to the fact that the company is unable to give advertisers reliable numbers concerning actual viewership. In order to be successful in Asia, plans are underway to begin developing several customized language channels. News Corp. has announced its future intentions to begin a DBS service in both the United States and Japan.

Newspapers and Magazines

News Corp. has grown far beyond its newspaper origins. At the same time, newspapers and magazines will continue to provide a strong foundation for future growth. News Corp. continues to be the largest newspaper producer in the world. News Corp. is responsible for 60% of all Australian newspapers, which includes a newspaper in every major city. Similarly, *The Sun, News of the World,* and *The Times* of London maintain a commanding share of the British market. In the United States, *TV Guide* remains the top weekly magazine in terms of both circulation and revenues. It is expected that newspapers and magazines will generate an estimated $3.7 billion for fiscal yeay 1995. News Corp. will reinvest some of its surplus capital into existing media properties and investments including New World Communications, the Fox FX Cable service, Star Television, and the company's recent purchase of the Vox pay television channel in Germany.

Convergence

In the years to come, News Corp. will become a preeminent global supplier of media software. The company's operating philosophy is that all media are one. The strategies used in the development and fostering of creative software

are synergistic and transferable regardless of whether the format is newspapers, television, magazines, films, or books. Murdoch, for his part, has long believed that by the 21st century, there will be only a handful of TNMCs. And although Murdoch, himself, is not a technologist, he fully recognizes that the TNMC of tomorrow will be vertically integrated and have the ability to own both software and the means of distribution. Murdoch has every intention of being one of them. In April 1995, News Corp. announced a partnership agreement with U.S.-based MCI Corporation to provide an integrated communication service. Under the terms of the announced agreement, MCI will infuse News Corp. with $2 billion.

NOTES

[1] The News Corporation Limited, US Securities & Exchange Commission Report, (Form 20-F. - Com. File No. 1-9141), (News Corporation Ltd., Sydney, Australia, 1993).
[2] Tom O'Hanlon, "Forbes on Murdoch," *Forbes*, 30 January, 1984.
[3] William Shawcross, *Murdoch*, (New York: Simon & Schuster, 1992), pp. 62–76.
[4] "The Fourth Network," *Business Week*, 17 September, 1990, pp. 114–121.
[5] "$3B Deal puts TV Guide in Murdoch Fold," *Boston Herald*, 8 August, 1988.
[6] Kathryn Harris, "A Big Dose of Realism," *Forbes*, 2 September, 1991, pp. 40–42.
[7] "Murdoch's Kingdom," *The Economist*, 18 August, 1990, p. 62.
[8] The News Corporation Limited, US Securities & Exchange Commission Report.
[9] News Corporation Ltd., *1994 Annual Report to Stockholders*, (Sydney, Australia: News Corporation Ltd., 1994), p. 32.
[10] Ben Bagdikian, "The Lords of the Global Village," *The Nation*, 12 June, 1989, pp. 805–820.
[11] Wolfgang J. Koschnick, "As I See It: An Interview with Rupert Murdoch," *Forbes*, 27 November, 1988, pp. 98–103.
[12] "The Wonder's Still in the Wireless: An Interview with Rupert Murdoch," *Broadcasting & Cable*, 24 January, 1994, p. 26.
[13] "Murdoch, Turner: A Study in Contrasts," *Washington Post*, 7 September, 1986, pp. D3–D5.
[14] Shawcross, *Murdoch*, pp. 38–39.
[15] Koschnick, "As I See It: An Interview with Rupert Murdoch," pp. 98–103.
[16] Shawcross, *Murdoch*, pp. 256–275.
[17] "Foreign Ownership Waiver Likely for Fox," *Broadcasting & Cable*, 8 May, 1995, p. 16.
[18] Harris, "A Big Dose of Realism," pp. 40–42.
[19] "Murdoch Unbound," *Business Week*, 29 May, 1995, p. 29.
[20] News Corporation Ltd., *1995 Annual Report to Stockholders*, (Sydney, Australia: News Corporation Ltd., 1995), p. 3., News Corporation Ltd., *1994 Annual Report to Stockholders*, (Sydney, Australia: News Corporation Ltd., 1994), p. 3.
[21] "The Thinking Man's Media Barron," *Broadcasting*, 13 April, 1987, p. 69.
[22] "New Star Over Asia," *Time*, 9 August, 1993, p. 53.
[23] News Corporation Ltd., *1995 Annual Report to Stockholders*, p. 32.

Postscript

The world has become a series of economic centers consisting of both nation states and TNCs. The clear lines that once separated countries and corporations are no longer visible. The combination of international deregulation and privatization trends, coupled with advancements in computer and communication technology, has transformed the conduct of international business. The result has been a consolidation of players in all aspects of business, including banking, aviation, insurance, and mass media.

Today's TNMCs are taking advantage of worldwide deregulation and privatization trends to make ever-larger combinations. Starting in 1995, we have witnessed a new round in transnational economic consolidation, evidenced by Walt Disney's $19 billion purchase of Capital Cities/ABC and Time Warner's purchase of Turner Broadcasting for $8 billion. The reasons prompting such mergers and acquisitions are the same today as they were 10 years ago. The goal, simply put, is to possess the size and resources necessary in order to compete on a global playing field. Let us consider, for a moment, three reasons that help to explain the new round of mergers and acquisitions. They include vertical integration and complementary assets, expanding into new global markets, and the strategic necessity of owning both software and distribution links.

Vertical Integration and Complementary Assets

The desire to control most or all of a company's operational phases and thereby create internal synergies, is a primary goal for any company or organization. Murdoch is a master of the vertical integration game. In April 1987, Murdoch launched the Fox Television Network with 108 affiliates. In the years that have followed, Murdoch has steadily improved the position of Fox television by combining a steady source of programming with greatly improved distribution outlets. In 1993, for example, News Corp. acquired the rights to televise the NFL. The NFL established Fox as a highly credible player in the field of television entertainment. Shortly thereafter, News Corp. negotiated with New World Communications for 12 VHF stations in key markets throughout the United States thus improving affiliation and direct viewer access. News

Corp. has taken the philosophy of vertical integration and elevated it to a global level. The result is that News Corp. is able to produce films and television programs that can be shown on the Fox Television Network in the United States, Sky Television in the United Kingdom, or Star Television in Asia.

Today's TNMC also wants to obtain complementary assets, which, in the case of Disney, means partnering with a company that provides an altogether different set of resources and strengths. The purchase of Capital Cities/ABC means the addition of a well-established news organization, as well as a ready-made distribution link into people's homes. The ABC television network is the most highly rated television network in the United States. The combined Disney–Cap Cities/ABC will operate in the top tier of a converging media industry with a full complement of media entertainment and news assets.

Expanding Into New Global Markets

A second consideration is the obvious need to expand into new markets. Some TNMCs invest abroad for the purpose of entering a foreign market and serving it from that location. The market may exist or may have to be developed. The ability to buy an existing media property is the easiest and most direct method for market entry. This was the strategy employed by Bertelsmann A.G. when it entered the United States in 1986 and purchased Doubleday Publishing ($475 million) and RCA Records ($330 million). One year later, Bertelsmann consolidated its U.S. recording labels by forming the Bertelsmann Music Group, which is headquartered in New York City. Today, the United States is responsible for 24.4% of the company's revenues worldwide.

Alternatively, the Sony Corporation had to create a market that, heretofore, did not exist. The Sony Corporation entered the United States in 1960 with the formation of the Sony Corporation of America. Throughout the 1960s, the Sony Corporation achieved a number of firsts in product design and innovation, including the portable videotape recorder, the integrated radio circuit, and the Trinitron television set, to name only a few. Starting in the 1970s, Sony began work on a contract for CBS television that would lead to the development of modern-day electronic newsgathering equipment. In 1979, Sony pioneered the development of small personal tape players that became the now-famous Sony Walkman. Sony's early entry into the United States enabled the company to become well established as a leader in the field of consumer electronics. Sales of broadcast and consumer electronic equipment in the United States account for nearly 31% of company sales by geographic location.

The Strategic Necessity of Owning Both Software and Distribution Links

The clear lines and historic boundaries that once separated broadcasting, cable, media entertainment, and telephony are becoming less distinct. A natural convergence of industries and information technologies are blurring those distinctions. The main driving force behind convergence is the digitalization of media and information technology. Digital technology improves the quality and efficiency of switching, routing, and storing information. It increases the potential for manipulation and transformation of data. Research and development in home entertainment and information systems is undergoing a major transformation. The future is moving toward multimedia or modularity of design whereby, components can be easily interfaced to create entirely new forms of media use and application.

The emergence of cable television has given consumers greater choice and made television viewing far more specialized. The cable industry, like the magazine industry, has moved toward highly narrowcasted programming, evidenced by such internationally recognized cable services as CNN, HBO, ESPN, and MTV. In addition to cable, U.S. and international telephone companies want to be the major architects in designing tomorrow's broadband television future. Although such companies have not been traditional television players in the past, they are currently positioning themselves for the new world of video dialtone and expanded cable services. Such companies are pursuing joint partnerships with media programmers and cable operators in order to bring financing and technical expertise together.

Open video systems and expanded cable represents a logical progression in narrowcasted services and specialization. The real value of a broadband residential service is the ability to provide consumers with entertainment, information, and utility-based services on demand. The future of broadband residential services will include a whole host of electronic media services including home shopping, video on demand, energy monitoring, and security systems, to name only a few. In a multichannel universe, the origins of entertainment, information, and utility-based services will become virtually indistinguishable to the user. The primary carrier that manages tomorrow's broadband residential system will become the equivalent of an electronic supermarket that features both in-house as well as competitive software products.

International Privatization and Transnational Media

Government-supported broadcasting is now giving way to the private sector. The high cost of television production has caused many of the world's leading PT&Ts and regional economic coalitions (i.e., the EC) to reassess the amount of money they are willing to spend on television production. For government policymakers, the continued privatization of television is not only attractive, but inevitable. The result will be an explosive growth in new commercial ventures.

Privatization will affect the market for international television and film in two ways. The first is the large-scale increase in the volume of programs purchased from commercial sources. Much of the program software is likely to be produced by several of the well-established TNMCs. The second effect of privatization will be significant competition for software products among potential program buyers. The newly emerging broadcast, cable, and DBS services will soon outnumber those channels that are presently government supported. As a consequence, state broadcasters will increasingly find themselves having to bid against commercial broadcasters for many of the same programs. The ensuing competition will bid up the price for program software.[1]

Issues of Size and Marketplace Realities

The TNMC is more likely to view transnational expansion and its effects in the context of whether it makes good business sense. Strategic decision making is based on the profitability of the market, growth potential, regulatory climate, and existing competitive situation. The TNMC is arguably better able to invest in the development of new media products and services than are smaller, national based companies or government-supported industries. The TNMC does not operate in all markets of the world. Instead, the TNMC tends to operate in select markets with an obvious preference and familiarity toward one's home market.

Business Strategies and Corporate Culture

One of the prevalent myths concerning TNMCs is that such companies are monolithic in their approach to business. In fact, just the opposite is true. The business strategies and corporate cultures of a TNMC are often a direct reflection of the person or persons who were responsible for developing the organization and its business mission.[2] Most of the highly successful TNMCs are managed by a handful of players who have had an extraordinary effect in determining the shape of the companies discussed in this book. Such notable persons as Morita, Turner, Murdoch, Eisner, Levin, and Mohn have given a unique brand and identity to the companies they manage. All of these men are risk takers without question. And all of these men possess an interest in media and telecommunications that goes well beyond the issue of straight profitability.

The Marketplace of Ideas

A second prevalent myth concerning TNMCs is that the consolidation of media companies into the hands of a select few has had an adverse effect on the marketplace of ideas. There is no evidence to support this claim. In fact, just the opposite has occurred. Since 1984, there has been a proliferation of new media technologies and services. The development of such mainstream technologies as personal computers, facsimiles, electronic mail, VCRs, DBS, and video games are all technologies that are the direct result of increased competition among large and small companies alike. During this same period of time, there has been a corresponding increase in new software combinations, including multimedia, the Internet, video rentals, home shopping, and online database services, to name only a few.[3]

In assessing the potential dangers of media concentration, the TNMC is unlikely to use its creative and/or editorial facilities to promote a corporate agenda. TNMCs like Time Warner or Bertelsmann are far too diverse in their media holdings to succumb to a single corporate ideology. At the same time, there are the exceptions. Murdoch has a long history of using the power of his news media to support political candidates. But even Murdoch, although admittedly conservative, is first and foremost a businessman. News Corp.'s primary objective is profitability and not the worldwide imposition of Murdoch's viewpoint. The combination of worldwide privatization trends coupled with advancements in new media technologies precludes any one company or person from dominating the marketplace of ideas.

Global Competition: What It Really Means

What are the real problems that face the TNMC in the years ahead? The answers to these questions are not unique to the TNMC. Rather, the problems have to do with all companies planning to operate in an increasingly privatized and deregulated world of business. There was a time in recent history when government and the private sector provided a secure home to millions of men and women. Government and business communication entities such as British Telecom, the German Bundespost, AT&T, IBM, and Time Inc. offered relative job security in exchange for hard work and loyalty to the company. All this has changed. Global competition has engendered a new competitive spirit that borders on obsession. A new form of economic Darwinism abounds, characterized by a belief that size and complementary strengths is crucial to business survival. In all areas of business and commerce, companies are announcing mergers and acquisitions at an unprecedented rate. The relentless pursuit of profits and the fear of failure have made companies around the world ferocious in their attempts to rightsize, reorganize, and reengineer their business operations. No company, large or small, remains unaffected by the intense drive to increase profits and decrease costs. In the words of Amanda Bennett, "the corporate world has become a cold, hostile war zone."[4]

Paradoxically, the TNC is becoming bigger with fewer people. Today's TNC recognizes the value of size as the basis for FDI, manufacturing, and research. At the same time, it also recognizes the value of self-managing teams and the entreprenurial spirit that leads to new product development and increased productivity. It is not surprising, therefore, that such companies as Bertelsmann, Sony, and Time Warner are undergoing a major reorganization that allows subsidiaries greater autonomy in the management of their operations.

Today's TNC has become ever more reliant on computer and communication technology. Companies are putting more effort into preparing workers for the new world of work. Advancements in communication and manufacturing technology have contributed to a significant increase in organizational productivity and efficiency. The intelligent network is at the heart of the new organizational efficiency. The intelligent network makes it possible for the TNC to operate on a global level. It provides the basis for the seamless integration of information and communication, both internal and external to the organization.

What is becoming increasingly clear, however, is that such productivity has its price in terms of human cost and labor. For the middle manager with years of seniority, it can mean being fired or forced into early retirement. For employees, it can mean one person doing the work of five. Promotions lie stagnant, as do real wage earnings. Productivity for productivity's sake is not enough. There comes a time when a company has to reexamine its larger mission in the context of why the company was created in the first place.

What distinguishes the TNMC from other TNCs is that the principle commodities being sold are information and entertainment. It is a business mission that requires a greater degree of responsibility, given the media's unique power to inform, persuade, and entertain. A TNMC without a core business ethic is simply an organizational machine producing highly efficient products without considering the consequences. The direct fallout of such machinelike thinking is content (software) neutrality; that is, the complete disregard for the media content or message. Profitability and organizational efficiency supersede the need to look at the value of the product and its potential impact on the audience. The pursuit of profits can sometimes blind senior management from exercising critical judgment when it comes to product quality.

When Mergers and Acquisitions Fail

During the decades of the 1980s and 1990s, there were an unprecedented number of mergers and acquisitions in all fields of business. As companies become increasing global, there is a presumption that size makes better. Yet, on closer examination, it is discovered that not all mergers and acquisitions are successful. Often, the combining of two major organizations may create problems that no one can foresee. Transnational size provides no assurance that the newly merged company will be well-run or that the presumed synergies will occur. Worse still, the failed merger can be highly disruptive to both organizations in terms of lost revenue, capital debt, and job performance. The inevitable result of such mergers is a corresponding decrease in professional staff and personnel as the combined company attempts to find cost savings. There are four reasons that help to explain why mergers and acquisitions can sometimes fail. They include the lack of a compelling strategic rationale, failure to perform due diligence, postmerger planning and integration failures, and financing and the problems of excessive debt.

The Lack of a Compelling Strategic Rationale

The decision to merge is sometimes not supported by a compelling strategic rationale. In the desire to be globally competitive, the merging parties go into the proposed merger with unrealistic expectations of complementary strengths and presumed synergies. The pressure to move ahead can sometimes obscure the fact that both companies do not provide the right strategic match.

The result can be costly to the acquiring company. In 1991, AT&T spent $7.5 billion to purchase NCR Corporation. The purchase of NCR Corporation was based on the assumption that NCR would be able to strategically match computers and telecommunications. The strategy, thus far, has proved unworkable. NCR has cost the parent company $144 million in pre-tax losses.

Failure to Perform Due Diligence

In the highly charged atmosphere of intense negotiations, the merging parties fail to perform due diligence prior to the merger agreement. The result is that the acquiring company only later discovers that the intended acquisition will not accomplish the desired objectives.[5] Very often, the lack of due diligence results in the acquiring company paying too much for the acquisition. It is the principal reason that prompted Bell Atlantic to cancel its proposed acquisition of TCI corporation. Once Bell Atlantic examined TCI's finances and the existing regulatory climate surrounding cable, it became clearly obvious that it would take 10 years before the company could expect to see a return on investment.

Postmerger Planning and Integration Failures

One of the most important reasons that mergers fail is due to bad postmerger planning and integration. If the proposed merger does not include an effective plan for combining divisions with similar products, the duplication can be a source of friction rather than synergy. Turf wars erupt and reporting functions among managers become divisive. The problem becomes further complicated when there are significant differences in corporate culture. Some companies are conservative with rigid hierarchies whereas other companies are more entreprenurial in spirit. Combining the two entities under the same roof can be difficult at best. IBM has a long history of buying small entreprenurial companies and then suffocating the would-be start-ups through its rigid hierarchy. Such companies as Rolm, SBS, and Lotus Development Corporation have all suffered under the weight of IBM's system of management.

Financing and the Problems of Excessive Debt

During the 1980s, an estimated $1.3 trillion was spent in the transfer and sale of corporate assets worldwide. Much of the financing was accomplished through easy credit by the world's leading financial institutions and corporate willingness to assume major amounts of debt. As we have seen, problems of debt financing ultimately brought about the collapse of Maxwell Communication Inc. In the case of News Corp., the company's excessive debt financing almost resulted in near bankruptcy. Today, there is a resurgence in debt financing. Starting in 1995, more than $270 billion worth of mergers and acquisitions have been announced in all areas of business and commerce.[6]

What does it mean for tomorrow's TNMC? The need to remain financially solvent may prove to be one of the most critical business issues in the years ahead. The dilemma is twofold. On the one hand, a company wants to avail itself of the opportunity to pursue mergers and acquisitions that represent a strategic fit. Such pursuits require extensive financing. On the other hand, the same company needs to have the reserve funds to maintain its business operations while simultaneously investing in new product development.

Time Warner's proposed purchase of Turner Broadcasting is fraught with a number of problems not the least of which is the $8 billion price tag. At a time when Time Warner should be stabilizing its existing $10 billion debt, the company is going after another acquisition that will bring the combined debt to $18 billion. Wall Street's immediate reaction to the announced deal was a 6% downturn in Time Warner stock.

There are a number of financial implications that need to be taken into account. Is the proposed merger good for stockholders when the value of their stock has been diluted? Is the proposed merger good for employees when the newly combined company will have to eliminate jobs in order to avoid duplication and contain costs? Will such changes have a direct or indirect impact on the quality of Time Warner products and services? Critics fear that Time Warner's purchase of Turner Broadcasting will only complicate what is already a large and unwieldy organization by adding undue financial pressures. In the final analysis, excessive corporate debt and financial instability is not good for business.

TNMCs and Nation States

The TNMC is the most powerful economic force for global media activity that the 1980s has produced. Through a process of FDI, the TNMC actively promotes the use of advanced media technology including cable television, DBS, and online database services. Such efforts have ignited the transborder flow of media products worldwide. The TNMC possesses a level of power and influence that is second only to nation states. As such, the TNMC raises the specter of policy issues considerably, given its unique ability to influence national politics, economic priorities, and social opinion. The resulting globalization of media activity will force both governments and policymakers alike to consider the long-term implications.

The geopolitical and cultural walls that once separated the nations of the earth are becoming more difficult to maintain. The world of global television, albeit CNN, MTV, Disney, and Bart Simpson, is quickly eroding the barriers. At the same time, there is not likely to become a single, unified market for television entertainment. Differences in culture, including language, shared common experience, and social values will preclude that possibility.

Tomorrow's television programmers are likely to program toward several countries at once. More and more, programs will be produced for regions of the world where there is a commonality of language and experience. The importance of the TNMC and coproduction ventures are going to foster a programming philosophy based on the assumption that the world can be broken down according to cultural zones. With the increase in channel capacity, it is expected that the next generation of television viewers is likely to be composed of people who can simultaneously appreciate World MTV and still have a decided preference for the locally originated dramatic series or sporting event.

As a social force, television and films, in combination with advanced communication, will continue to homogenize culture. In a transnational economy, cultural trespass is well beyond anyone's ability to reestablish the lines of separation. There is no global organization that can impose uniform regulation on those media companies whose products are deemed inappropriate for public consumption. However, sovereign nations do have a right and a responsibility to exercise appropriate controls on media and other product imports when such products are deemed harmful or hazardous. Such rules, however, should be consistent and uniformly applied to all commercial traders. International deregulation and privatization is admittedly a delicate balancing act that will require government and its representative agencies to properly function as the nation's defenders of the public interest while simultaneously participating in an interdependent global economy.

NOTES

[1] Steven S. Wildman and Steven E. Siwek, "The Privatization of European Television: Effects on International Markets for Programs," *Columbia Journal of World Business*, Fall, 1987, pp. 71–73.

[2] Richard A. Gershon, International Deregulation and the Rise of Transnational Media Corporations, *Journal of Media Economics*, (6)2, 1993, pp. 6–7.

[3] "What's Going On," *Broadcasting & Cable*, 25 September, 1995, pp. 23–25.

[4] Amanda Bennett, *The Death of the Organization Man*, (New York: Morrow, 1990), pp. 13–27.

[5] "The Case Against Mergers," *Business Week*, 30 October, 1995, pp. 122–126.

[6] "Land of the Giants," *Business Week*, 11 September, 1995, pp. 34–39.

Author Index

A

Allen, William T., 142
Anderson, Michael H., 61, 62
Ang, Ian, 128
Auletta, Ken, 143

B

Bagdikian, Benjamin H., 5, 8, 29, 117, 202
Barrett, O., 118,
Baudot, Barbara, 72
Beltran, L. R., 118
Bennett, Amanda, 216
Boyd, Douglas, 118, 126
Bruck, Connie, 137

C

Cardoso, F. H., 120
Carveth, Rod, 14, 48, 49
Childs, Julian B., 81
Chorafas, D., 81
Clurman, Richard M., 140
Compaine, Benjamin, 30

D

Daft, Richard, 83, 86
De Cardona, E.F., 118, 120
Dupagne, Michel, 45
Dymsza, William A., 5

E

Egan, Bruce, 99

F

Faletto, E., 120

G

Gallagher, Lynn, 111
Gershon, Richard A., 49, 87, 108
Goldhar, Joel D., 88
Grosse, Robert, 7
Guback, Thomas, 44

H

Halberstam, David, 135, 136
Hatfield, Dale, 111
Howard, Donald, 72

I

Irwen, Manley, 122

J

Jacoby, Neil H., 3
Janus, Noreene, Z., 62, 119

K

Kagan, Paul, 136
Kujawa, Dwayne, 7

L

Launer, Michael, 27
Lee, C., 118
Lei, David, 88
Lengel, Robert, 83, 86
Lerner, Daniel, 120
Lieberman, Ira W., 21
Litvak, Sanford M., 192

M

Mayo, Michael, 72
Merenda, Michael, 122
Morita, Akio, 158
Moscow, Vincent, 29
Mowlana, Hamid, 117

N

Nordenstreng, Karle, 118

O

O'Hanlon, Tom, 195

Oliveira, Omar S., 72, 120
Owen, Bruce M., 39
Ozanich, Gary, 14

P

Paldan, L., 120
Picard, Robert G., 39
Poole, de Sola, Ithiel, 30, 90, 105, 127

R

Rheingold, Howard, 86
Roche, Edward M., 4, 77
Runde, Helmuth, 173

S

Salinas, R., 120
Schiller, Herbert I., 118
Sepstrup, Preben, 39
Shawcross, William, 203
Smith, Ralph Lee, 101
Steinman, H., 81
Studemann, Frederick, 166, 171

T

Toffler, Alvin, 82, 94
Tunstall, Jeremy, 118
Turow, Joseph, 34

V

Varis, Tapio, 42, 118
Vernon, R., 3

W

Waterman, Robert, 14
Wells, L., 3
Wildman, Steven S., 39
Wilson, Gary, 188
Wilson, Mark, 7
Wirth, Michael, 14

Y

Young, Marilyn, 27

Subject Index

A

AT&T, 13, 23, 33, 60, 97, 156

B

BBDO Worldwide, 62–66, 69, 216, 218
Bangemann Report, 28–29
Bell Atlantic, 32, 106–107, 218
Berlusconi, Silvio, 8, 47, 124
Bertelsmann A.G., 4, 5, 31, 35,46, 138, 151, 166–176, 213, 216
    Bertelsmann Music Group (BMG), 168, 170, 174–176, 213
    business strategy and philosophy, 171–174
    decentralization, 13–14, 166, 169, 171, 173
    financial performance and analysis, 174–175
    Gruner and Jahr, 167, 171, 173, 175
    historical overview, 166–168
    organizational structure, 169–172
Bonification, 68–69
British Broadcasting Corporation, 24
British Telecom, 24, 32, 97, 216
Broadband residential services, 97–113, 214
Business communication model, 86–87
Buying influence, 123–124

C

Cable television, 30,49–52, 97–113, 137–138, 214–215, 219
    expanded cable (enhanced services), 97–113
    international cable development, 49–52
    interactive cable television, 101, 107–108, 138
    multiple system operators, 30
    program distributors, 49–52
Canal Plus, 46, 176
Capital Cities/ABC, 104–105, 138, 143, 182–183, 185, 191–192, 199
Clinton, William J. and Gore, Albert, 97

Columbia Broadcasting System (CBS), 105–106, 138, 143, 157–158, 208, 213
Comparative advantage, 10–11, 79, 127
Continental Cablevision, 104–105, 147
Convergence of modes, 31, 105, 112, 213
Craxi, Bettino, 124

D

Database marketing, 89
Davis, Marvin, 141
Decentralization, 4, 13–14, 77–78
Deregulation, 20, 22–23, 27, 29, 35–36, 45, 97–98, 212, 216, 220
Deutsche Telecom, 176
DDB Needham Worldwide, 62, 69
Digitalization, 107, 213
Direct broadcast satellites, 25, 51–56, 70, 210, 215, 219
    British Sky Broadcasting, 12, 25, 55, 197, 199–206, 209, 213
    Japan Satellite Broadcasting, 52–55
    Star Television, 56, 200–202, 209–210
Diller, Barry, 199, 204
Disney, Roy, 178, 180
Disney, Walt, 178–180
Dondelinger, Jean, 44

E

Education and distance learning, 110–111
Eisner, Michael, 8, 180–183, 186, 189, 191, 193, 215
Electronic funds transfer, 80, 121
Ericsson Corporation, 24
ESPN, 105–106, 214
European Community, 20, 27–29,43–48, 214
    deregulation and privatization, 27–29
    European television, 43–47
    television without frontiers, 8, 27, 43–44

F

Financial solvency, 14–16, 69, 219
Fisher, Mark, 44

224 SUBJECT INDEX

Foreign direct investment, 5–10, 38, 70, 73, 78, 82, 122–123, 129, 147, 156, 168, 176, 216, 219
    empire building, 8, 78, 195, 201–203
    foreign market penetration, 6, 78, 156, 168, 213
    overcoming regulatory barriers, 7–8, 47–48, 78
    production and distribution, 7, 78
    proprietary assets/natural resources, 6, 78
    in U.S. media corporations, 10, 168
Freccero, Carlo, 44

G

Gannett Company, 137
General Agreement on Tariffs and Trade, 47–48
Global custody (international banking), 82
Global inventory management, 89
Gorbachev, Mikhail, 26
Graham, Katharine, 33
Group broadcasters, 30

H

Hachette SA, 6–7, 33
Home shopping, 102, 107, 111–112

I

IBM, 13, 216, 218
Ibuka, Masaru, 154–155, 158, 160–161, 163
Idei, Nobuyuki, 161
Integrated community planning, 100–101, 147
    Singapore, 101
International media trade, 38–59, 118–119
    barter and syndication, 45
    coproduction ventures, 48–49, 57, 220
    cultural zones, 57–58, 220
    television and film, 38–42, 220
    U.S. television trade, 42–43
Intellectual property and copyright, 124–128
Intelligent networks, 78–95, 217
    decision support systems, 79
    electronic messaging networks, 82–87
    financial networks, 79–82
    global manufacturing networks, 87–90
    research and online database networks, 90–94
    strategic planning issues, 78–79
Internet, 30, 93–94, 161, 216
Interpublic group, 62
Itoh, C., 147, 149

K

Katzenberg, Jeffrey, 182, 189

Kirch Group, 46, 176

L

Lagardere, Jean Luc, 6, 8, 33
Levin, Jerry, 8, 136–137, 139, 141–143, 148–149, 152, 215
Lintas, 62
Lowe Group, 62
Luce, Henry, Robinson, 135–137, 195

M

Malone, John, 16, 99, 148–149
Maxwell, Robert, 5, 8, 25, 32, 197
Maxwell Communication, 15, 138, 199, 219
McCann Erickson, 62
Medical infomatics (telemedicine), 109–110
Microsoft Corporation, 30
Microwave Communications Inc. (MCI), 32, 105, 202, 211
Milliken, Robert, 88
Miyet, Bernard, 46
Mohn, Reinhard, 4, 166–168, 171, 173–174, 215
Morita, Akio, 155–156, 158, 161, 215
Motion Picture Association of America, 42, 47
Multimedia (modularity of design), 105, 112, 213
Munro, J. Richard, 137, 139–141
Murdoch, Keith, Sir, 195–196, 203–204
Murdoch, Keith Rupert, 8, 16, 25, 32–33, 35, 55–56, 124, 195–208, 210–212, 215–216
Murphy, Tom, 182–183
Music Television Network (MTV), 52, 58, 105, 138, 214, 220

N

NASDAQ, 81
National Broadcasting Company (NBC), 105–106, 143
News Corporation Ltd., 30–31, 35, 105, 138, 151, 195–211, 213, 216, 219
    British Sky Broadcasting, 12, 55, 197, 199–206, 209, 213
    business strategy and philosophy, 196–197, 201–205, 210–211
    debt financing and risk, 16–17, 199–200, 204–207, 219
    financial performance and analysis, 205–208
    Fox Television Network, 12, 198–199, 201–209, 212–213
    historical overview, 195–200

SUBJECT INDEX 225

New World Communications, 208–209, 212
organizational structure, 200–201
publishing (publications), 195–205, 208, 210
Star Television Network, 56, 200–202, 209–210, 213
vertical integration, 11–12, 198, 211–213
NHK, 155, 164,
Nicholas, Nicholas J., 137–142
Nippon Telegraph and Telephone (NTT), 25–26, 97
NYNEX, 105–106

O

Ohga, Norio, 155–156, 158, 161
Omnicom Group, 62, 69
Open video systems, 97–113, 214

P

Paramount Communications, 105–106, 138, 141–142, 149
Pay-per-view/video on demand, 101–102, 105, 107, 112–113, 136, 209
Perestroika, 20, 26
Program quotas (regulatory barriers), 35, 43, 47, 127–128
Privatization, 12–29, 35–36, 40–42, 53, 56–58, 60, 70, 97–98, 212, 214–216, 220

Q

Qube, 101–102, 137–138

R

Reagan, Ronald, 22, 32, 124
Ross, Steven, 5, 137–141, 143

S

Saatchi and Saatchi, 69
Schulof, Michael, 6, 159–161
Smith, Ray, 107
Sony Corporation, 4, 6, 30, 154–165, 213, 216
Betamax VCRs, 157–158, 160, 164
business strategy and philosophy, 6, 156, 158–161, 163–165
electronic news gathering, 157–158, 213
financial performance and analysis, 161–163
historical overview, 154–158
organizational structure, 158–159
research and development, 160–161
transistor radio, 156
Trinitron television, 157, 158, 163, 213

Walkman portable cassette player, 154, 158, 161, 213
SWIFT, 80

T

Telecommunications and organizational planning, 83–87,
Telecommunications Inc. (TCI), 16, 32, 148, 218
Thatcher, Margaret, 24–25, 32, 124, 204
Time-based competitiveness (quick response), 88–90, 187
Time Warner Inc., 5, 31–32, 135–152, 206, 212–213, 216, 219
business strategy and philosophy, 145–149
financial performance and analysis, 15–17, 149–151
Full Service Network, 102, 143, 147, 151
historical overview, 135–145
Home Box Office, Inc., 49, 52, 105, 136–139, 145–147, 151, 213
merger with Turner Broadcasting, 16, 106, 147–149, 151–152, 212, 219
organizational structure, 144–146
Time Magazine, 135–136, 143
vertical integration, 11, 13, 144–145
Toshiba Corporation, 147, 149
Transborder data flow, 120–122
Transnational advertising agency, 45, 60–76, 119
client conflicts, 69–70
European advertising, 45
source control and self-censorship, 33–34
Transnational media corporation, 4, 16–17, 29, 35–36, 45, 48, 57–58, 62, 68, 71, 106, 116–120, 127–129, 142, 151, 154, 167–169, 171, 173, 176, 182, 195, 199–200, 206, 210, 212–220
consolidation (concentration), 29–35, 62, 135, 212, 216
cross media ownership and technology partnerships, 31, 104–106, 213–214
debt financing and risk, 14–17, 149–152, 199–200, 204–207, 219
foreign direct investment, 5–10, 38, 70, 73, 78, 82, 122–123, 129, 147, 156, 168, 176, 216, 219
mergers and acquisitions, 9–10, 104–106, 147–149, 151–152, 182–183, 185, 191–192, 212–213, 217–219
Transnational media influence, 70–74, 116–129

226　SUBJECT INDEX

content (software) neutrality, 34–35, 119, 127, 144, 217
cultural trespass, 5, 70, 73, 116–117, 127, 190–191, 219–220
dependency, 71, 73, 116, 120
homogenization of culture, 70, 117, 128, 220
host nations, 70–74, 119–123, 127–129, 219–220
marketplace of ideas, 4–5, 29–35, 117, 215–216
media imperialism, 71, 117–118
national economic priorities, 71–72, 119, 219
national sovereignty, 5, 71–72, 116–129, 219–220
politics and media influence, 32–33, 35, 124, 216, 219
privacy data, 122, 128
Tucker, C. Delores, 34
Turner Broadcasting Inc.
　Cable News Network, 50–51, 105, 136, 143, 213, 220
　merger with Time Warner, 16, 106, 147–149, 151–152, 212, 219
Turner, Ted, 8, 51, 136, 148–149, 215

U

UNESCO, MacBride Commission, 73
Universal product codes (bar codes), 88–89
U.S. Telecommunications Act of 1996, 22–23, 100, 103–104, 113

US West, 104, 147, 149–150

V

Valenti, Jack, 47
Vertical integration (complementary assets), 11–13, 68, 144–145, 148, 198, 211–213
Viacom, 105, 106
Virtual communication, 86

W

Walt Disney Company, 10–11, 17, 30, 178–193, 212–213
　business strategy and philosophy, 186–188
　comparative advantage, 10–11
　cross licensing and marketing, 7, 185, 187–189, 192–193
　financial performance and analysis, 188–189
　historical overview, 178–183
　organizational structure, 183–186
　purchase of Capital Cities/ABC, 104, 106, 182–183, 185, 191–192, 212–213
　theme parks, 180–181, 184–185, 189, 190–191
Wells, Frank, 180, 182, 191
Windowing, 39–40
Wossner, Mark, 168, 173, 176
Wriston, Walter, 82

For Product Safety Concerns and Information please contact our EU representative GPSR@taylorandfrancis.com
Taylor & Francis Verlag GmbH, Kaufingerstraße 24, 80331 München, Germany

www.ingramcontent.com/pod-product-compliance
Lightning Source LLC
Chambersburg PA
CBHW061442300426
44114CB00014B/1791